TROPHIES OF GOD'S GRACE

"...God gave the increase."

Episodes in the Lives of Real People

Chosen From 55 Years of Missionary Experiences

as related by

Elias Edward (Ed) Schwartz, D.D.

"Trust in the Lord with all thine heart..." PROV. 3:5,6
Ed. Schwartz 8-11-96

Baptist Mid-Missions

Cleveland, Ohio, U.S.A.

Baptist Mid-Missions
7749 Webster Road
P.O. Box 308011
Cleveland, Ohio 44130-8011

ISBN 0-941645-01-0

Cover design by José Ramírez

Printed in the USA

Dedicated

to

My Loving Wife Mildred,

My Constant Companion and Fellow Laborer

during

55 Years of Missionary Service

and continuing so to be in

Our Retirement Ministries

Acknowledgments

Many thanks are hereby given to those who have been of special help to me in writing this book of memoirs.

To Robert Collins, my Field Administrator, and to Leigh Adams, Vice President, for urging me to write a book of our missionary experiences.

To Bernice Hilliker for assembling the typewritten pages in proper order and encouraging me to proceed with the project and then doing the final proofreading with helpful suggestions and corrections.

To Edna Lionberger for typing the original manuscript into an office computer, enabling me to copy it into my home computer.

To Joan Stephens for the tedious work of editing the manuscript and for her wise counsel to delete from the manuscript all material which did not contribute to the main thrust of each chapter and to the book as a whole.

To the men who consented to review the manuscript and who commented so favorably on its content.

To Richard Meyer for formatting the manuscript with its photos and making suggestions for clarifying certain expressions. To Bob Owen, our printer, for making it all look so very professional.

To José Ramírez, of our Philadelphia ministry, for designing the cover which so aptly illustrates the central theme of the book—Missions are People.

Finally, to Gary Hilliker and Marvin Stephens, General Director and Business Manager respectively, for their wise counsel and advice as to proper procedures in making *Trophies of God's Grace* available to the public, and to the entire staff of our Spanish Publishing House (Editorial Bautista Independiente) in Sebring, Florida, for their patient labor of love in taking the final revision through the many details involved in its publication.

Gratefully,
Ed Schwartz

Contents

V
Venezuela Ministry - Part 2

VI
Philadelphia Ministry

VII
Dominican Republic Ministry

VIII
Venezuela Ministry - Part 3

IX
Puerto Rico Ministry

Focus of the Book

When you think of missions, do you think first of people or do you think first of places? Places have a way of capturing our imagination; exotic places with climates and creatures mysteriously different from those with which we are acquainted. In our mind's eye we have an image of the mission field. That mental portrait may include people, but they are generally faceless and do little more than blend into the background of some idyllic setting worthy of the cover of *National Geographic*. And yet if asked which is more vital to missions, people or places, we would all say people.

Ed and Mildred Schwartz, throughout their 54 years of missionary service, have been driven by their concern for the eternal welfare of people. Their orientation to missions occurred in the skid-row district of their home town, Philadelphia, Pennsylvania. They learned early that anywhere they encountered people who needed Christ constituted their mission field. What they learned at home they faithfully practiced in places like Venezuela, Puerto Rico and the Dominican Republic. But they were not as fascinated with those foreign venues as they were with the marvels of seeing people come to Christ everywhere they proclaimed the Gospel. *Trophies of God's Grace* chronicles Ed and Mildred's missionary endeavor in a manner that magnifies the importance of people and minimizes the significance of places.

Trophies of God's Grace should impress us with God's interest in lost people everywhere. It should also convince us that God takes pleasure in using servants who are totally surrendered to Him. Ed and Mildred have modeled what we should all think of when we use the term *surrender*. They can identify a specific time when they gave up any right to choose for themselves how they would live their lives. They placed themselves, all of themselves, on the altar, understanding they were to be living sacrifices over which God would exercise sole direction. Their memoirs then become a testimony of what God has been pleased to do with two lives totally surrendered to Him.

Rev. Gary L. Anderson, D.D., President
Baptist Mid-Missions
7749 Webster Road
Cleveland, Ohio 44130-8011

Endorsements

I am delighted to see in print the marvelous missionary stories I first heard recounted by Ed and Mildred Schwartz while visiting them in Puerto Rico. Leigh Adams and I sat enthralled for hours listening to living testimony as to the faithfulness of God in behalf of His missionary ambassadors to Latin America.

The blessing and encouragement we received will now be shared with many others who will rejoice to know that "faithful is he that calleth you, who also will do it" (I Thessalonians 5:24).

Robert C. Collins

Rev. Robert C. Collins, is a veteran missionary of 54 years, having served in Bolivia, Brazil and as our Field Administrator. Rev. Collins now serves on the staff of our Spanish publishing house.

********** ********** **********

It has been my privilege to read the manuscript, *Trophies of God's Grace*. Having served with Dr. and Mrs. Schwartz in Venezuela (challenged by Ed Schwartz personally), I can attest to the scores of anecdotes they recount. To which, I aver, "To God be the glory, great things He hath done."

It is my candid observation that every veteran missionary will want to read this volume. Every prospective missionary ought to read this treatise. And, every student preparing for a life of missionary service should be required to read, *Trophies of God's Grace.*

Every church library should carry this text. The pastor's personal library should include it. And, educational institutions developing full time Christian workers should adopt Dr. Schwartz's book as a "must" to be read. Congratulations, Ed and Mildred, on a job well done.

Dr. Edward Morrell, Jr.

Founder, General Director Emeritus, Field Representative, Evangelist with the Committee On Missionary Evangelism.

It has been my privilege to review *Trophies of God's Grace*, an interesting resume of fifty years of missionary service, written by Ed Schwartz. It reviews their testimony and work from the days of their personal experience with Christ in salvation to the completion of their ministry in Venezuela, Dominican Republic, Puerto Rico and in the Philadelphia Spanish-language work.

This book will also be an encouragement to Christian families interested in the missionary challenges and opportunities of our time. Young people in our homes may read it and learn the meaning of God's call to service. It will likely become a missionary textbook and a source of collateral reading in our Christian colleges. Missionaries now on the field will find many helpful and encouraging words in these pages. It is my privilege to encourage the reading of this exciting missionary report.

Sincerely in Christ,
James T. Jeremiah
Chancellor of Cedarville College
Cedarville, Ohio

Dr. James T. Jeremiah, after pastoring a number of churches, served for many years as President of Cedarville College.

********** ********** **********

Fifty years of loving service to your Lord is a very great tribute to your unqualified love and profound dedication to Him. This commitment to your Master has not only brought Him great glory but it has also conveyed much blessing to those to whom you have ministered. You have been very effective and exemplary instructors of the Word of God. You have taught what and how to reach both the unsaved as well as nurture those who have already entered the Lord's family. You have very clearly demonstrated over more than half a century what is implied and included in being the children and servants of our wonderful Lord.

You have not only received the Lord's gifts but you have also exercised them through your unstinted and unselfish devotion and dedication. Sinners have been reached and saints have been edified. Many of them with the enabling of the Holy Spirit have emulated you, resulting in their serving our Lord devotedly and effectively.

Several passages of Scripture come to mind which relate and describe your loving service. I have selected a few of them for their appropriateness in relating to your personal dedication and devotion. May they remind you and all who read these memoirs to always faithfully fulfill our high calling and holy privilege.

"His lord said unto him, Well done, thou good and faithful servant; thou hast been faithful over a few things, I will make thee ruler over many things" (Matthew 25:21).

"Therefore, my beloved brethren, be ye steadfast, unmovable, always abounding in the work of the Lord, forasmuch as ye know your labour is not in vain in the Lord" (I Corinthians 15:58).

"But as we were allowed of God to be put in trust with the gospel, even so we speak; not as pleasing men, but God, which trieth our hearts" (I Thessalonians 2:4).

"For God is not unrighteous to forget your work and labour of love, which you have showed toward his name, in that ye have ministered to the saints, and do minister" (Hebrews 6:10).

By the divine assistance of the Holy Spirit of God, like you, may all of us who know and love Him, aspire to and attain the lofty standard set forth in John 8:29, "I do always those things that please Him."

Dr. William A. Mierop, Quarryville, Pennsylvania

Dr. William Mierop pastored churches in the Philadelphia-New Jersey area, then as President of the Bible Institute of Pennsylvania managed the union with the Philadelphia School of the Bible, resulting in the formation of the Philadelphia College of Bible.

********** ********** **********

Missionary E. E. Schwartz has done us all a great service by recording God's wonderful works in the lives of many people. He rightly gives all the glory to our Lord Jesus Christ.

We trust that God will use this book to challenge His dear people to give their lives in service to Him.

Joseph M. Stowell, D.D.; D.Hum.

A pastor with more than 30 years as a member of the General Council of Baptist Mid-Missions.

Forward

The apostle James wrote, "Elias was a man subject to like passions as we are, and he prayed...." He was emphasizing the fact that God does indeed impact common people and use them in a significant and unique way for His glory. This principle is illustrated so beautifully in the lives of Ed and Mildred Schwartz who for over fifty years have been on the cutting edge of world missions.

With an easy-to-read and captivating writing style the author rehearses details of the call to ministry and of God's perfect timing in getting them into Venezuela just before Pearl Harbor and the United States involvement in the second world war. It was at this point Venezuela closed its borders to all foreign missionaries but through divine intervention Ed and Mildred were on the field with full credentials starting their career service.

Throughout the book fascinating narration reveals their personal experiences with the country, culture and people. With sincere openness they speak of their adjustments to the difficulties and joys of missionary work. *Trophies of God's Grace* shows missions just as it is lived and experienced. It is the story of two people who in the yoke of the Great Commission ploughed fertile ground in Latin America. The harvest will be eternal.

Ed and Mildred Schwartz have served with honor and distinction as valued members of the Baptist Mid-Missions family. I commend to you this book for it will inform and inspire as it reveals the greatness and faithfulness of our God.

Allan E. Lewis, President Emeritus
Baptist Mid-Missions

Born in Africa of missionary parents, after graduating from Moody Bible Institute and Northern Baptist Seminary he pastored 2 churches. He was the President of Baptist Mid-Missions for 23 years until retirement.

Introduction

That God should be praised and glorified is our first and foremost motive for writing these stories. Whatever success we experienced in our missionary service is because our Lord and Savior Jesus Christ, by His Holy Spirit, worked in and through us. The Lord enabled us to go forth to sow the precious seed of God's Word (Matthew 13:3), and water it with our tears in prayer (Psalm 126: 5,6). In due time, **God gave the increase** (I Corinthians 3:6). Thus, the title of the book: *Trophies of God's Grace*.

Concerning the stories you are about to read, we have been asked, "How have you remembered all the details?" Good question, but not too hard to answer. First of all, Mildred kept a casual diary, recording the dates of important events and I kept notes of the most interesting happenings. I did this because of advice given to me by Dr. William A. Mierop, then President of the Bible Institute of Pennsylvania.

Having been invited to speak at a chapel service, I arrived early, and was sitting in Dr. Mierop's office. After some chitchat, Dr. Mierop gave me the following advice.

"Now, Ed, when you speak to our students today, please don't preach. I repeat, please don't preach. We hear good messages from excellent preachers who visit us from time to time, and we don't need you to bring us another sermon or Bible study. What we want from you are stories of **how God is working** on the mission field, about souls saved, lives changed, and victories won. We need to be encouraged to pray more for missions and to support them.

"And, Ed, I advise you to follow this practice when you visit your supporting churches or when you get into new ones. Of course, if there are problems on your field, we should hear about them also so that we can pray for you more intelligently.

"But you must always **emphasize the positive**, the successes. No church likes to support a loser. Success breeds success even in the Lord's work. We want to be able to praise God for what **He is doing** out there through your ministry."

Needless to say, I had to hurriedly change the subject of my talk, for I had indeed planned to preach. The Lord gave complete freedom as I related some of our experiences during our first term in Venezuela. The students showed much interest as I spoke. Many gathered around me in the free period after chapel to ask questions. Some complemented me on what had been accomplished. I thanked them for the compliments but quickly passed them on to Jesus with a "Praise the Lord, He did it all." By doing this, I was remembering Dr. George Mundell, one of my beloved professors at the Bible Institute of Pennsylvania. He counselled us to graciously accept such compliments and then immediately pass them on to the Lord.

At home after that chapel service, I started to write down, while still fresh in my mind, all the things that were said and done during our years of training at the Eighth Street Wayside Rescue Mission and during our first term on the foreign mission field. I then started to keep an even more detailed record of our work. As the years have gone by, I have repeatedly related our experiences to anyone who would listen. I have used them as illustrations for messages in church services, in missionary conferences, and in studies given in Bible institutes. Thus, the details have become fixed in my mind in computer hard-disk fashion. Of course, it is impossible to remember every word spoken in past conversations, but, with a little sanctified imagination, we have been able to fill in with the obvious ones.

The incentive to compile the stories came from many of you who encouraged us to do so. Quite often, after you heard one or two related in a meeting, you would say to us, "You ought to write a book," or, "These stories ought to be preserved." Encouragement also came from Rev. Robert Collins and Rev. Leigh Adams, our Field Administrators, as you read in Rev. Collins' endorsement.

Some of the people we tell about were brought to a saving knowledge of Christ apart from our personal ministry. Our contact with them came as we became their missionary-pastor-teachers, helping them in their spiritual growth. Some of them also became avid soul-winners. Now, after so many years, we rejoice to see that our children in the Lord have remained faithful.

One example is brother Solórzano who was 84 years old when I baptized him in 1971. In January 1991 we returned to Venezuela to speak at the annual conference of our independent Baptist churches. As I approached the open door to our church in Bella Vista, I saw him sitting in one of the pews. With eyes still bright at age 104, he saw me and couldn't wait for me to get to him, but got up from his seat and hobbled in my direction.

He greeted me with the typical Hispanic embrace. He is grandfather to the seventeen children of Rafael Ascanio (a former pastor) and his wife, all members of the Peña de Horeb Baptist Church in Bella Vista, suburb of San Félix. **To God be the glory**!

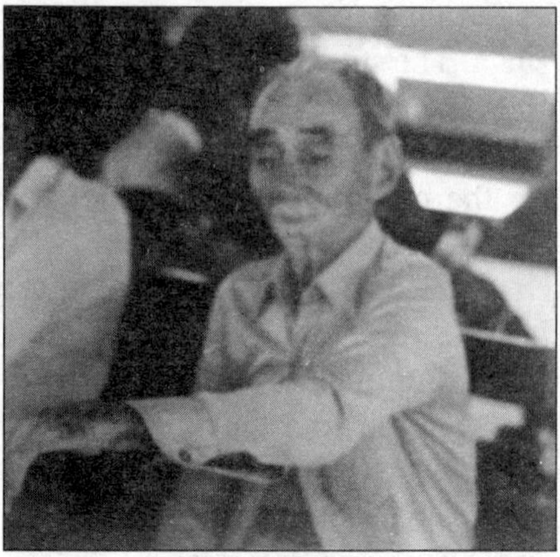

Don Solórzano

We thank the Lord also for the conditional promises He gives us in Psalm 37:3-7 and Proverbs 3:5,6, which became our "life verses". Though not always very successfully, we have tried to follow the advice they give: *"Trust... Delight thyself... Commit thy way... Rest in the LORD, and wait patiently for him...." "Trust in the LORD with all thine heart; and lean not unto thine own understanding. In all thy ways acknowledge him,..."* and then, the **PROMISE**... *"HE SHALL DIRECT THY PATHS."*

October 17, 1995 — Ed and Mildred Schwartz

I
Rescue Mission - Pre-field Training

Chapter 1

Christ Saves an Alcoholic

"Therefore if any man be in Christ, he is a new creature: old things are passed away; behold, all things are become new." (II Corinthians 5:17)

An open-air Gospel service was in progress on the corner of Ninth and Race Streets in Philadelphia, near the Eighth Street Wayside Rescue Mission. My friend George Toms and I were standing on opposite corners giving out Gospel tracts to passers-by, inviting them to stop and listen to the message being preached.

That summer Mildred and I had been accepted as missionaries by Baptist Mid-Missions to work in Venezuela, South America. We had one more year of Bible college to complete before preparing to leave for the field. We continued to help out at the Rescue Mission whenever time from studies and our secular work permitted.

I noticed a man standing in the shadows of a doorway. He began to slowly walk towards me. He looked like the typical tenderloin derelict, unshaven, hair uncombed, trousers unpressed and soiled, suit coat buttoned to his neck, probably to hide the fact that he was shirtless. I caught the body odor of the typical "flop-house bum," the smell of insecticide used by the cheap hotels. "Young man, maybe you can help me." His voice was thick and trembly, but had a certain tone of refinement. Surprisingly, I did not catch the odor of the cheap rum these poor decrepit men usually drank. As the man spoke, I thought, "This man seems to be sober. How strange! Even more strange, he is not immediately asking for a handout."

I replied, "Well mister, I'll try. What is your problem?"

"Something happened to me today."

The man paused as he reached out his hand and caught me by the arm as if to steady himself. Under the street light, I could see his face. It was wan and pallid. The man was trembling. No, he wasn't drunk. I was sure of that, but it was quite evident that he was not well.

"I think maybe God is trying to tell me something."

The man tried to continue, but his knees buckled under him, and he grabbed me with both hands. Thoughts again raced through my mind, "What is this? Am I about to be mugged?" But the man recovered himself, straightened up and backed off.

"I'm sorry, young man, I just feel awfully weak. I haven't eaten anything today. I only had one drink. Is there some place where we can go sit down and talk? Maybe you can explain something to me."

The street meeting was almost over and most of the church group would be going up town. I motioned for my friend George to come over. George was about ten years my senior and as my spiritual counselor, had helped me out of my doctrinal liberalism. On that particular night, George was in charge of the inquiry room at the Mission.

"George, this man is a bit shaky on his legs, do you think it would be all right if I took him over to the Mission?" Leaning closer to George, I whispered, "He is stone sober. I'm sure of that. He is just very weak and not too well."

George agreed and accompanied us to the Mission. We had barely entered through the rear door, when the door leading to the meeting hall opened and John Dobbs, the superintendent, exclaimed, "Am I ever glad to see you, George. One of the church groups did not show up tonight. Will you please lead the next service?"

This left me alone with the man. I was inexperienced in rescue mission work and felt very nervous. I had the man sit down and I served him a cup of coffee and one of the sandwiches a visiting church group had provided.

I had been silently praying for guidance, and hoped that I would not hear the usual sob story from just one more "mission stiff." Even as I was thinking this, I wondered why the men who attended the services at the Mission were so nicknamed. Looking at the man now in the lighted inquiry room, I thought, "Maybe it's because of their clothes. They are actually stiff. I guess it's from getting them rained on and then drying on their bodies."

As the man finished his coffee, I turned to him, "Now let's hear your story."

"My name is Harvey Trainer. I am from Cincinnati, Ohio. I had a wife and three lovely children, a boy and two girls. I was a partner in a prominent law firm. We had to do a lot of entertaining with many parties and much drinking." The man paused to get his breath. "But, I guess you've heard a lot of stories like mine. There's lots of men like me on skid row."

"Yes, I have," I answered, "but the Lord has helped many a man like you right here in the Mission, and He can help you also. But, go on with your story, please."

"Well, it wasn't long until I found that I was an alcoholic. I just couldn't leave the bottle alone. I lost my partnership. I lost my wife and children. The mortgage company took my house. I just couldn't stay there any more. I've been wandering for... I don't know... I've lost track of time... it seems like ages, but I guess, about three years... Baltimore, New York and now here for maybe six months. Like the rest of us, I wash dishes, and clean bathrooms in cheap rat-infested hotels. I beg... I borrow when no one is looking... do anything to get enough for the next drink... But I'm fed up. I just can't go on."

"But Harvey, you're not drunk now. How come?"

"No... that's because of what happened to me today." Harvey shook his head in disbelief. "I can't understand it."

"So, what happened?" I asked as I pulled up a chair and sat down closer to Harvey.

"Last night I didn't have the quarter for a cot in the flop-house. Some man told me to go over to the Galilee Mission. Sometimes they will let a man in for free if they aren't already full. I didn't think they would do it, but that lady over there they call Mother Bachman let me in. I don't know why, but she looked into my eyes... I could feel her looking into my very soul. She said a little prayer for me in the little room in back of the chapel... like this one here... then she gave me a ticket and sent me upstairs to the dorms. As I left the room, I could hear the people singing in the chapel. I remembered the song. It was one we sang in Sunday School when I was a boy. I remember the music well, but I only remember a few of the words, "What a Friend we have in Jesus."

"I couldn't sleep... just kept thinking about what a mess I had made of my life. I hadn't felt like that before... I guess the booze had numbed my mind. Anyhow, I thought, 'Nobody can help me now, not even Jesus!' The more I thought about my condition, I couldn't see any hope... no use going on... no other choice but to end it all."

I couldn't help thinking, "How melodramatic he sounds... yet, he does sound different from the others." Aloud, I said, "Well now, friend Harvey, suicide is not the answer. Jesus can help you if you will let Him. But, what happened to you today?" I offered the man another cup of coffee. "What stopped you from taking your life?"

Harvey, sipped the coffee and continued, "Well, as I was saying, I didn't sleep at all last night. The other men were snoring away, some were talking in their sleep and one of them had a terrible nightmare... screamed out loud. I just lay there, making plans. I finally decided that I would throw myself under one of those trucks coming off Ben Franklin Bridge.

"This morning I hurried out to the street. I felt weak and was shaking like a leaf. I had to have my eye-opener first. I went up Tenth Street and into Fred's saloon. I guess you know that we always get our eye-opener drink free so we can get out on the street again to beg, borrow or steal. We gotta get some cash so we can pay good old Fred for the next ones."

As Harvey said those last words, he was looking down at his worn-out shoes and shaking his head. He was really disgusted at the degradation into which he had sunk. "No doubt about it," I thought, "this man is really repentant."

"Yes, I know how you must feel, Harvey, but please go on."

"Okay. I left the bar and walked down to Race Street, turned east to Sixth Street. I stopped and watched the traffic coming off the bridge. Then I turned down Sixth Street a short distance and waited on the west side for the right truck to come along. As they come off that bridge, some turn down Sixth to make deliveries on Market Street. They come around pretty fast and I wanted a big loaded one that would be hard to stop, in case the driver would see me.

"So I waited," Harvey continued, "and pretty soon a big one came around the corner running low on its springs. It was heavily loaded. This is it! I rushed to the curb to throw myself under the wheels and then I saw it." Harvey stopped to wipe perspiration from his forehead.

"Saw what? What did you see?" I asked.

"The vision, that's what... Oh, I don't know... I guess it was a vision... or something. Anyhow, it stopped me dead in my tracks. Just as I reached the curb, I glanced up and through the windshield of the tractor's cab, I saw the driver... a young fellow... and along side of him was a pretty young woman holding a baby in her arms."

Harvey paused. "You know," he continued, "sometimes those drivers of private rigs take their families along on short trips just for the ride... Well, you know how they say that a dying man sees his whole life pass in front of him in just a matter of seconds... Something like that happened to me, only not my past, but the future.

"My thoughts raced so fast when I saw that lady with the baby. I thought, if I should throw myself under the wheels of that tractor-trailer, the driver might see me and try to stop... his truck could jackknife, maybe turn over... maybe he and the lady and baby could be killed. Or if only I were killed, the trouble I would cause him and his wife would be inexcusable.

"Like I said, it all happened in a split second. Then, while I paused on the curb, the truck flew past. As it did, I looked into the cab... no lady... no baby, just an old bearded truck driver. I staggered back. I didn't know what to think. I leaned against the building. I was shaking like a leaf and felt sick to my stomach. What did it mean? It must have been a vision. Who sent it? Was it God or was it the devil?

"Funny what things a person thinks of in a situation like that," he continued. "I remembered something my mother used to say about an old wicked drunk who lived in our village and who had survived a number of serious accidents. She would say, 'If God don't take you, the devil must!' I thought that must be my condition, even the devil doesn't want me. I felt frightened and began to tremble. I don't know why, except maybe because I had heard that people who kill themselves go to hell.

"Anyhow, I was pretty shaken up. I walked over to Seventh Street, turned and entered Franklin Square. I wanted to talk to somebody and the skid row crowd usually ended up there about noon to rest in the shade of those big trees. You can always catch a nice breeze coming up from the river and across the open area of the bridge entrance.

"I talked to a few of the men I know. They thought I was crazy when I told them about the vision. I tried to find someone who could answer some questions about religion. Finally, one of them suggested that I wait until night and go talk to those religious fanatics that were holding street meetings that summer on the corner of Ninth and Race streets or at Eighth and Vine.

"Something unusual is happening to me, that's for sure," he said, looking at me. "I haven't had any craving for drink. I felt hungry, but knew if I tried to eat, it wouldn't stay down. So I just hung around the square, thinking... thinking. Oh, how stupid I have been to let liquor get a hold on me like it did. If I could only go back... I know I could make it... things would be different.

"I was standing in the shadows, watching you while the meeting was going on, waiting for a chance to speak to you. Once, a voice seemed to say, 'Harvey, you're crazy. The booze has your mind seeing things that aren't there. These people don't want anything to do with you. Go get yourself a drink and forget the whole thing.'

"But something the preacher said has given me some hope again. He talked a lot about sin and damnation, but then he also said that Jesus came into the world to save sinners, and that He would save from the gutter anybody that came to God through Him. I don't understand all that about coming to Jesus, but, one thing I know, I am in the gutter."

I couldn't help smiling. "Friend Harvey, about that *gutter* you say you are in. The preacher didn't say *gutter*, he said *uttermost*. He was quoting a verse from the Bible."

I opened my Bible to Hebrews 7:25 and showed it to Harvey. "Wherefore he [it's talking about Jesus] is able also to save them to the uttermost that come unto God by him, seeing he ever liveth to make intercession for them."

"Anyhow, you have the right idea. There isn't a sinner so bad that the Lord can't save him... Yes, Harvey, Jesus comes right down to the gutter and will lift you up. He'll save your soul and straighten out your life, if you'll let Him. Look, here's another verse, Romans 10:13. See what it says, 'For whosoever shall call upon the name of the Lord shall be saved.'"

Harvey looked at me, confusion written all over his face. "How can that be? Why would God be interested in me? What have I ever done but badness? That lady, Mother Bachman... after she prayed for me last night, she said, 'My son, God loves you.'"

"That's true, Harvey. God does love you. Look what Jesus said over here in John 3:16, 'For God so loved the world, that he gave his only begotten Son, that whosoever believeth in him should not perish, but have everlasting life.'"

"But, surely that must mean that He loved the good people. How could He love a sinner like me?"

"Well, Harvey, I can't explain why, but I do know that He loves us all. We're all sinners, you know. The Bible says, 'All have sinned, and come short of the glory of God.' The Bible also says here in Romans 5:8... look, read it for yourself... 'But God commendeth his love toward us in that, while we were yet sinners, Christ died for us.' You see that, Harvey? It says 'while we were yet sinners.' You see, Christ died for us sinners."

Harvey began to express more doubts, ask more questions. But now there was hope in the tone of his voice. For the next fifteen minutes, I took Harvey along what the Christian worker calls "the Roman Road to Salvation." These were all verses from the book of Romans. They showed how all men are sinners, condemned to eternal death, how Jesus came and died on the cross for the sins of all men, and He rose again "for our justification," and how that, if the sinner believes in his heart these truths about Jesus, and receives Him as Savior, he will be saved. The last reference I showed Harvey was Romans 10:9,10, emphasizing the words, "...and shalt believe in thine heart... thou shalt be saved."

"Well," exclaimed Harvey, "I've never heard such wonderful news! I think I believe... I want to believe. But how can I be sure that I'm saved? Don't I have to do something more?"

"No, there is nothing more that you can do. Jesus has done it all. All you have to do is ask Him to save you. Look at verse 13 again... read it for yourself... 'For whosoever shall call upon the name of the Lord shall be saved.' It says anybody... no matter how bad you are."

"How do I do that?"

"Easy... All you have to do is ask God to forgive you and save you. He'll do it... Wouldn't you like to do it right now?"

"Yes, I would... Will you help me?" he asked. "I've never prayed before."

"Okay... let's kneel down by our chairs. I'll pray first, then I'll say a prayer that you can repeat after me."

I prayed for Harvey, asking God to make clear the way of salvation. Then I led Harvey in the sinner's prayer. To my surprise, Harvey continued on his own.

"I thank you, Lord Jesus, for saving my soul. But could you do a little bit more for me? I want so much to make things right with my wife and my children. Please straighten out my life and help me get home again. I beg you, Lord, with all my heart. Anyhow, whatever you do, I thank you for saving me."

"Praise the Lord!... Amen!" and a few "Hallelujahs!" came from the doorway behind us. The service in the hall had ended and George and the other workers had quietly entered the inquiry room and had listened to our prayers. What a time of rejoicing we had over that one sinner who had gotten saved. They all congratulated Harvey, patting him on the back and giving him words of encouragement.

George, having had more experience in rescue mission work, took over. He, with brother John, began to counsel with Harvey Trainer. Though not an ordained minister, John Dobbs, because of his dedication to rescue mission work and his loving concern for the "down-and-outers," had become known as "brother John." It would not be easy for him in his new life in Christ, they told him. "Your friends out there will do everything in their power to get you back. But," brother John assured him, "you can count on us. We're your family now. We're brothers in Christ and we'll do everything we can to help you."

On the second floor of the mission building there was a room where a new converts' Bible class was conducted each Monday night. George quickly got Harvey's promise to attend. There was also a small kitchen, a bathroom and two small bedrooms, one of which was occupied by the caretaker.

"Harvey," offered brother John, "you may sleep in the other room tonight. Tomorrow, I will be here early and we'll see what we can do about getting you some clean clothes. I'm sure I can find a job for you."

Harvey kept wiping tears from his eyes as he kept thanking me, then George, then brother John. He just couldn't imagine that there were still people in this world who could love a skid row bum. Not only that, but God had saved him. He said he felt so different, like a million pound load had been lifted from his back.

Joe, the custodian, took Harvey by the arm. "Let's go upstairs. We'll have another cup of coffee before hitting the sack. I think there's a doughnut or two left over."

Chapter 2

Was He for Real?

"Being confident of this very thing, that he who hath begun a good work in you will perform it until the day of Jesus Christ." (Philippians 1:6)

"What do you think, George? Is Harvey for real?" I asked as we left the Mission.

The excitement of leading the man to Christ was over and I was feeling a bit let down. I was new in rescue mission work, but I had seen several disappointing cases. The "converts" would last about a week or two, maybe a month or so, and then fall back into their old ways as if they had never made a profession of faith in Christ.

George knew how I was feeling. He had gone through the same feelings. "Ed, let's not dwell on the failures. Let's remember the successes. Many of the saved men never get out of skid row, but they aren't skidding any more. They support themselves with jobs in the cheaper hotels. They do janitorial work in some of the office buildings down on Chestnut and Walnut Streets. And they still live down there in the district in some of the cleaner, but cheaper hotels or in one of the numerous rooming houses. Many still give good testimony to the saving grace of Jesus even though they never can quite return to the world they once knew."

George began to reminisce. "Remember old Nate? I was there the night he got saved. I dealt with him myself. I almost got drunk just from the smell of his breath. But we got through the prayer of acceptance of Christ and got him bedded down over at Galilee Mission. I never thought for one minute that his profession of faith was real. But, there he was in the mission service every night. He hadn't breathed a sober breath for more than fifty years. He was seventy when he received Christ and its been three years since he last drank.

"Did you hear what happened to Nate again last Sunday morning? It has happened several times. Every Sunday morning the police are out rounding up the drunks left over from Saturday night. They want to clean up the streets before the church people start out for their worship services. Last Sunday morning they picked Nate up again. The police were so used to seeing him drunk for so many years, they can't get used to the idea of him being sober.

"The desk sergeant knows him well, and when he sees them leading 'old Nate' in, he yells at the policemen, 'Let 'im go; he got religion a couple of years ago. He's as sober as my sainted mother, bless her departed soul.' So saying, he crosses himself.

"Nate gets a kick out of it. He doesn't let on at first so that he can witness to the police. He carries some Gospel tracts in his pocket and stuffs them in the pockets of the drunks, praying that they will read them in their cells when they sober up."

"I guess I need more faith when dealing with these men. By the way, George, what about that vision that Harvey had? I thought that God doesn't speak to men today through visions."

"That's right, Ed. Like Professor Smith told us, when the Apostle John finished writing the book of the Revelation, the Bible was complete. There will be no new revelation from God. Remember those verses in Hebrews, the first chapter? In olden times, God did speak to men in many different ways; visions, dreams, and even a donkey spoke to the prophet Balaam. But now, in our age, God has spoken to us by His Son Jesus, and we have His Word the Bible.

"Ed, you notice that the vision that Harvey had did not reveal any truth to him, it didn't teach him anything, it didn't preach the Gospel to him nor lead him to Christ. What it did was stop him long enough to keep him from throwing himself under that truck to commit suicide. Maybe God did send the vision to him. I don't know. Or, maybe it was just some mental picture conjured up by his poor sick mind, poisoned by all that liquor he had consumed. Anyhow, God did use it to make him think, and eventually brought him to someone who could show him God's Word and lead him to accept salvation in Christ. God does work in some marvelous and mysterious ways. One thing sure, Ed, we who have His Word should not seek to put our faith in visions, dreams, or horoscopes."

By this time, we had arrived at George's home. As was our custom, we both prayed short prayers and said good night. Before George closed the car door, he remarked, "I'm no prophet, so I can't say for sure whether Harvey Trainer will hold out or not. Only the Lord knows, but time will tell."

And TIME DID TELL.

Harvey Trainer did hold out, and he always gave the glory to Jesus, his Savior. He would testify of how Jesus had changed his life completely and how he never again had a taste for alcohol. Brother John had fitted him out with a good clean suit, shirt, tie and shoes. Then, after a shave and haircut, Harvey felt so good that he started out on his own to look for a job. No one recognized him. They thought he was just a "good guy down on his luck."

Harvey's first job was that of a waiter in one of the restaurants frequented by the men who had their businesses nearby. Harvey attended George's Bible study class for new converts every Monday night and his spiritual growth was beautiful to see. He rented a room near the Mission and attended the meetings every night; later on he helped with the singing and kept order.

It wasn't long until one of the Christian business men who helped to financially support the Mission took notice of Harvey. The man offered Harvey a job as a salesman in one of his electrical appliance stores in the city. Harvey made a good appearance and through his pleasant way of treating the customers, began to break records with his sales. The owner found out that Harvey had been a lawyer and tax consultant, and began to use his expertise in this field.

In spite of his new success in the business world, Harvey never gave up his attendance at the Rescue Mission. In the pre-meeting prayer services, he would be heard praying, not only for the church groups that came to help in the meetings, for the salvation of the men, but also that the Lord would in some way unite him with his family again. He had been in touch with his wife several times by phone but she was incredulous. She had been only a nominal church member for years, so just could not believe that anything could have changed her husband.

One night, in the Bible study class, Harvey announced that he had gotten a leave of absence and was taking a trip to his home town to see his wife and children. After class, George and the men prayed that Harvey might be reunited with his family, if it were the Lord's will.

George, and I especially, continued to pray for Harvey Trainer, but wondered why we did not hear from him. We heard from the owner of the appliance company that he had received letters from Harvey at two different times asking for an extension of his leave of absence. Then finally, a letter came, addressed to George, John and me. George and I were at the Mission on a Bible college off-night, so we read the letter together. The letter was full of praises to God.

"My dear brothers in Christ: I thank my Lord every day of my new life for how He, through you, rescued me, a lost drunken sinner on his way to hell and a Christless eternity."

Then Harvey proceeded to tell all that had happened since he arrived in his home town. He found a room in a hotel near the offices where he once worked. He called his wife to arrange to see her and the children at the Sunday morning worship service of the church where she attended occasionally. This had to tell her something for he had always refused to go to church.

Harvey then went to the law offices to see his former partners. They were glad to see him and immediately noted the change that had come over him. He told them how he had been saved, and how his life had turned completely around. They were more ready to accept him again than his wife was. He did not blame his wife for she had more to lose and certainly had gone through a lot more grief because of his former life style.

As he talked, the change in Harvey became even more apparent. His arrogance had been replaced by a sober humility. There was none of the former boastfulness. This was indeed a new Harvey who continually gave God the glory. These men were not religious, but had respect for a man's convictions though they might be different from their own.

When they heard that Harvey was once again practicing law as representative of the appliance company in Philadelphia, they did not hesitate to invite him back into the partnership. Harvey confessed to them that this was what he had hoped and prayed they would do. A few preliminary agreements were made and one of the men reached for the ever-present bottle of champagne and, with a mischievous wink of the eye, proposed, "Let's make a toast to Harvey's return to the good life."

"None for me," Harvey spoke firmly. "That good old life, as we called it, thank God, is gone forever. Christ has replaced it with better things. I will accept the truly good things which God will give me, but not those things which before ruined my life. Men, I'm not a preacher, but I must read you a verse from the New Testament which explains what happened to me when I received Christ as my Savior.

"I took my Testament from my pocket. I've never been without it since you gave it to me, my brothers. I read II Corinthians 5:17 to them. I changed it a little bit and gave them my version so my friends would better understand it. 'If any man receives Christ as his Savior, he becomes a new person; the old things of his life are finished for him, because he now is a new person in Christ and wants to please Him.'

"The fellow who suggested we drink a toast said, 'Hey guys, it looks to me like we all need some of what Harvey's got. Anyhow, welcome back, Harv, and good luck with your wife.'

"Well, I wasn't depending on luck to help me with my wife, but they didn't understand that. I was depending upon my Lord to work it all out for me... and He did.

"Sunday came, and I met my wife and children at church. After the service, I took them to lunch and then to the zoo. This gave me a chance to talk to Betty as the children ran on ahead. Betty was very reserved; didn't have much to say. I could see that she doubted and was wary of where I might lead the conversation. I couldn't blame her. I decided not to mention anything at that time about the possibility of getting back together again. I did tell her that I had been invited to rejoin my law firm partners and that I would be staying on in the city.

"Betty was working as a secretary in an office not far from ours. I found out where she usually had her lunch and went there, making it look casual, and got to talk to her again. There were other opportunities also, but I'll make the story shorter for I see that this is already quite an epistle. One day she invited me to her folks' home for dinner after church. I had always tried to carefully witness to her about what the Lord had done for me and it must have made some impression upon her for she began to attend church services more regularly.

"It was great to be with the children again if only for a few hours. My in-laws treated me very coolly at first, but they soon saw the difference Christ had made in me. I had an excellent opportunity to witness to Betty and her parents that afternoon, but I did not press them to make a decision. Toward the end of that week, Betty called me at the office to invite me to visit them on Saturday. By that time I had found a good fundamental church to attend, and when I determined from Betty that they wanted to hear more about what Christ had done for me, and how I could have given up my drinking habits, I asked if I could bring Pastor Blake with me.

"By now, you must be jumping ahead to the obvious conclusion. And you are right. Praise the Lord, Betty, her dad and mom, received the Lord that Saturday night. Pastor Blake was wonderful. I have no problem telling people about what Christ has done for me, but I don't feel capable of dealing with people who are satisfied with their nominal Christian beliefs.

"Thank God, we are a family again. The Lord is blessing in my old profession. Former clients have come back to me again. The Lord is blessing me financially, and I trust that I will be faithful in returning to Him a proper portion. Which reminds me, please find my check enclosed. It is a little offering for the work of the Rescue Mission.

"Two weeks ago, Betty and I found a nice little house that we can rent and later buy. It's not very luxurious like our old one, but adequate for us to establish our home again. The old house became available as we were looking around, but neither one of us wanted to be reminded of the things that had happened there, the drinking parties, and the arguments. That old life is behind us forever and we want to keep it that way. We want our children to see in us a real Christian mom and dad. As soon as we moved in, we started to have family devotions so as to be spiritually in touch with our Lord and with each other. Please pray for us that we will be able to lead our children to also trust in Christ as Savior.

"So, good bye for now, my dear brothers. One of these days we plan to visit Philadelphia to show the children the Liberty Bell and other historical buildings. Lord willing, we'll come by the Mission."

The letter ended with, "Yours in God's marvelous grace," and signed, "Your brother in Christ, Harvey Trainer."

Brother John broke the silence that followed the reading of the letter. "Brethren, let's join hands and pray for Harvey and his family."

I knew that each of us was praising the Lord in our heart, so I suggested, "Let's sing the *Doxology* first."

George, John and I joined hands there in the inquiry room of the Rescue Mission where Harvey had received Christ as his personal Savior. We sang the *Doxology* and George prayed.

Afterward, as George and I were driving home, he remarked to me, "So, now you have your answer. Time has proven to us that **HARVEY WAS FOR REAL!"**

Chapter 3

Three Trophies of God's Grace

"For what is our hope, or joy, or crown of rejoicing? Are not even ye in the presence of our Lord Jesus Christ at his coming? For ye are our glory and joy."

(I Thessalonians 2:19,20)

The experience that Mildred and I gained helping out in the Rescue Mission work along with activities in our home church were good preparation for our future service on the mission field in Venezuela. There were great victories as well as some disappointments. Every incident did not have a happy ending, and this too prepared us for the spiritual battles ahead.

The street meetings on skid row continued all through that summer. We were not taking classes so, along with George and his wife, we were able to attend almost every night that there were no services in our own church. George and I would help first in the street meeting, and then go over to the Mission hall for the late meeting.

One night while the street meeting was in progress, we heard a voice from a loud speaker a few blocks away. Wondering who it was, George and I walked down Race Street toward the sound. We began to understand some of the words, they were certainly not religious.

There was a young man standing on a box, belting out his message of hate of capitalism and extolling the virtues of Karl Marx. He had a small amplifier turned up to full volume. It was ridiculous for there was only a small group of men surrounding him. It is true that poverty makes a fertile field for communism to take root and grow, but the people of skid row consisted of drunks, prostitutes and drug addicts, not very good candidates for party members.

His speech finished, the young man handed out some pamphlets and copies of the *Daily Worker*, which George and I refused. George explained, "We have right here in the Bible the answers to all the social problems you can think of or make up. Jesus Christ is the answer."

The young man defended his work, claiming that he had studied the New Testament. "I have no objection to the teachings of Christ. After all, He taught the brotherhood of all men, social justice and the principles of Marx and Lenin."

"No way did Christ teach economic socialism," denied George. "True, He did condemn exploitation of the poor, but never did He teach political involvement for His disciples. Never did Christ teach that you can change society through revolution or the legislation of moral laws. Christ taught that all men should come to Him and receive Him as their Savior. Then their heart would be changed and they would love their fellowmen no matter what their race or creed might be and they would begin to deal justly with all men. Young man, I tell you, change a man's heart and you will change his attitude and life."

"Hey, that sounds good. I'd like to discuss this with you some more, preacher."

"I'm not a preacher," corrected George, "but I can and will be glad to show you what the Bible says, if you'll let me. We're on our way over to the Mission hall. Why don't you come with us and we can talk some more."

On the way to the Mission hall, we learned that the young man's name was Mike. A part time shipping clerk, Mike supplemented his income by preaching and passing out literature for the local communist cell. He also had to attend their meetings regularly.

At the Rescue Mission, we soon discovered that Mike really wasn't interested in hearing more of the Gospel message. He just wanted to argue the teachings of socialism and political revolution. Later, on our way home, George remarked to me that Mike had some far deeper problems not related to communism.

"What do you mean, George?"

"Mike's on drugs," revealed George.

"How can you know that?"

"Didn't you notice his nervous twitching, his agitation over the most simple points in our discussion, his lack of concentration? But, most of all, I could tell from his eyes."

"His eyes?"

"In the better light of the inquiry room I noticed how dilated his pupils were. They didn't even change when I put on the bright overhead light. I guess I'm accustomed to look for things like that. Then too, Ed, didn't you wonder why, on such a hot humid night like this, he had on a long-sleeved shirt? You would have thought he would have unbuttoned the sleeves at the wrist and rolled them up. I can't be sure, of course, but I would say that he wanted to hide the needle marks. Did you notice he got more nervous and had to leave suddenly, and couldn't wait one minute more though we offered to drive him to where he lived?"

I was surprised at George's observations. I hadn't noticed anything. But George had a lot more experience than I with the people on skid row. I was silent for a time as I continued to drive north on Fifth Street. Then, "From what you've said, George, and from the way Mike reacted, I don't have much hope of ever winning him to the Lord."

"Frankly, neither do I, Ed, but all things are possible with God."

********** ********** **********

There were quite a few women of all ages who attended the Mission services. These were, as were many of the men, permanent residents of skid row. Though they had made a profession of faith in Christ, for many physical or personal reasons, they felt they could not leave. They worked as waitresses or cleaning women. Some sold notions from little stands they set up along the curb on east Market Street. They attended the Mission more or less faithfully, considering it to be their church. Often, one or two would come back into the inquiry room to ask prayer for some problem they were experiencing or to seek advice. The superintendent was glad that almost every night that the church groups came down to help, they included some women who could help counsel and in this way help some of their less fortunate "sisters." These mission women came to know and respect Mildred and Loretta, George's wife, because of the love they showed, and almost always came to speak with them when they were there.

It wasn't always easy for the uptown church women to help in the services of the Mission. Sometimes they heard remarks from the men that caused them embarrassment, or they saw things that they did not want to see. Often, when quite a number of women were present in the congregation, Loretta would sing several solos and Mildred would give her testimony.

It was on one of those nights that Betty and another woman came into the Rescue Mission. It didn't take a prophet to know from their dress and manner that these two were "ladies of the night," of walking. They sat down and listened attentively through the service, and when the invitation was given, they responded by coming forward. They were invited into the inquiry room where Mildred and Loretta began to deal with them. I was already there with one of the men who had come forward earlier.

Betty's friend did the talking, changing her wad of chewing gum from one side of her mouth to the other.

"This here's Betty. She don't belong here, no way. I mean, yes, she should be here in the Mission, because that's why I brung her. What I mean is, she don't belong here in Skiddy-town, and she don't belong in our business. Ya know what I mean?"

Betty kept her head down and was nervously twisting her hanky. Mildred took one of Betty's hands in her own to make her feel more at ease, but Betty began to sob. At that, her friend put her arm over Betty's shoulders, drew her close, and continued speaking.

"Like I said, Missus, Betty don't belong here, that's all. Look at her. She's so depressed, cries a lot, and Madam is about to kick her out. Ain't that Madam's a hard woman, but Betty ain't no good this way. I been close to Betty, and it breaks my heart to see her so sad... so I told her I was going to bring her down here. I know you good people can help her."

Then Loretta spoke up, "Now I remember you. You're Patty, aren't you? You came back here, and I talked with you one night last year, right?"

Patty acknowledged, "Yeah, that was me. I tried to do what you told me, missus. I started to read the little Bible you gave me, and I even tried to pray and all that. But I guess I just don't take to religion, or maybe religion don't take to me. I don't know. Anyhow, the other girls made fun of me, and I just couldn't break away from Madam."

The room was very quiet. Patty continued, "But maybe it can be different for Betty here. I hope so. Betty don't belong here, like I said before. It was an accident, that's what it was. She got in trouble with a boy in school, and her folks kicked her out, as if they never did no wrong. Well, Betty was wandering around out there like in a daze. Madam saw her and felt sorry for her. She took Betty in and when she saw her condition, she let her stay for free. But then, Betty lost the baby. After a bit, Madam put her to work, but she's no good at it. Her heart just ain't with it... Try to help her, will ya?"

Patty stopped, took a deep breath. "I gotta get outa here, gotta get a smoke!" With that, she jumped up and almost flew out of the inquiry room door, ran down the aisle of the meeting hall, and out into the street.

Loretta turned to Betty, "How old are you, girl?"

"Nineteen... almost."

"How long have you been with a... Madam?"

"About a year."

A gasp from Mildred. "Why you were just a child when you got into trouble with that boy, poor dear."

Loretta and Mildred began to talk to Betty. They prayed with her, and showed her from the Scriptures how to be saved. "One good thing about working in a rescue mission," thought Mildred, "you have no trouble trying to convince people that they are sinners like when you're dealing with the uptown people. These people here on skid row know what they are. The problem here is that most men and women just don't care about their condition."

The two women talked to Betty for about a half hour. Betty cried a lot and kept saying, "I'll do whatever you say, only get me out of here!"

"But Betty," urged Mildred, "what you need to do first and above anything else is receive Christ as your Savior."

"Yes, yes, I'll do it. Anything. Show me how."

That wasn't exactly what they wanted to hear. Betty just wanted to escape the life she was living. They could tell that she felt nothing in her heart about Christ. Finally Loretta spoke, "Well, Betty, it won't do any good to accept Christ with the only motive being just to escape. We understand how you want to get away from life down here, but unless you receive Christ into your heart, I'm afraid you'll be right back here tomorrow."

Mildred suggested, "Why don't we lead Betty in prayer anyhow, and trust the Lord to make her understand. Maybe she will yield to Him when she has more time to think it over."

So Mildred led Betty in the repentant sinner's prayer, ending with, "And Lord, help me to understand. I want my soul to be saved as well as my life. In Jesus' name, Amen."

Loretta and Mildred again prayed for Betty, thanking the Lord for saving her. However, they confessed to each other later that they doubted if they had really "gotten through" to her.

Brother John had come in and had listened to the last part of the interview with Betty, and now Loretta filled him in with the rest of the story.

"Well," said Brother John, "we can't let her go back to Madam, nor can we send her out into the streets... let me make a phone call."

Brother John slipped into the tiny side office, and called a very dedicated Christian couple whose ministry had been to help girls like Betty. They had a small house, with just one extra bedroom which they always reserved for cases like this one.

"It's all arranged," Brother John told them. "Mildred, if you and Ed will take Betty and drop her off on your way home... here is the address... it won't take you much out of your way. It's in North Philly, on Third Street. Brother and sister Greene will be waiting for you. They have clothing Betty can use, so there is no need for her to go by Madam's house."

The Greenes knew from experience just how to treat a girl like Betty. They did not press her to talk. They let her get her bearings first. Whenever Betty did want to talk, they were there. They were willing and patient listeners as well as wise counselors. The workers at the Mission prayed for Betty, and the Lord answered their prayer. After several weeks in the Greene's home, Betty really opened her heart and asked the Lord to save her. There was no doubt about it now. Betty was a completely new and changed person, "a new creature in Christ."

But this is not the end of the story. One hot and humid night toward the end of August, George and I were down on Race Street, helping in the nightly street meetings. During testimony time Mike appeared. There was a woman with him who appeared to be much older than Mike, maybe thirty-five or forty. She was very heavy. They began to sing in loud voices, mimicking the special music sung earlier. When I spotted Mike, I joined George on the other corner. George remarked, "Mike and his girl friend are really *high* tonight. Looks like we might have trouble with them."

"But I thought Mike was attending your Monday night Bible study?"

"He does, but just to argue. Sometimes I wish he didn't come, but then... one never knows just how deep the Sword of the Spirit is penetrating into his heart and mind."

That night they had the largest group ever of men and women gathered around to listen. The amplifier was turned up a bit louder than usual so that those on the outside of the group could hear the speaker over the raucous noises Mike and his friend were making.

The preacher was a dynamic young evangelist who was being used mightily in the city in evangelistic campaigns and young peoples' rallies. Many souls, especially among the youth, were being saved. The noise didn't seem to bother the preacher. His strong stirring voice, along with his message of God's judgment and eternal hell-fire, caused many hearing him to shudder. That night, there on the street corner, several men came forward in response to the invitation and were later dealt with in the inquiry room of the Mission.

Mike and his friend became terribly agitated and almost ran down Race Street to escape the words of the preacher. Later on that night the two of them showed up at the Mission during the last service. The woman was shaking as Mike helped her to a seat. He was very pale and seemed terribly concerned for his friend.

Brother John began to give the invitation, interrupted by verses of the invitation hymn. The woman, still trembling, struggled to stand, and with Mike's help, stumbled forward toward the platform. It took Mike and another man to get her up the steps, she was so large. Brother John opened the door to the inquiry room and directed them inside.

George and I were just finishing dealing with the men who came over from the street meeting. We gave them instructions about following through with the Lord, a copy of the New Testament, and a personal invitation to the Monday night new converts' Bible study. Dismissing the men with a word of prayer, we turned our attention to Mike and his friend, who by this time was gasping for breath. Mike was crying like a baby.

George whispered to me, "These two have about had it. They must have had alcohol on top of the drugs they are into."

Brother John, coming in and, seeing at a glance what was happening, spat out the words, "Can't talk to them in this condition, and we don't have the equipment to take care of them... we just gotta pray." And pray we did.

Little by little the two grew calmer, and Mike's friend was breathing normally again. Realizing that George and I were getting ready to talk to them, Mike grabbed his friend by the arm and said, "Come on, Rosie, let's get out of here!"

George pushed him back into his chair. "No you don't, not 'til after you listen to what we have to say! You came in here tonight in need of help, and we're going to try to give it to you in spite of you, Mike. You listen and listen good! We know your condition, and you know that you can trust us. We're not going to turn you over to the cops. We do want to tell you about Christ. He is the only One who can help you and your friend."

George gave a brief presentation of the Gospel story. Rosie began to cry and, through her sobs, I barely heard her say, "Please, if you can help me... if Christ can help me... I want Him to do it."

Rosie listened attentively as she was told how a sinner could receive Christ as Savior and be saved. Then she said, "Yes, I will accept Christ as my Savior." She followed us as we helped her pray the prayer of repentance. Mike still resisted and now that the crisis was over and he was feeling better, he began to assume once again his braggadocio attitude.

"Come on, Rosie, we've had enough of this Gospel thing. Let's go get us another drink!"

"Are you crazy, Mike, we just nearly killed ourselves. Besides, I mean business. I haven't had enough of this Gospel, I want more."

Mike remonstrated, "Aw, you don't want to stay here. Come on, let's go over to my place. You'll feel different tomorrow."

Rosie saw that she would have to get tough with Mike. "Get lost, kid! No way am I going back into drugs. I'm sticking right here. Finally, I know who my real friends are, who really care about me and can help me, not someone who just wants to get from me. How about it, you mission guys?"

"That's right, Rosie; it is Christ who will help you. But, how do you feel? You almost had it, you know," George told her.

There was a loud bang as Mike slammed the inquiry room door behind him, and ran out into the street. The mission workers didn't see him again for over a month.

Rosie had been a tough character. We were all surprised to learn that she was only twenty-eight years old. From her appearance, she could have been at least forty. She had worked as a barmaid in a saloon over on Arch Street near the burlesque theatres. She had to be tough and know how to handle herself with the kind of men that came into such bars after a night in one of those theatres. On the side, she was a drug pusher as well as a user. She was the one from whom Mike got his supply, mostly for free, since she had a warm spot in her heart for him.

Rosie lived out on 20th Street, not far from where brother John and his wife had their apartment, so she went home with them. They talked until long after midnight over coffee and buns. It just didn't seem possible that such a person as Rosie could change so much and so quickly. But then, our Lord has been known to perform miracles.

Chapter 4

Mike, Rosie and Betty - Sequel

"For whosoever shall call upon the name of the Lord shall be saved." (Romans 10:13)

Rosie's testimony in the skid row neighborhood was tremendous. People could hardly believe it was the same person. She quit her job at the bar immediately, and being well-known in the area, soon got a job as a waitress in a restaurant down on Market Street. The marvel of it all was that the Lord took Rosie through the withdrawal period without any medical help.

Rosie attended the services at the Rescue Mission every night that she did not have to work. She spent much time with the workers, praying with them and learning more about Christ and His Word. She confided to the ladies that she had a husband and three little girls living out in a suburb of the city with his parents. She talked with him by phone, and told him what had happened to her. He informed her that after she had fallen into sin and was found to be living and working on the edge of skid row, he had divorced her. She hadn't contested. She had completely lost interest in him and the girls.

But now, things were different, with her heart changed by Christ, Rosie longed to see them again. Brother John called and convinced him that a great change had come over her since she had received Christ as her Savior. Her husband was indifferent, but did agree to arrange for his mother to take the children to the zoo on a certain afternoon where she could see them.

What a joy it was to see them and to hold her babies to her breast, if only for a few moments. They really didn't know her and their grandmother told them that she was an aunt visiting the city. Rosie was a practical person and knew that she would probably never be able to return to her family and the life she once knew as a respected wife and mother in a better than middle class family.

One night Rosie confided to the workers at the Mission that she was being threatened by her former drug suppliers. They would "take care of her," they said, if she didn't leave off this religious kick and come back into the business again. They told her frankly that now she was a Christian they were afraid that she would make some kind of a confession to the narcotic agents and implicate them regardless of her promises not to do so. The brethren prayed continually for her and her influence for the Gospel continued to grow in the community.

Then one day, very early in the morning, brother John received a call from the Community Hospital. The police who took Rosie to the hospital had found John's card in her purse and since there were no other identification cards, they called him. He and his wife hurried to the hospital and found Rosie barely conscious, but able to give them a brief story of what had happened to her.

There had been a number of men to be dealt with after the mission service, so it was later than usual when John and his wife dropped Rosie off at her apartment house. Rosie opened the door to enter the house, but hesitated. The hall and stairway up to the second floor were in complete darkness. She thought it strange and something seemed to tell her not to go in. But since she knew her way up to her apartment so well, she decided to go in anyway. She had taken but a half dozen steps when she felt a sharp jab in her right thigh. Her heart leaped into her throat. She knew immediately what it was. "Why didn't I check before entering the dark hall? Oh why?" she thought.

Someone, hidden in the darkness, had given her a shot of drugs. She swung her right arm out in a circle toward the hidden enemy, made contact, heard a voice crack out an oath, a scuffle and then the slamming of the front door. She felt a rush like hot water inside her leg. Her knees buckled under her, and she fell to the floor unconscious.

The next thing Rosie knew she was looking up into the faces of brother John and his wife from her hospital bed. The police had explained before they went into the room that another tenant had entered the hall and, striking a match, saw Rosie lying there. He found the light switch further down the hall, tried to rouse Rosie and when he couldn't, called the police. They didn't know how long she had lain there before the man found her.

Brother John and his wife barely had time to have prayer with her when her body was wracked with several spasms, and holding tight to their hands, Rosie gasped, "Jesus... Jesus..." and was gone.

Brother John had Rosie's former husband's phone number still in his wallet so he called to inform him of the tragedy. Her husband wanted nothing further to do with Rosie, alive or dead, but said he would pay for the funeral expenses since he still had a paid-up insurance policy on her. Brother John was well known by the police for his mission work so there was no problem getting the body released to him. Of course, there had to be an autopsy first. The cause of death was a massive overdose of morphine.

The funeral service was held in the Rescue Mission. It seemed like all of skid row crowded into the Mission hall and overflowed out into Eighth Street with the police keeping the traffic moving. Many of the business men were present as a result of Rosie's testimony during the short period of her life as a believer. The mission workers all gave short testimonies, each ending with an assurance of seeing Rosie again some day in glory. Clifford, the young evangelist, still in the area, gave a powerful and stirring message after which a number of people came forward to make a public profession of faith in Christ. Mike was spotted trying to conceal himself behind a couple of tall men standing in the doorway.

Rosie's body was buried in an old cemetery out on New Second Street. There Mike appeared in time to drop a flower on the coffin as it was being lowered into the ground. He looked terrible, unshaven, unkempt, shivering and crying audibly. In fact, George and I had to take him in hand or he would have fallen into the grave. We led him off to one side as the pastor from one of the Mission's supporting churches gave his closing remarks. Then after a short prayer for the unsaved friends that were present, he closed with, "Until the morning, Rosie. We'll see you up there with our Lord Jesus."

George and I almost had to carry Mike between us toward my car. He was shaking so he could hardly walk. Through his clenched teeth he was repeating over and over again, "I want to be saved too." Truly Rosie's death would not be in vain. For Mike it was like a last call from God to come to Him. At last he realized that he had come to the end of himself and he cried out, "Lord help me! I am a sinner!"

"The Lord is willing and ready to save all who call upon His name," we assured him. And He did!

Mike was feeling better and back at the Mission that night he gave testimony to his new found faith in Christ. Mike's soul was saved, but his body was in a horrible condition. After Rosie was saved, Mike lost his source of drugs. With no money to buy "good shots," he had to take whatever stuff was available on the street—weak, mixed with talc, contaminated. It is a wonder he had not ended up in the morgue. But now Mike was willing to do anything—anything—just to get that "monkey" off his back, and get his health restored.

George and I took Mike to the Colony of Mercy, a Christian Rehabilitation Camp in New Jersey. He spent three months there. With the help of dedicated believers operating the camp and several of the lay workers who had come that way before, Mike grew in grace and in the knowledge of his Lord and Savior. He was freed from the drug habit, never to return to it.

During the yearly Christmas banquet that was given by the Eighth Street Wayside Rescue Mission to the "down and outers," Mike appeared again. He was a changed man—robust and healthy looking, cheeks glowing red from the cold wind hitting them on his walk from the bus station. And what a wonderful testimony he gave that night. "I recommend Christ to you, my friends. My Jesus saves and keeps and satisfies."

During his stay at the Rehabilitation Camp, Mike heard the Lord's call for full time Christian service. He was sure that the Lord wanted him to become a Rescue Mission worker, to help others who were helplessly lost as he had been. Mike always contested the use of the word "helplessly." He said that he, and others like him, felt "helpless," but that there was **help** to be had. "And," he added, "thank God for those who bring us **help**, preaching salvation in Jesus Christ!"

The superintendent of the camp had made contact for him with the Bible Institute of Pennsylvania in the city, and it was arranged for Mike to enroll there beginning with the spring term. In return for his board and keep, he would do janitorial work and help in the kitchen. His tuition was guaranteed through a scholarship donated by an association of business men. Mike was later assigned by the practical work department of the college to the Eighth Street Wayside Rescue Mission, where he was to assist in the work as often as his studies and work load would permit.

Meanwhile, Betty was growing into a beautiful character, growing in grace and in the knowledge of her Savior under the loving care of brother and sister Greene. She had gotten a job as a sales clerk in a department store in Center City. That fall she had enrolled in the night courses offered by the Bible Institute.

On occasion, Betty and Mike met at the Rescue Mission services, for the Greenes often accompanied the group from their home church that went there to hold a service. Mildred and I watched a romance blossom and grow to full bloom until Mike and Betty were married the following summer. With the financial support of several of the more affluent supporters of the Mission who knew of Mike's call to rescue mission work, the happy couple spent a honeymoon in the Pocono Mountains at a Christian family camp, and then were able to move into a utility apartment near the college.

Several years went by and Mildred and I were on the mission field in Venezuela. A letter came from George who wrote about Mike's graduation and how a group of Christian business men, seeing the need in another depressed area of the city, financed the opening of a rescue mission and named Mike as Superintendent with Betty in charge of the ministry to the women.

After reading George's letter, we had a praise and prayer meeting all by ourselves and thanked the Lord for allowing us to have a small part in Mike and Betty's salvation. If Rosie in heaven knew about the events that followed her tragic death, she must also have thanked her Savior and rejoiced that the blessed work of saving souls among the "down and outers" was going on in the new Rescue Mission under Mike and Betty's ministry.

Chapter 5

Positive Faith and a Good Sense of Humor

"A merry heart maketh a cheerful countenance...."
(Proverbs 15:13a)
"A merry heart doeth good like a medicine...."
(Proverbs 17:22a)

Though some Christians seem to think so, life in the Lord's service is not entirely somber and serious. There are times of diversion, fun and laughter, laughter at comical situations which occur at unexpected moments, and laughter at one's self after making some cultural or language faux pas. A sense of humor is definitely an asset to any Christian worker whose ministry brings him into contact with the more sordid side of life.

A servant of the Lord with a good sense of humor is usually one who also thinks positively, has an optimistic faith which very often is contagious. Remember the "merry heart" and the "cheerful countenance" spoken of in Proverbs. Smile when you are making purchases and soon the clerk waiting upon you will be smiling too and will more readily listen to you when you speak a word for the Lord. We have found that the words of that old popular song are true: "When you're smiling, the whole world smiles with you."

A veteran missionary to Africa, member of our home church, remarked to mutual friends that he had no fear for our well-being out on the mission field. He said, "Ed and Mildred are optimistic, they usually think positively, and they have a good sense of humor. If they can maintain this attitude on the field, it will help keep them from getting depressed and becoming missionary casualties." We praise the Lord for this and, though we don't always succeed, we try to obey the apostle Paul's admonition, "Rejoice in the Lord alway: and again I say, Rejoice" (Philippians 4:4). We take this to mean: rejoice, glory, boast, and be happy in the Lord always.

Those days of preparation for missionary service were busy ones. The U.S. and the rest of the world were just coming to the end of the Great Depression. I had a full time job as salesman for our brother-in-law's barber supply business in which I had a small financial interest. We attended the Bible Institute of Pennsylvania on Monday, Tuesday and Thursday nights. The Eighth Street Wayside Rescue Mission was known as a late mission. The services began at 8:00 P.M. and often lasted until 11:00 P.M. On school nights, we would go to the Mission after classes.

But one Friday night in the winter, we went to the Mission with George and Loretta. Parking our car out back, we entered through the door leading into the inquiry room. As we were hanging up our coats, we heard someone singing a solo in the service—but what singing!

"Who in the world is that and what is he singing?" Mildred asked. "It sounds terrible."

The man's voice came in stronger now as he reached the chorus. The accent made it difficult to understand the words. As we quietly opened the door to the meeting hall and found seats among the young people who were conducting the meeting, the words came clearer.

"I am not unter law, I am unter grace. It vas grace dot lifted me. It vas grace dot set me free. I am not unter law, I am unter grace...." His voice faded out as if he had forgotten the last line. Whether he was out of tune, or was making up his own music, I could not tell.

The singer was a man about forty years old, slight of build. Did he have a beard, or was he just unshaven? I couldn't tell. His suit did not fit very well, but it was clean and pressed. Several of the young people were giggling, and I admit that it was all I could do to keep from laughing. This was a normal reaction the first time anyone heard "Jew Charlie" sing in his German accent.

The song finished, the man began to talk, "I praise mine Gott in himmel (God in heaven), dot I am no more unter dee law dot vas condemning me as a sinner. My Messiah found me und He said, 'Charlie, I am Jesus. You come now to me already, und I vill safe you.' I beliefed on Him und I am now safed forever since. Oh, how I luff my Jesus. Und He vill do dot for you too, mine sinner friend... just you come to Jesus now."

Concluding his testimony, he left the platform and took his seat in the congregation. Before Charlie was very far into his testimony, the giggling had stopped, and at least in our eyes, some tears welled up. They were tears of joy for "Jew Charlie's" beautiful testimony—beautiful in spite of his accent and mispronunciation. His tone of voice full of love for his Lord and Savior made the difference. Later in the evening, while the men were being served hot chocolate and sandwiches, brother John explained to us about the man.

"Brother Charlie has a little business selling fruit and vegetables from a pushcart which he parks in the street along with many others at the curbside market up on Marshall Street. He is an immigrant Jew who got out of Germany just before the Nazi Party began to take over. Through the ministry of the Philadelphia Evangelization Society he was given a Gospel tract in his native language and through further contacts was finally won to the Lord. As you have heard, his English is far from perfect, but he really loves the Lord. I don't know if he knows any other chorus. The one he sang tonight is the only one I have ever heard him sing."

"How is it that we have never seen him before?," I asked.

"Well, he only comes to the Mission on Friday nights. It seems that his orthodox Jewish custom of beginning the Sabbath on Friday at 6:00 P.M. has carried over into his Christian life. I don't know if he still really keeps the Jewish Sabbath—he doesn't talk very much—but he is here every Friday night unless he is sick, and, if given the chance, will come to the platform to sing the same chorus and give his short testimony. He stays until we close. Then you won't see him again all week unless you go to the Marshall Street curbside market."

"What is his full name?" asked Mildred.

"We don't know. When I asked him one time, he said, "Just call me Jew Charlie like everybody else. Dot ish O.K. mit me."

"The O.K. makes him a true American," John explained, with a twinkle in his eye.

We recall another comical fellow who attended the Mission services quite regularly. The workers loved him dearly in the Lord, but his actions always brought smiles to their faces. He acted like a punch-drunk boxer with the sniffles. The mission workers knew him and always called him brother William, but the mission people called him the sniffer.

When we first began to help at the Rescue Mission, we noticed a peculiar action on the part of a number of men sitting in the services. They seemed to be always sniffling.

I remarked to brother John, "Quite a number of the men out there seem to be suffering from colds; they're always sniffling. Couldn't we get some vitamins or something to give them?"

Mildred added, "Yes, and maybe we could get them some small packages of Kleenex. It turns my stomach seeing and hearing them sniffle. They ought to learn to blow their noses."

With that, brother John burst out laughing. Getting control of himself, and between some continued ha-ha-ha's, he explained.

"My dear brother Ed and sister Mildred, please excuse me for laughing, when it really isn't a laughing matter. Those men are not sniffling—they are sniffing. You see, a good many of the men use a weak kind of drug in powder form like men used snuff years ago. They rub the powder into the soft skin of their hand between the thumb and index finger. Then every little while they raise their hand to their nose and take a little sniff. It gives them a light kick, but it is habit forming and, if done in excess, can be dangerous."

He continued, "William, in his younger years, took some very severe beatings in the ring from superior boxers who used the poor guy as a punching bag, and this accounts for the jerks of his head from time to time. He also had the drug-sniffer's habit, but kicked it after he got saved. Now, even after several years, his hand will go up to his nose from force of habit."

"Oh no," exclaimed Mildred, "live and learn. This is such a different style of life down here. We really need a guide book, and we thank you, brother John, for the explanation. Please, any time and in any way you can, help us to understand."

"Yes, I will," agreed brother John. "We who have worked on skid row for so many years get used to such things and sometimes take too much for granted. It is good for you young folk to come down to help us remember. Any question you might have, don't be embarrassed, I'll try not to laugh as I did before, and I'll explain if I can."

Chapter 6

A Demon Possessed Salesman

"And he [Jesus] *said unto them, This kind can come forth by nothing, but by prayer and fasting."* (Mark 9:29)

One winter Thursday night something occurred at the Rescue Mission which the Lord used to open our eyes to the powers of darkness which Satan would always activate to hinder our ministry and to keep souls from coming to Christ. It was a valuable learning experience never to be forgotten and served to convince us of the urgent need of **continuing prevailing prayer**.

That night, George and I got there early. At the close of the first service a young man in his late twenties came forward when the invitation was given. Brother John motioned to me to take him into the inquiry room and deal with him. The young man's name was James. He was from New York City, just passing through on business. Looking for some excitement, he came down into the "red light" district. Seeing the Mission's sign outside, he came in.

I asked James if he had come forward to receive Christ as his Savior or if he had some problem for which he wanted counsel. He said that he was a Christian, but as the conversation continued, it became obvious that, while he may have been a member of some church, he certainly was not a believer in the true evangelical sense of the word. He wanted to argue with me over every truth that I presented in explaining the Gospel.

Finally, in an angry voice, James said, "I really don't believe that God exists. If He does exist, He certainly isn't a God of love. I don't believe He is interested in us down here on earth, and furthermore, He doesn't answer prayer."

"Why do you say that?" I asked.

"Because my mother has been an invalid now for four years and is in continual excruciating pain. I have prayed and prayed for her healing or, at least, that God would take away her pain, and He doesn't do it, that's why."

I tried to explain. "Now wait a minute, I want to say this as kindly as I can, but it is evident from what you have told me that you have never been born again. You may be a Christian in the generic sense like so many others are, but by your own confession, you have never accepted Christ as your Savior."

I had hardly gotten the last words out of my mouth, when James became extremely agitated and began to curse and swear. However, quickly regaining his composure, he said, "Excuse me, please, I just feel angry with God because of my mother's condition. It isn't fair."

I tried to continue. "Well, what I was going to try to explain was that before God will answer your prayers, you must first get the sin question settled. Like I was telling you before, you must repent of your sins and ask God to save you. The Apostle John said in his Gospel, chapter 1 verses 11 and 12, 'He came unto his own, and his own received him not. But as many as received him, to them gave he power to become the sons of God, even to them that believe on his name.'

"Now you are a lost sinner, at enmity with God. But after you become a child of God, you will be able to pray for your mother with more assurance. God will answer your prayer, if it be His will. Right now God wants to hear you pray—'God be merciful to me a sinner, and save me in the name of Jesus Christ, the Lord.'"

Again James became very agitated and seemed to be trying not to say anything. I looked up from my Bible and saw George standing just inside the doorway where he had been listening.

"Hi, George—meet James. I have been trying to explain the Gospel to him, but I can't seem to find the right words.— James, this is George. He has had more experience than I. Maybe he can help you."

I vacated the chair where I had been sitting, assuming that George would take over.

George sat down in front of James, opened his Bible and got right to the point. "The Bible says in Romans 3:23 '...all have sinned, and come short of the glory of God,' and again in Romans 6:23 it says, '...the wages of sin is death; but the gift of God is eternal life through Jesus Christ, our Lord.'"

James started to shake and to swear at George and me, accusing us of trying to force our religion on him. We were astounded at James' sudden reaction. But he immediately calmed down and again apologized for the outburst.

George began again, showing James from the Bible the Gospel truths. George placed his open Bible in James' hands and had him read for himself several portions. Finally, George turned to Romans 10:8-10, and pointing to it, asked James to read it aloud, explaining that this was what he had to do to be saved.

James started to read. He got through verse eight and started on verse 9, "That if thou shalt confess with thy mouth the—the—the..." and couldn't go any further. Again he started to tremble.

George took up the reading. "...confess with thy mouth the Lord Jesus."

James again began to swear and curse and threw the Bible to the floor. Just at that moment, the outside door opened and in walked Mother Bachman.

"Good evening, my brothers. It has been a good day. Praise the Lord." She smiled and nodded to us as she removed her coat and scarf and hung them up on the rack. Then, as she started to walk past us to go into the meeting hall, she paused and looked intently at James.

"Son," she spoke sharply to George, "son, hold everything. I suggest prayer before you go any further. Here at the Mission, we always kneel down when we pray."

Thus saying, she took James by the arm, and to him she said, "Young man, you kneel down right down here in front of your chair—there, that's right."

Then whispering to George, "You stand here in back of him. Put your hands on his shoulders, and press your knees into his back, and no matter what happens, don't let him get up!"

Without taking a breath or even waiting for George to take his position, Mother Bachman started to pray. There were no flowery introductions, just the same short sentence repeated over and over again. "Lord, rebuke the devil and send the demons away, in the name of the Lord Jesus Christ... Lord, rebuke the devil and send the demons away, in the name of our Lord Jesus Christ."

George had quickly taken the position as instructed, and as Mother Bachman continued to pray, James started to tremble and shake all over and then tried to get up. George was a big man, muscular and strong, but it took all the strength he had to hold James down. George pressed his knees hard into James' back. His knuckles were getting white from the pressure he was putting on James' shoulders. No one was aware of how much time the battle against the powers of darkness continued, but just as George thought he would have to let James go, Mother Bachman prayed, "Thank you, Lord Jesus!"

James relaxed completely, his head dropped to his clasped hands on the seat of the chair, and he began to sob like a child. George released his hold on James, stood up straight while he tried to unbend his fingers.

"Now go ahead, George, lead the boy to Christ," said Mother Bachman, squeezing George's shoulder as she passed by, and went out into the meeting hall to see if there were any women needing counsel.

I helped James up to a sitting position on the chair as George sat down in front of him with his Bible open. I continued to pray silently as George began again to explain the Gospel to the young man. There was no further erratic reaction on the part of James when the name of Jesus Christ was mentioned. After a time, James bowed his head, confessed himself a sinner before God and asked Christ to come into his heart and save him. George and I both prayed for James, asking the Lord to guide him through his problems and to protect him from any further Satanic attacks.

James stood up and clasped George's hands in his and then mine, and then embraced us both. Then standing back and looking at us, he exclaimed, "Oh, wow! How different I feel. I can't explain it. It feels like a big cloud of—what can I call it?—confusion has gone from my head. I feel like I have been so mixed up—like I didn't even know who I was. Oh boy! How depressed I have been. I often thought of taking my life. But was that me, or somebody else? Anyhow, I have never felt so good in all my life!"

I then gave him some further words of encouragement, quoted a few more verses of Scripture, and then said, "Brother James, you know you are now our brother in Christ. You can now pray for your sick mother, God will hear you for you are now His child."

"My sick mother?" asked James, a perplexed expression on his face. "Oh my—of course—I lied to you—or was it me? Mother passed on years ago. I guess I was just trying to make excuses for not wanting to believe. But that is all different now. Please forgive me. My mind is clear now and I know what I must do. I've got to get back to my hotel and pack. If there is a bus out of here tonight for New York, I'll take it—gotta get home!"

Brother John joined them in prayer as we committed James into the Lord's hands. There was no doubt in our minds that James was now a saved man, freed from the demons that had been tormenting him.

As I drove up Fifth Street to drop George off at his house, we were silent, absorbed in our thoughts about the new and strange experience we had. Finally, I broke the silence.

"George, I never expected to see anything like that here in the States. I have been reading up on spiritism and demonism as reported by missionaries out in Africa and China. But here in good old Philadelphia, Pennsylvania?"

"Well, Ed, I guess the devil is busy all over the world, but I have been thinking about Mother Bachman. She is something else again. Somehow or another she must be able to tell when a person has an evil spirit. You know it is rumored that she also has the gift of healing."

We continued in silence, just thinking, until we arrived at George's house. Then I said, "The next time Mildred and I visit with Mother Bachman, I'll ask her about this incident with James."

Chapter 7

Mother Bachman

Part 1 - A question of healing

"My son, attend to my words;... keep them in the midst of thine heart. For they are life unto those that find them, and health [medicine] *to all...."* (Proverbs 4:20-22)

We want to dedicate this chapter of our memoirs to Mother Bachman. She was a wonderful and beautiful person, dedicated to her work as a volunteer at the Galilean Rescue Mission, located just about three city blocks away from the Eighth Street Wayside Rescue Mission. The Galilean Rescue Mission held early services each night, closing about 9:00 P.M. Then the men who had been previously registered were allowed to go upstairs to bed down. Mother Bachman, then in her late sixties, was in charge of the registry on four nights of the week.

Quite often, after her work was done and she had counseled with the women attending the service, she would walk over to the Eighth Street Wayside Rescue Mission and help in the service there. When this mission closed for the night she usually got a ride home with one of the church groups. Whenever Mildred and I were there, we would take her home.

We were always happy to be with this elder sister in Christ, who always had a wise word of counsel and encouragement for us, urging us to continue our preparation for the foreign mission field. If we left the Rescue Mission early, we would stop in and visit with her for a little while over a cup of tea. Sometimes we would see her at the Berachah Church when we visited there for some special service and then take her home. On one occasion we saw her as we were leaving the service, and Mildred suggested we hurry to overtake her and offer her a ride home.

"Praise the Lord," cried Mother Bachman as she saw us. "I was wondering how I would get home tonight. During the service the Lord told me to give a dollar to that poor lady with all those children. I did, and then I realized that it was the last dollar I had. I told the

Lord that He would have to get me a ride or give me the strength to walk. I determined not to tell anyone. And here you are, dear young folk. The Lord sent you."

Mother Bachman had quite a reputation among the people of her home church as well as with others who knew. She had been a private practical nurse most of her life. Since her retirement, she had devoted her time as a volunteer worker at rescue missions.

Mother Bachman had such patience and a spirit of tranquility that the doctors liked to use her, especially in cases where the patient had some terminal illness. Her very presence seemed to work miracles. There was always marked improvement in the patient's condition and in some cases complete healing.

Mildred and I had determined that on some convenient occasion we would ask Mother Bachman about her reputation of having the gift of healing. Such an occasion came the night we met her at Berachah Church and took her home. We accepted her usual invitation to stop in for a cup of tea. The missionary speaker to whom we had just listened in the church service had told a story of miraculous healing resulting in a whole tribe coming to the Lord for salvation. We spoke about that and then asked Mother Bachman frankly about the reputation she had.

Mother Bachman told us that she never claimed to have the gift of healing. How then, we asked, were there so many cases, through the years of her nursing career, in which the patient was healed when the doctor had said there was nothing more he could do?

"My dears," replied Mother Bachman, "that is something we will have to ask our Lord Jesus when we are in glory with Him. I'm sure I don't know."

"But there must be something different about you, Mother Bachman," urged Mildred. "Can't you think of anything that you do differently than other nurses? George told us one day that many of the doctors prefer to have you as the nurse on their most difficult cases."

"Well, Mildred dear, I am, of course, a child of God through faith in His dear Son, but not many nurses take religion seriously. I believe in praying about everything. So, when a doctor calls me, I pray about it first to see if it is the Lord's will. When I am sure of that, I go, asking the Lord to help me win the patient for Christ if he is not already a believer. I try to do my best to care for the patient, but my first concern is always his spiritual well-being. If he allows me to do so, I will read verses to him from the Bible. I try to get the patient to commit his life and physical problems into the Lord's hands, and to ask God to do His will whether for better or for worse. I take every opportunity to talk to the patient about his need of a Savior. Many of my patients have gotten saved, some have not. Many have gotten healed and some have not. Whatever good work was done, the Lord did it."

So, we had the answer. No question about a special gift of the Spirit, unless you mean the gift of a beautiful, tranquil soul in the body of a motherly practical nurse. Mother Bachman simply went about her chores as efficiently as possible. Her sweet character, her wonderful quietness, and faith in God gave assurance to the patient, producing in his heart a tranquility and restfulness that did as much as the medicine to effect the cure. The doctors observed this and made the most of it. When Mother Bachman was younger, she was in constant demand. The doctors apparently believed that, "A merry heart doeth good like a medicine..." (Proverbs 17:22a).

Many of her patients appreciated her for her counsel and honored her, some as their spiritual mother in the Lord. Mother Bachman did admit that in her lifetime there had been some twenty-three cases that were pronounced terminal, but which the Lord had healed. There were other cases that she remembered when the patient died after accepting Christ as Savior, and these cases too were cause for much rejoicing. God always received the glory.

In those days, I did not have the biblical knowledge to be able to say yes or no to such an assertion. Now, after years of Bible study and research, I am able to categorically declare that the gift of healing and other similar gifts ceased to exist with the close of the apostolic age. This, of course, is not to say that God does not heal. He certainly does, if He so chooses. But, in this day and age, God does not give to any person in particular any of the special gifts of the Spirit that were used to empower the apostles and their fellow-disciples to prophesy and to write the Sacred Scriptures. These gifts were for a particular time in history.

Part 2 - A question of discernment of spirits

> *"For we wrestle not against flesh and blood, but against principalities, against powers, against the rulers of the darkness of this world, against spiritual wickedness in high places."* (Ephesians 6:12)

It was a severely cold night in January. I stopped our car in front of Mother Bachman's home. Instead of the usual short word of prayer, Mother Bachman said, "You have to come in for some tea. It's not too late and it will warm you up a bit. The Mission hall was really cold tonight. Besides, I baked some fruit cookies I'm sure you will like. It's my own recipe. It's like fruit cake, only small like a cookie and very short. They melt in your mouth."

It didn't take any urging for us to accept for it was really cold and I also wanted the chance to ask Mother Bachman about that incident with James. Removing our overcoats, we sat at the old-fashioned round table. It did not take long to brew the tea and soon we were enjoying the cookies. The room was made more pleasant and colorful by the light reflecting from the stained-glass lampshade hanging over the table. Then Mother Bachman reached for a small package and handed it to Mildred.

"Mildred dear, do you remember telling me how cold your feet get during the night in the winter? Well, here is something to warm them up."

Mildred opened the package and removed a pair of beautifully knitted foot warmers. They were like booties, only larger, of course. "How thoughtful," exclaimed Mildred as she leaned over to kiss her on the cheek. "They will surely come in handy tonight. Those sheets get awfully cold."

"Mother Bachman, there is something I would like to ask you to explain, if you can. Do you remember that young man, James?"

Mother Bachman nodded.

"How did you know that James was demon possessed?"

"Son, I don't know how I knew. I just knew. When I entered the inquiry room that night, I felt kind of a chill. I felt that there was an evil presence there. When I looked at James, I just knew that the devil was controlling his life. I can't explain any more about it. I just knew that we had to pray the demons away or the boy would never get saved."

"But you took over like—what shall I say—a professional. I don't like that word, but what I mean to say is that you knew just what to do. Has that ever happened before?"

Mother Bachman thought for a few moments, and then said, "Well, yes, it has happened, maybe two or three times in my life." And then, with a twinkle in her eyes, she continued, "I know what you are thinking, my dear Edward. No, I do not have the gift of discernment. But I do have the Lord living in my heart and sometimes He gives me feelings—urges, maybe—about the brethren or the unsaved with whom I come in contact, and I try to act upon them.

"But that is neither here nor there, dear young folk. It is the "right now" that is important. I have been praying for you, and feel that now is the time to tell you what is on my heart. You are preparing to go out as missionaries to Venezuela, but before you go you must know what missionary work is all about, whether here at home or out in a foreign country. My dears, we are engaged in a war—a spiritual war against Satan and the forces of darkness. You have to know this. Of course, the devil is a defeated foe. Christ got the victory over him when He shed His blood on Calvary. But the devil doesn't give up. He continually tries to hinder the Lord's work and keep lost souls from coming to Jesus.

"In his war against the Lord's work, what he likes to do most is attack the personal lives of the missionaries. He will attack you when you are all alone out there so you must be prepared and know what to do. You must always spend time in prevailing prayer or the devil will stop you and send you home defeated. Don't let this happen. Now just in case you think this is nothing more than the ramblings of a scared old woman, see what the Lord says about it in Paul's letter to the Ephesians. Look here in chapter 6, verses 10 through 20."

Mother Bachman opened her Bible and we read the portion together. She pointed especially to verse 12. "For we wrestle not against flesh and blood, but against principalities, against powers, against the rulers of the darkness of this world, against spiritual wickedness in high places."

"I don't want to think of you two out there like babes in the woods, not knowing what to do or where to turn. Study God's Word, put on the whole armor of God. This will not only protect you but will enable you to penetrate the enemy's territory, win souls and gain victories. You think the work is hard here, just wait until you're in Venezuela. Satan isn't going to like your going into territory which has been his for many centuries.

"Do you know, Ed and Mildred, I think that this is why you had that experience at the Mission with James, so that you would ask me about it, and we could have this talk together. Now go on home. Thank you for dropping me off and coming in for tea and my cookies. God bless you and go with you."

"Thank you so much for the booties," Mildred said as she embraced Mother Bachman and kissed her on the cheek.

"Thank you for the advice, Mother Bachman. I am beginning to realize that we really are in a great war. Please continue to pray for Mildred and me, that we do not fail our wonderful Lord and Savior. I'll never forget what you told us tonight. Thank you again."

I never did forget it and, in fact, I began to study more about the Christian's warfare and how to engage in it. Mildred and I were to have more than one occasion to thank the Lord for this truth that began to be taught us in such a practical way while we were still preparing to go out on the foreign mission field in Venezuela.

II
Spiritual Preparation

Chapter 8

Personal Testimony
Salvation and Call to Missionary Service

> *"Jesus... said... Verily, verily, I say unto thee, Except a man be born again, he cannot see the kingdom of God."*
> (John 3:3)

> *"My sheep hear my voice, and I know them, and they follow me: And I give unto them eternal life; and they shall never perish, neither shall any man pluck them out of my hand. My Father, who gave them to me, is greater than all; and no man is able to pluck them out of my Father's hand."* (John 10:27-29)

Before we relate to you how the Lord dealt with us in that transition period while Mildred and I were getting ready for full-time service, between our Bible Institute days and our first term as missionaries in Venezuela, you ought to have a clearer picture as to where we came from, where we were going, and how we got there, spiritually speaking. I like to call it "**Our Theological Pilgrimage**," a journey from uncertainty to a positive assurance in God.

Mildred and I came from families devoted to two different protestant churches. Each family, though not spiritually inclined, was religiously loyal to its particular denomination. Neither of us can remember ever hearing the Gospel preached. My church Sunday School had us repeat in unison, Sunday after Sunday, the beatitudes, the Ten Commandments, the Apostles' Creed, the "Lord's Prayer," and certain selected statements from the catechism. I memorized many verses of the Bible.

I was a young teen when my family moved to another neighborhood. Since my denomination had no church there, I started to attend an even more liberal church. Mildred was attending this church rather than her own because her girl friends went there. In that church we met and began to date. A few years later, we married.

We were married a little over a year, when we attended several meetings of an evangelistic campaign conducted by Gypsy Smith in the famous old Baptist Temple on North Broad Street in Philadelphia. On the night of November 5, 1931, we both stood in answer to the invitation to accept Christ as our personal Savior, and hand in hand we descended the stairs from the balcony, along with some 150 others.

There were no workers prepared to deal with us personally, to help us understand better from the Bible the step we had taken. Gypsy dismissed the congregation and then gave the group standing before the platform a short word of exhortation about being faithful to Christ, and sent us home. We were happy about what we had done and the next day told our pastor about it. His reply was, "What did you do that for? You've always been good kids."

Our pastor was a "good" man, lovable and faithful in exhorting us to live the "good life" and to be faithful in church attendance. But, in all the conversations I ever had with him, he never mentioned anything about being "born again." Some months later I felt called of God to study for the ministry. My pastor was overjoyed, gave me some pastoral studies prescribed by our denomination, and obtained a limited scholarship for me to attend classes in the denomination's college and seminary located in Westminster, Maryland.

After we had made that profession of faith, Mildred and I gave up our worldly habits and diversions. But, during that first year of college, we returned to some of our former vices, weakly following the example of some of our fellow ministerial students. But we lasted only a year in college due to lack of funds. We had to get secular employment. Later, we praised the Lord for this; otherwise, if I had continued in that program, I would doubtless have ended up as a modernistic liberal preacher.

During that time of uncertainty as to our future, the Lord sent a special blessing. On December 30, 1933, our first son, Elias Edward V,

Ed and Mildred with Eddie, 3 weeks old
(Elias Edward Schwartz V)

was born. After about two years we moved back to Philadelphia where I took a salesman's job in Mildred's brother-in law's business. It was back in the old church where we met George and Loretta Toms. George, a preacher's son, along with Loretta, had accepted Christ as Savior about two years earlier. We began meeting in their home Wednesday and Sunday nights after our church service to study the Bible together following Dr. Scofield's notes.

One of the first things we experienced as a result was the **positive assurance** of our eternal salvation. Prior to this time we thought that even after we professed faith in Christ, we could be lost, and that we would have to get saved all over again. Now **we knew** the truth, that it was **Jesus Christ** who had saved us and not we ourselves, and that He would keep us eternally saved (John 10:27-29). What a marvelous peace flooded our souls, a peace "which passeth all understanding," a peace based upon a positive assurance in our hearts and minds that we now possessed an eternal salvation that could not be lost.

The second truth that was made real to us was our need to be Scripturally baptized. Mildred had been christened as a baby and I had been sprinkled when I joined the church. Now we wanted a believer's baptism, which we obtained in Berachah Church. Though we understand things a bit differently now, and since Berachah did not require us to become members, we elected to remain in our own protestant church.

We continued our study of the Bible with the Scofield notes, but soon felt the need for more formal Bible training. George, Mildred and I, enrolled in the evening school of the Bible Institute of

Pennsylvania, which later, joined with the Philadelphia Bible School to become the Philadelphia College of Bible. That first year, during a Victorious Life Conference, we yielded ourselves fully to serve the Lord whenever and wherever He directed.

The Lord's call to full-time missionary service didn't come to us through visions or night dreams. He didn't send a message from heaven in flaming letters written across the sky. His will became known to us gradually, over a period of time, through very normal circumstances as we listened to missionaries from various parts of the world give reports of their work.

Moreover, we knew a young couple, the Fletchers, working as missionaries in Venezuela. We contributed small amounts toward their support and received letters from them telling us of their needs and the need for more missionaries. As we prayed for them the conviction gradually grew that the Lord wanted us to serve Him in Venezuela. It was then in the late fall of our second year in Bible college.

So, when Mildred and I were sure about our call to foreign missionary service we applied to Baptist Mid-Missions, the agency under which the Fletchers were serving. But there was a problem. We were not prepared for the letter that came to us from the mission office, along with initial forms to be filled out. The letter stated that we had to be members of an independent Baptist church.

By this time, we were without a home church. As we attended Bible College, we began to teach in our Sunday School classes and Youth Society, the Bible truths we were learning. The pastor became very disturbed with us for teaching that salvation was by grace, through faith, without works, and that the believer's salvation was eternally secure. It wasn't long before the four of us were asked to give up our classes and withdraw our membership.

Loretta joined Fellowship Church, a fundamental non-denominational church in her neighborhood. George joined Berachah Church, one of the first of the separatist churches in the area, where he was given the opportunity to teach the Men's Bible Class of the Air. Mildred and I began attending different churches in search of one that preached the true Gospel and taught that the Bible was the Word of God. As yet we had not found one.

We did work, however, for almost a year in a small evangelical church. It was conveniently located across the street from our apartment in lower Nicetown. We taught Sunday School classes and organized a young people's society for the student pastor. When a permanent pastor was appointed, we were asked to join the church or else we could not continue serving there. When we examined their doctrinal statement we discovered that it was essentially the same as the church from which we had separated. Of course, we excused ourselves from that work.

So when the letter came from Baptist Mid-Mission telling us that in order to proceed with our applications we had to be members of a Baptist church, we were very disappointed. We had decided never to become members of a denominational church, and at that time we thought that Baptist was just the name of another religious denomination.

"I don't understand it. I was sure that the Lord was leading us to apply to Baptist Mid-Missions," I complained to Mildred.

Mildred agreed, "So was I. Where did we go wrong? I was sure that some day we would be in Venezuela under the same mission agency as the Fletchers... Now what do we do?"

I re-read the letter. Suddenly it dawned upon me. "Wait a minute. Look, Mildred, the letter says 'an **Independent** Baptist Church.'"

"So... what's the difference between an Independent Baptist Church and a regular one?"

"That's a good question and may be the answer to our problem. I am just as sure as you are that we are to go out under Baptist Mid-Missions. If the Lord is really leading us, and I believe He is, He will give us the answer."

We were both silent for a few minutes, then, when I was just about to suggest that we have prayer about it right then and there, Mildred spoke first.

"Ed, didn't you tell me one time that a fellow who graduated with you from high school had gone to seminary and was a pastor? I think you said he was a Baptist."

"You're right, maybe he can help us. He should be in the Yellow Pages under clergy."

Leafing quickly through the telephone directory, I soon found my friend's name and phone number. I was able to arrange a meeting with Rev. Charles Dear for the following evening. After Pastor Dear listened to our explanation about our call and that we had expected to go to Venezuela under Baptist Mid-Missions, he admitted that he did not have all the answers.

"But," he said, "there is a difference between a Baptist church that belongs to the Convention and an Independent Baptist church. My home church, which ordained me, belongs to the Convention. The church which I pastor is an independent church which was started only about two years ago. My pastor was angry with me when I accepted the call to this church."

We then asked, "But, what is the difference?"

"Well, I don't think there is any difference in what is taught. I think that we teach essentially the same doctrines that you are learning down at the Bible College. I am not sure of all the ramifications, but I think that a number of Baptist churches withdrew from the Convention, because liberal theologians are allowed to teach in the Baptist colleges and seminaries. Many pastors tried to get the Convention to remove those men but to no avail. So they took their churches out of the Convention. Now my church is a new one—never was in the Convention—and it was started by an independent missionary."

Mildred spoke up, "Ever since we left our former church, we have been looking for a church whose doctrine and practice is as close to the teachings of the Bible as possible."

"Like I said when I talked briefly with Ed on the telephone last night, I think that Baptist churches are as close to the New Testament church as they can possibly be. If this were not so, I would not be pastoring one of them."

Pastor Dear gave us a copy of the constitution and doctrinal statement of his church. After careful study of this document and several little prayer meetings about the matter, we applied for membership in the Crescentville Baptist Church. Pastor Dear and the members of the church accepted our baptism by immersion done in Berachah.

A week or so after this, we filled out the rest of the forms and sent them in to the Baptist Mid-Missions office. We were examined and accepted as missionaries to Venezuela in August of 1940, between our second and third year of Bible College.

Note:

Our **Theological Pilgrimage** was by no means ended when we graduated from Bible College and were on the mission field. It was especially there that we became Bible-believing Baptists, not for convenience, but by **conviction**. As we worked to lead souls to

Christ, disciple them, teach them the Word of God and get them organized into a local church, we ourselves continued to learn more and more sound Biblical doctrine. As yet, we have not "arrived," our **pilgrimage** continues. After 54 years of missionary church-planting, and teaching in Bible institutes, we find ourselves still learning. There are many things we do not understand. Some day, when we are with the Lord in glory, we plan to ask Him about them. Meanwhile, we are content with what the Lord has permitted us to learn.

> *"The secret things belong unto the* LORD *our God; but those things which are revealed belong unto us and to our children forever, that we may do all the words of this law."*
> (Deuteronomy 29:29)

Chapter 9

"The Battle Is The Lord's"

Faith for financial needs - Raising missionary support
Out to the field in a hurry -
"The King's business requireth haste"

> *"Wherefore take unto you the whole armour of God, that ye may be able to withstand in the evil day, and having done all, to stand."* (Ephesians 6:13)
>
> *"Commit thy way unto the Lord; trust also in him; and he shall bring it to pass."* (Psalm 37:5)

"Ed, what you have to do is get as many as possible of God's people praying for you. I mean people who really know the Lord and believe that He hears and answers prayer. I mean, and listen Ed, this is important. I mean people who know God's Word and understand that there is a spiritual war going on, that Satan is our enemy who is fighting against us and that if victories are to be won on the mission field, the missionary must be upheld with prevailing intercessory prayer."

We had just informed George and Loretta that we had been accepted by Baptist Mid-Missions as missionaries to Venezuela. In the course of our conversation, we had mentioned our concern about financial support. I, for one, had not yet learned to wait upon the Lord and commit future needs into His hands. George proceeded, as was his custom, to lecture us. We listened carefully for we appreciated very much the counsel given by this older and more mature brother.

"Your financial needs," continued George, "are the least of your problems. Our heavenly Father is rich, He owns the cattle on a thousand hills. All the silver and gold are His, and when you need it, He will send some your way. It is the spiritual aspect of your call and preparation that is of utmost importance.

"What you need **first** of all is **prayer**. You need a goodly number of prayer warriors holding you up before the throne of grace, especially when you are out there on the front line of the battlefield. So, get busy, Ed and Mildred, and tell as many believers as you can about your call to the mission field and ask them to promise to **pray** for you. The Lord will supply your needs, get you to the field, take care of you out there, and use you in His service."

Right then and there, in the living room of George and Loretta's home, we had a prayer meeting. The main prayer request was that we would have the wisdom needed to prepare ourselves for missionary service. Later on, at home, Mildred and I covenanted with the Lord that, with His help, **we would not mention our financial needs unless we were specifically asked about them.** We would just ask God's people to become our prayer partners.

A few nights after that conversation, I couldn't sleep. I whispered, "Hon,... are you awake?"

"Yes, I am," Mildred replied sleepily, as she rolled over, and looked at the clock on the bedtable. The dial read 2:00 A.M. We had stayed awake until after twelve talking about our plans to get to the mission field. Now, after two hours, I was still awake thinking.

"Mildred, I have been thinking about what Mother Bachman said the other night, and what George counseled us to do about getting financial support. The advice they both gave us was pretty much the same and makes good sense."

"Yes," agreed Mildred. "How can I forget what Mother Bachman said about us going into Satan's territory. It's scary. She said that we would be engaged in a real spiritual warfare as we try to win souls to Christ."

"That's right, and George's advice coincides when he said that we need as many prayer warriors as possible to intercede for us as we go. I have been trying to think of what we should do. Our church knows about our call and has promised to back us up, but until now we have just casually mentioned it to our fellow students and a few others who have promised to pray.

"Our brother-in law already knows that I'll be leaving the business after graduation and devoting my time to contacting churches. We will not mention finances, just ask them to pray for us. We'll just trust the Lord to put it in the hearts of God's people in the churches to ask us about our needs. Hopefully, some will take us on for financial support.

"Do you remember that tract I showed you the other day, the one I found at the college book store, called *Intercessory Foreign*

Missionaries? Well, I think that we should write to the author and get a quantity of them to give out when we give our testimony in the churches. In fact, I am thinking of using what the tract says as the outline for my messages when I appeal to people to pray for us. The tract really shows from God's Word how missionaries **urgently** need believers to dedicate **definite periods** of time each day to pray for the **definite needs** of their missionaries, and shows how they should go about it."

"What about our prayer cards, Ed? Will Dick Ward have them printed soon?"

"Yes, he is going to have them finished this Friday."

"Well, we had better get to sleep, Ed. Exams are coming up soon and, what with going down to the Rescue Mission so much, we haven't spent much time in studying."

"Right you are, Mildred. I just hope now that we have talked a little, I can stop thinking and get to sleep."

Our first prayer reminder card

In a short time we had secured a quantity of the *Intercessory Foreign Missionaries* tract. Early in March, we started to get opportunities to speak in some local churches. Invitations came without asking for them. Wherever we spoke, a copy of this tract was given along with a copy of our prayer-reminder card to all who would promise to pray for us on a regular basis.

Hundreds of copies of the tract were distributed. We emphasized our need to have believers pray for us at definite periods each day. We promised to keep our intercessory missionaries, as the tract called them, informed of specific needs for ourselves and for the work. We would let them know when and how their prayers were answered and tell them also of victories won and souls saved, for praise and thanksgiving.

George began to set up a special prayer band for us among the members of his various home Bible classes. By the time we left for the field he had more than a hundred believers willing and ready to pray at a moment's notice. Once on the field, whenever we had an emergency problem, we could write to George, or send him a cablegram. When he heard from us, George would contact some key persons who would in turn call those on their list of prayer warriors, so that within a matter of minutes more than a hundred intercessors would be at work.

We testify here and now that whatever success we have had on the various mission fields was not due to any special ability on our part, but was rather due to the many faithful prayer warriors interceding on our behalf. All the glory goes to God who gives the increase.

Well, it was Spring of 1941, final exams at the Bible College were over, as was graduation. We had finalized our plans, so we thought. I gave up my work as salesman in my brother-in-law's company to devote full time to deputation work. We would trust the Lord to supply our needs. He had already done so in part through a small interest in the business which we now cashed in. This would help pay our living expenses during the year of deputation.

Graduation - George, Mildred and Ed, May 1941

We began to pray in earnest that the Lord would open more doors for us to give our testimony in churches. We figured that it would take us at least a year, maybe eighteen months, to raise the necessary monthly support to go to Venezuela. This was the average time needed during the late 30's and early 40's. But then the Lord took over! He began to work so rapidly that even the thirst of my "hurry-up" spirit was soon to be more than satisfied.

The minimum support which the Mission had advised us as necessary was $100.00 a month for us as a couple and $25.00 additional for our son, Eddie, Jr., now 7 years old. This must make our readers smile for it seems like such a ridiculously low amount compared to what missionaries need now. But then, when we could buy a loaf of bread for five cents, and three pounds of hamburger for a quarter, a dollar went a great deal further than it does today.

We had $20.00 monthly support promised by our home church, plus $5.00 additional promised by a businessman friend of ours. This support began at once to help us through the period of deputation. It was a blessing because many churches do not begin their promised support until the missionary is on the field.

Then, Monday of the last week in May, we received a letter which began to change our plans considerably for that summer. The letter was from Dolores Finley in Elyria, Ohio. We had met Dolores in August 1940, during a Baptist Mid-Missions conference held in the Madison Avenue Baptist Church in Patterson, New Jersey. At the time of this conference, Dolores had just returned to the U.S. from Venezuela for a year's furlough.

In her letter, after a brief introduction, Dolores gave us the reason for writing to us. She was due back on the field sometime toward the end of the summer. Dolores explained, "It is neither proper nor safe for a single lady missionary to travel alone, overland through wild country from Caracas to El Callao. So, that is why I urgently need you to accompany me."

"This year?" Mildred gasped.

"Yes, she means this year... Why, here it is almost June and she expects us to get ready in three months! There's no way that we could possibly do it."

Mildred agreed. "Why we have only 20 per cent of our support promised."

"Right. It's impossible! Impossible! Out of the question."

So saying, I sat down right away to write to her, explaining that, in view of the time we needed to raise our support, her suggestion was too preposterous to consider.

In about a week we received another letter from Dolores. First she reminded us that nothing is impossible with God. Then she told us that when she received our letter she made a few phone calls to pastors she knew to tell them about us. Some agreed to invite us to give our testimony in their churches.

"So," Dolores said, "if you are free to make the trip right away it just might result in some support for you." Dolores then listed a proposed itinerary that she had worked out for us with the help and influence of her father, Dr. H. K. Finley, then editor of the Ohio Independent Baptist magazine, and pastor of the First Baptist Church of Wellington, Ohio.

After reading the letter, we remained silent for a few minutes, mentally reviewing its contents. Mildred broke the silence. "Dolores is a persistent one, isn't she? But I still can't see how we could do what she suggests."

"Neither do I. It just seems so...." As I paused, trying to think of an adequate word, it suddenly dawned upon me what was happening.

"Mildred, what are we doing? What has happened to our faith and our commitment? Here we have been praying for the Lord to open doors to churches and now we are complaining when He does. Dolores has been trying to convince us that the Lord can make possible what we think is impossible. We ought to thank her for her efforts, and also believe that the Lord can make it happen.

"But she means we have to go out west this week already," protested Mildred.

"I know, but we have nothing to keep us back. Eddie can stay with your sister Viola, he loves to play with his cousins. At least we can make the trip and trust the Lord to make it worthwhile."

The trip was a fast one by train to our first stop, Pana, Illinois, for the Sunday services, then up to Fremont, Michigan for Wednesday night, then back to Elyria, Ohio, where we stayed with Dolores and her parents. She took us to Spencer for a special missionary meeting on Friday and then to Xenia for the Sunday services. In all, the trip took only ten days.

We had hardly reached home again when another letter came from Dolores. Again, she urged us to plan for an early departure for

Venezuela. Dolores wrote, "I agree that this will be a great step of faith for you, but our Lord is a great God and I feel sure that He will make it possible. Let us remember the words of Hudson Taylor—I think it was he—who said, 'Expect great things from God; attempt great things for God.' Or was it the other way around? It's been a long time since I studied Missions, but you know what I mean.

"I have," Dolores continued, "selected three possible dates for our sailing to Venezuela. You know we sail on the Grace Line Luxury ships—nothing too good for God's servants. They have servants' quarters that we can reserve at prices we can afford. They sail every Friday and I suggest either August 29, September 5 or September 12. Why not, by faith, choose one of these dates? Let me know the one you choose and we'll work toward that one."

"She's crazy—positively crazy—to think that we can raise our support and get our equipment together in only two and a half or three months," Mildred emphatically stated.

I agreed and I was a bit perturbed that Dolores would put us on the spot this way. "Of course, we have faith in the Lord, but we also have to be practical. We still only have that $25 promised support. Those churches we visited were friendly enough and quite a number of people took a copy of the tract and prayer card. Many promised to pray for us, but they didn't make any promises about financial support."

"Well, Ed, let's pray about it. I'm sure the Lord will lead and tell us what to do."

We did have prayer right then and there and afterward felt better about it. I called George who made his calls and started our prayer partners praying. Nevertheless I determined to write to Dolores and tell her that "there was no way we could do it." We didn't have time that day to write. In fact, a few days went by before we had time to think about it again.

Toward the end of the week a letter came from the secretary of the Mission. We were informed that letters had been received from the churches which we had visited on that trip and each one promised monthly support in varying amounts. The secretary of the Mission commented that the churches had told her to let us know right away. There seemed to be a spirit of urgency in the letters from the churches. She also commented that she had never seen such quick response from deputation meetings, ending with, "The Lord must want you on the field in a hurry."

The newly promised support amounted to $60 a month, so with the support we already had, the total was $85 toward the needed $125. We had another prayer meeting to praise and thank the Lord for what He was doing and to ask forgiveness for our very weak faith. We re-read Psalm 37:3-7, the portion of God's Word through which He had spoken to us that day when we first yielded ourselves to the Lord.

We prayed: "Lord help us to trust you completely. Help us to make your will the desire of our heart. Help us to renew our commitment and to again put all our ways entirely into your hands. Help us to rest completely in you."

When we finished praying, Mildred suggested, "The Lord is working so fast for us, Ed, maybe we ought to select one of Dolores' dates. What do you think?"

"Yes. While we were praying I received the same impression and September 5 kept coming into my mind."

"Sounds good," Mildred agreed. "Then let's write to Dolores and tell her." Mildred went to the desk, took out paper and began to write. Needless to say, Dolores was delighted.

Near the end of June, an invitation came to speak to the young people's group in a church in the area of Pottstown, Pennsylvania, Limerick Chapel. A fellow-graduate of the Bible College, John Lenko, a member of this church, had arranged the meeting. As was now our custom, we emphasized our need for prayer partners. John had urged the pastor of the church to attend. Impressed with our testimony, Pastor Clarence Didden asked us to remain for the evening service. He had us give a brief testimony before the whole congregation.

At the close of the service, they had a prayer circle of the deacons with us in the center. After this, the entire congregation passed in front of us, shaking our hands and wishing us Godspeed. As they did so, quite a few slipped money in various amounts into our hands. It was a material expression of their interest in us, and many told us that they would be praying for us. We had never had such an experience before. It seemed that the brethren of Limerick Chapel took us under their wings the first time we met them. It was Christian love at first sight.

We had gone to this meeting by train, but no trains were running after 8:00 o'clock. So after the service Pastor Didden drove us in his car down Ridge Avenue to City Line Avenue where we could get a trolley car which would take us right to our street. As we said our good-byes, we thanked Pastor Didden for going out of his way for us, for the opportunity of giving our testimony, and for the monetary gifts we received from his people. We told him, "What a blessing it was to hear so many say that they would be praying for us."

"Yes, and they really mean it. It is not just an idle promise. And our people really know how to pray. We believe the truth of our church's motto, 'Where Prayer Rises, Power Falls.'"

Then to add to our rejoicing, Pastor Didden told us, "Not only will we be praying for you, but, Lord willing, we'll be helping you financially. While the brethren were coming forward to shake your hand, I met with the Missions Committee and they agreed by faith to give $25.00 a month toward your support."

"Praise the Lord!" we both shouted.

"Yes, the praise does belong to the Lord." Then, after a short prayer, committing us to the Lord, "God bless you, Ed and Mildred, and give you wisdom as you pack. Just keep trusting the Lord according to the verses you quoted tonight from Psalm 37:3-7. Those are my life verses also."

With this last event we were now sure that we had made the right decision on the date to leave for Venezuela, September 5, 1941. But, Mildred expressed how we felt, "Oh wow! How can we ever get ready in time? There are so many things to find and buy."

I told her, "Well, money won't be a problem. We can now use the money from the business, that was to carry us through the year of deputation, to pay for our passage and purchase our equipment."

We already had many items on the list the Mission had sent us. There remained only to buy some special items which would be needed in the tropics and, of course, clothing for Eddie in various sizes to fit him as he would grow during our 3 to 4 year term of service.

Our total promised support was now at $110. The Mission gave us clearance to leave for the field because a number of small gifts for us had been coming regularly into the Home Office. Experience had shown that these gifts would probably continue. Counting these, the total being received for us was a little over the required amount.

But again we wondered how we would get everything ready in time. And again the Lord provided through our good brother in Christ. George obtained strong wooden boxes from the factory where he worked, then took an early vacation to help. It was a very hectic time as we made last-minute purchases and worked to get our boxes packed and ready to ship.

Further complicating our lives, I had to spend a lot of time at the local office of the Selective Service Program. In preparation for possibly entering the war, the U.S. had begun to register all men who might be called up for military service. As an unordained minister of the Gospel, I had been classified as 4-F. Even so, it took a lot of arguing back and forth before they finally excused me from military service and gave me permission to leave the country.

Then, early in August, the Venezuela Field Council of Baptist Mid-Missions requested that I be officially ordained before leaving the States. This was deemed important because of the religious-cultural ideas of the Venezuelan people and in dealing with the government. So with all the work before us, I had to prepare a doctrinal statement and myself for examination by an ordination council. The council, besides several pastors, included the president of Baptist Mid-Missions, Dr. M. E. Hawkins, who was holding a Bible conference in our church, and Pastor Clarence Didden from Limerick Chapel.

On August 28, 1941, just one week before leaving for Venezuela, I was ordained to the Gospel ministry. Three days later, on September 1, our boxes were on a truck on their way to the pier in New York City to be loaded on the ship on which we would sail on September 5.

Dolores had spent a lot of time helping us get our entry permit from the Venezuelan government and getting other legal papers in order. But, in the preoccupation of getting us ready to go with her, she had neglected to check on her own re-entry permit! So on Thursday, September 4, when we went to the Venezuela Consulate to get our visas on our passports, Dolores discovered that her re-entry permit had ceased to be valid on August 31!

On September 5, 1941, a delegation from our home church and our friends from the Eighth Street Wayside Rescue Mission, including George and Loretta, came to have a prayer meeting on board ship and to wish us "bon voyage." Poor Dolores sadly waved us goodbye from the dock as the ship moved out into the harbor. She had to wait in New York City for two weeks until her permit could be renewed by cablegram. We would wait for her in Caracas.

Chapter 10

Arrival in Venezuela

"The Lord shall preserve thee from all evil; he shall preserve thy soul. The Lord shall preserve thy going out and thy coming in from this time forth, and even for evermore." (Psalm 121:7,8)

The trip to Venezuela was a very pleasant one. The Grace Line ship was truly a luxury liner. In addition to being a cruise ship, many businessmen used the line to travel to and from the principal South American seaports and New York City. It was as Dolores had said, and even though we occupied servant's quarters, we were accorded the same courtesies and services that the wealthy passengers received, including the variety of delicious food. The Lord really does take abundant care of His servants.

We sat in our deck chairs, basking in the sun which grew warmer day by day. Sailing into the tropics, the very calm waters were disturbed only by the flying fish as they, in silvery streaks, flashed in and out of the water a few yards away from the ship. In the relaxing atmosphere of the luxury liner, we had time to rest and to rethink the events of the last few months. We couldn't believe that so much had happened in so short a time. Here we were on our way to Venezuela at least a year ahead of the schedule we had planned for ourselves. At that time, only the Lord knew why. We could only marvel at what He had done.

However, there was among the passengers a little feeling of anxiety. The pursers tried to keep our minds occupied with all sorts of social activities and diversions most of which we passed up. Eddie enjoyed the shuffle-board, ping-pong and the many table games. The Santa Paula was the fastest of all the Grace Line ships and it was traveling at full speed. The U.S. was not yet involved in World War II, but German subs had been spotted in the Atlantic waters and our captain was taking no chances.

Mildred, Eddie and I were not afraid. We remembered the Scripture portion which George had read in the little Godspeed farewell service our friends gave us aboard ship right before the gangplank was pulled in. "The LORD shall preserve thy going out and thy coming in from this time forth...." The Lord had called us for missionary service in Venezuela, had worked wondrously and rapidly to get us on our way, and He would take us safely there.

The trip provided an extra blessing when we were able to lead the ship's nurse to the Lord. She came to us after the protestant service that I, as an ordained minister, had been asked to hold on Sunday during the voyage. She had all kinds of problems which she was able to turn over to the Lord once she had accepted Him as her Savior. We felt that in this way the Lord had put another stamp of approval on our call to Venezuela.

We arrived at the coast of Venezuela during the night of our fifth day. Coming up on deck we looked out upon La Guaira, the picturesque but bustling little port city of Caracas. It stretched out for several miles nestling along the narrow ledge of flat land between the Caribbean Sea and the four thousand foot high eastern branch of the rugged Andes Mountains. These served as a theatre-like backdrop behind the varied colored buildings housing the stores and homes. The houses in the background seemed to climb further up in an attempt to conquer the precipitous slope, some supported by skinny columns of wood or cement, while others seemed to just cling precariously to each other.

Needless to say we were anxious to get ashore for a closer look at life in our adopted land. But we had to wait for officials to come aboard to check our passports and documents. Then there was the unloading of all our baggage and boxes, one of which I saw burst open as the net carrying it and other packages was lowered too quickly to the wharf. The Lord must have sent some special handlers, for we saw our things all gathered up and the box nailed shut again, without anything being lost or broken.

We also had to wait for our contact from another mission who was going to help us through customs. We had planned to study Spanish during a year of deputation work, but the Lord saw fit to send us to the field, so obviously, we would need help. Soon Rev. Davenport came to help and to take us to his home in Caracas where we were to stay until Dolores arrived.

Mildred had a very upsetting experience. While Rev. Davenport and I, and Mr. Ghent, an English-speaking commission agent, spent several hours getting our baggage through customs, she and Eddie were sent from La Guaira, up and over the mountain, to Caracas. The taxi was full of people and not one of them spoke English. The driver had been given the address of the missionary's home where we were to stay, but the streets and numbers on the houses were quite different from the way the address was written. They rode around the streets for over an hour until Mildred was sure she would spend the night in a police station. Finally, quite by accident, humanly speaking, the driver stopped at a house to inquire. Imagine Mildred's relief when she saw in the doorway a little blond-haired girl who responded to the call of her name. One who has never been in such a predicament cannot appreciate how it feels to be lost (?) in a strange land, and unable to speak the language.

The two weeks of waiting in Caracas were pleasant and educational. We had not expected to stay in a modern comfortable home with modern conveniences. Our hosts were very solicitous of our needs and taught us many things about the country and the customs of the people. When Dolores arrived, we started the journey inland. The agent who had helped us through customs also had our boxes and trunks loaded on a truck that would take them interior to the gold-mining town of El Callao, our Mission's field headquarters.

The first day of our trip was comparatively easy. We made it by commuter plane, a service that had been recently scheduled to accommodate oil company people. We arrived in El Tigre in the eastern oil fields and stayed with missionary friends. The rest of the trip interior was made by station wagon.

These cars were usually loaded way beyond their legal capacity. But it was a lot better this way for the traveler. The roads were so bad that the cars would bump and sway and sometimes lean so far sideways that the passenger at the window could almost touch the ground. Packed in like sardines, we did not have to use our muscles to maintain an upright position. Traveling with only a few passengers, you had to strain to keep from bumping your neighbor and usually arrived at your destination with sore muscles and an aching rib-cage.

We got a late start the next day. The road from El Tigre to Soledad and Ciudad Bolivar was very bad, in fact, there just wasn't any road. Erosion had worked havoc on what had once been a road, almost completely wiping it out. Our driver followed the trails made by the big trucks that carried supplies to the interior towns. Although the driver forced the car to its limit, about 10 miles an hour over the best parts, we arrived at the Orinoco River just minutes too late to get on the last *chalana* [ferry boat] that would have taken us across to Ciudad Bolivar.

We had expected to stay in the comfortable home of missionary friends in Ciudad Bolivar, but we were stuck in Soledad for the night. The name of that little village means "a lonely place," and it really was. There was nothing we could do but try to find the hotel. Hotel? Not really. It was a one-story building with low ceilings, like all the rest of the houses there. The roof was of *moriche* palm leaves laid overlapping to carry off the rain water. It was the home of rats, and non-poisonous snakes which fed on the rats. Fortunately, the rooms with ceilings gave some protection for the human guests.

The exterior mud-plastered walls, whitewashed, were the worse for wear. The elements had done their best to peel off the surface and some of the mud was gone, exposing, in a number of places, the poles and saplings placed crosswise as lathings for support. Above the front door was a sign, weather-beaten and hardly legible, identifying it as the Hotel Soledad.

There was the proverbial outhouse. No plumbing. The shower room was a three-sided structure placed against an outside wall in the patio of the hotel, open to the sky. It had a square cement slab to stand on to keep our feet from getting dirty from the surrounding sandy mud. We dipped the water for our shower with a gourd from an old fifty-gallon drum. When traveling, people always had their own towels. Dolores had forgotten this, so our towels were still in our boxes somewhere on the road between Caracas and El Callao.

The hotel had not expected paying guests, so the dining room was closed for the day. There was a little family grocery store still open, so we satisfied our hunger with a supper of sandwiches made with *pan de agua*. This is a bread which has aspirations of being something like Italian rolls, but doesn't quite make it beyond the stage of toasted air with a crust around it. On this bread, we spread some potted meat with a slice of *queso llanero* [native white country cheese] on top. Fortunately this country native cheese was fresh enough so as not to be interlaced with *gusanos* [maggot type worms]. For our beverage we had some nice cold, believe it or not, Coca-Cola. Even the tiny food stores way out in the "sticks" had kerosene refrigerators to provide cold drinks and ice. As we finished our meal a little girl entered our room carrying a tray with four tiny cups (demitasse) and a pretty china coffee pot. We had our first taste of the thick, syrupy, black and very sweet Venezuelan coffee. Delicious! It made our day, and we were ready for bed and, hopefully, a good night's sleep.

The proprietress had sent out to borrow another hammock. Hammock? Yes, for out in the country, away from the more populated areas, the majority of the people slept in hammocks. Only the well-to-do had beds in their homes. Every house had hooks in all the walls from which the hammocks were hung. Sometimes in small homes and large families, the children would hang their hammocks double-decker. In certain areas the hammocks were covered with mosquito netting to protect the sleeper from the malaria-carrying mosquito, mice or even rats that might wander in or fall from the roof in the homes without ceilings. In some areas, protection from the small vampire bats is still needed. Ugh! But wait, there's more.

The extra hammock was for Dolores. She found it already warmed up for her. The proprietress had to make one of her cousins who lived down the street give up her hammock and double up with her sister. The Venezuelan hammocks are large, usually seven or eight feet long and at least six feet wide, easily accommodating two persons as in the case of the matrimonial hammock. The strings are so intertwined that when one lies diagonally on the hammock, one's body lies straight and level just as in a bed—almost.

Mildred had the privilege of sleeping in the only bed in the hotel, but she had trouble getting to sleep for thinking about what Dolores had told her. Although almost everyone slept in hammocks, it was considered demeaning to die in one. So, whenever someone was dying, their loved ones would scrounge around among their friends and relatives to borrow a bed. Mildred kept wondering who the person was who had last died in that bed.

Finally, Mildred did get to sleep; but not for long. She was suddenly awakened by an unearthly roaring right outside the open window close to her head. The sound was hard to describe, you have to hear it for yourself. Mildred thought that some terrible wild beast was trying to get in. You see, only wealthy people had glass windows in their homes. The windows of the hotel were the usual open frame with vertical wooden bars spaced about three inches apart. They had wooden shutters for privacy, but they were open so the cool night air could come in.

Milded was sure that the wooden bars were not strong enough to keep the beast out. Mildred's screams woke Dolores who was able to calm her as she identified the sounds. Dolores pulled aside the gingham curtain, the kind that one sees in all the windows of the village homes. In the dim light of the sooty kerosene lamp that Dolores had lit, Mildred could see the dim form of a burro standing right outside. Donkeys roam the streets of the villages freely at night looking for whatever clumps of grass they might find. Their owners recover their burros in the morning.

The next morning at daybreak, we were up and ready when our car came for us. We crossed the Orinoco River on the very first trip of the ferry and were soon in the mission compound, glad to accept the invitation of the missionaries to have breakfast with them before continuing our journey. Thus we came to know Dr. and Mrs. Van Eddings who proved to be valuable friends and help to us on many occasions. In the middle of the morning our chauffeur came for us and we were off to Upata.

Upata is an Indian name which means "his house." Many of the Venezuelan towns have Indian names whose meanings have some bearing upon the history of the area. We met our fellow-workers, had a time of fellowship with them around the supper table and then to bed, or rather, to hammock.

We had only a few hours sleep. Very early in the *madrugada* [before dawn], we continued our journey to El Callao. The road-trails were dry, so we made good time. We arrived at our church just as the service ended and the members were coming out. This was a great surprise, especially to the missionaries, for we were not expected until Tuesday. In those days the trip from Caracas usually took the better part of a week, but we made it in three and a half days. The telegram advising them of our travel plans arrived two days later.

A few days later, our baggage caught up with us. We took the next week getting acclimated, unpacking our trunks and crates, sorting out and repacking our clothing according to the estimated dates it would be needed. We had brought enough to last us four years. There were also birthday and Christmas gifts to be secreted away and brought out at the proper time. Our household items were packed away until we would be in our own home. For the present, we would be living with our senior missionaries, Rev. Sylvan Hausser, his wife Eunice, and Dolores, who would be our Spanish language teacher.

Our schedule was a full one. In the mornings, we were with Dolores in language study. Dolores, a former school teacher, was trained in teaching methods, and her help was even more appreciated as time went on. In the afternoons, we took turns teaching Eddie the Calvert Course correspondence lessons which we had purchased and brought with us, years two through five. In our spare time we went out into the streets, visited the market place and listened to the people talk. We needed to get our ears tuned to the new sounds of Spanish and to talk with the people as we were able. Night times were spent doing our homework. It was fantastic how quickly Eddie picked up the language as he played with our neighbor's boys.

In those days, newspapers arrived days late, so we were quite unaware of what was happening out in the world. There were short wave radios, but the news was sparse. There was also so much static that the words were garbled and often misunderstood.

October and November went by quickly. Then late in the evening of December 7,—remember, this was in 1941—Mr. Hausser came into the large family room where we all were reading, studying or doing our homework. He had been across the street listening to the news on the short wave radio in the home of a member of the church.

Mr. Hausser excitedly announced, "The United States has just declared war on Japan."

"What!" we all exclaimed. "You mean we are at war?"

"It is all so strange," he explained. "It seems that some Japanese in Hawaii attacked a woman named Pearl, and President Roosevelt went on the air a few minutes ago and announced a declaration of war."

"Why, I never heard of anything so ridiculous," said Mrs. Hausser. "The very idea!"

"Yes," agreed Dolores. "It's an awful thing for a woman to be attacked, but to declare war over it... Who is this Pearl, anyway? She must be an awfully important person... daughter of some big diplomat or something."

Mr. Hausser replied, "I don't know who she is. We men were just talking about how they are fixing up the town plaza, when one of the men said, 'Listen to that.' We couldn't hear too well, but we understood that a lot of sailors had been killed. Someone remarked that they must have gotten into a fight that resulted in a riot. Then we heard the announcer say that the President declared war. The batteries were weak and we could hardly hear anymore, so they cut off the radio."

The news, of course, was about Pearl Harbor. It was not a laughing matter, but upon remembrance of that night, we missionaries cannot help but laugh a little at our ignorance of geography and of world affairs. The following day we knew the complete story.

It was during the next few months that Mildred and I understood what the war meant to us. It soon became evident why the Lord had gotten us out to the field in such a hurry. Tied economically to the United States, Venezuela declared itself on the side of the Allies though not actually at war, and closed its doors to the comings and goings of all missionaries.

As time went on we also understood the reasons for this. The Roman Catholic priests, were almost entirely Spanish. Spain was on the side of the enemy, the Axis, and the Spanish Falange could have been like a "fifth column" in the South American countries. Venezuela has hundreds of miles of wild, deserted coastline, but the army did its best to guard it. One day, at daybreak, five men were captured on one of the isolated stretches of beach. They were spies coming ashore in a dory from a submarine which had surfaced just off shore. Two of the men were Spanish priests in whose possession were found maps of Venezuela and other countries, detailing the military installations, airfields, the large and rich oil fields, and other strategic areas.

All the Catholic priests were placed under house arrest for almost a year, then, as things eased off a bit, they were allowed to circulate in their parish. American missionaries could travel almost at will with permission obtained from the chief of police of the town where they lived, or from the Governor of the State. When a protestant missionary had to leave on furlough, he was not allowed to return. The Venezuelan government had nothing against us, but for political reasons they could not show us special consideration and be accused of discrimination. But it was all for the purpose of controlling the movements of the priests who were mostly foreigners. Today, most priests are Venezuelans.

At last, we had the answer to why the Lord had gotten us to the field so soon. If the Lord had permitted us to work out the plans that we had, not to go to the field until the summer of 1942, we may never have gotten there at all.

BUT, the Lord had supplied our needs and had hurriedly gotten us out to the field in the Fall of 1941. Only He knew of the urgency for haste. We have often thought of God's promise to Israel in Isaiah

65:24: "And it shall come to pass, that before they call, I will answer; and while they are yet speaking, I will hear."

Even as we and our friends were praying, the Lord was working in ways we did not know, preparing for us to enter Venezuela. The Lord knew the need for us to be on the field before war was declared. The Lord got us there. To Him alone goes the glory.

The door for missionaries to enter or return to Venezuela stayed closed for three years. During those three years, the missionaries under Baptist Mid-Missions tried to stay on the field as long as they could, but little by little, with their health undermined by the severe climate, they had to leave on furlough even though they did not know when they would be allowed to return. Finally, during our fourth year on the field, furloughed missionaries began to return and we were able to leave on furlough.

III
Venezuela Ministry - Part 1 - Tumeremo

Chapter 11

A Fallen Angel

An experience in spiritism

"Put on the whole armor of God, that ye may be able to stand against the wiles of the devil... Stand therefore, having your loins girt about with truth...."
(Ephesians 6:11,14a)

Mildred and I were barely through the first quarter of the Spanish language course when we were moved to Tumeremo, which soon became our first solo mission assignment. It was an emergency situation. Robert Fletcher and his wife had been working in that town where a small congregation of believers had been established. The town was situated almost on the border of British Guiana (known today as Guyana) on the east. It had a permanent base for the National Guard whose principle work was to keep undesirables from crossing the border into Venezuela.

Because Mrs. Fletcher was pregnant and, in poor health, it was decided that she should return to the States. Robert was to remain in the work for at least six months. We were to take over the house and make a home for Robert who in return would help us with our language studies. Periodically we were also to send our exam papers to El Callao for Dolores to check. So, after just four months on the field, we moved "lock, stock and barrel" up to Tumeremo. The household goods we had brought from the States would be in use much sooner than expected.

The eight room Mission house was one story, built L-shaped on the corner of two streets. The doors of its seven private rooms all opened on to a wide covered veranda, which ran down two sides facing the inside patio. The patio extended all the way to the next street in back. It contained banana plants, seven coconut trees, several lemon, orange, tangerine trees, and a wild cherry tree. The main entrance from the street into the veranda was through a wide arcade at the end of one wing. This part of the veranda was used as a family room where guests were received and which was converted into a Bible study and prayer meeting area on Wednesday nights. A corner room with doors opening on each of the streets had been used as a grocery store. The Sunday services were held in this room; the Sunday School classes on the veranda.

This was a good arrangement for Robert and us, but it lasted only a month. Robert's wife's health continued to deteriorate, and was complicated by a tremendous homesickness for her husband. Late in February, a letter came for Robert from his wife begging him to join her. With the letter came prepaid airline tickets with reservations already made for a date just a week after the letter was received. In order to make it, he would have to leave immediately.

At dawn the following Monday we said good-bye to Robert as he left Tumeremo. We had had breakfast with him by the light of the gasoline pressure lamp. We read Psalm 121, and were praying, committing him into the Lord's hands, as the truck driver announced his arrival with blows of the horn. We watched until the truck turned into the third street from the house. Then we shut the door of the street entrance, and sat down on a bench on the patio veranda. We didn't say anything for several minutes.

We felt **really alone** and very inadequate to take over the work, especially since we were just beginning to speak Spanish. True, Tumeremo was only 27 miles from El Callao, but it might just as well have been a hundred. There were no constructed roads, only wagon tracks. Even in dry weather it took five hours to make the trip to and from El Callao. In the rainy season, only the largest and most powerful trucks attempted to go.

Finally Mildred spoke, "Well, let's have our devotions before you light the fire to heat the wash water."

I reached for our Bibles and the devotional booklet lying on the table. I opened the booklet and turned to the Bible reading for the day, Ephesians 6:10-12. "Finally, my brethren, be strong in the Lord, and in the power of his might. Put on the whole armor of God, that ye may be able to stand against the wiles of the devil. For we wrestle not against flesh and blood, but against principalities, against powers, against the rulers of the darkness of this world, against spiritual wickedness in high places."

"How about that, Mildred! Could the Lord have given us a better Scripture reading for today? Shades of Mother Bachman! She surely knew what she was talking about."

"What do you mean, Ed?"

"Satan will use this situation to try to wreck our missionary service our first year on the field. He knows we are going to be afraid that we won't be able to do the job. He'll try to get us to give up and run back to El Callao and leave this little congregation alone. Mildred, I think that we have to recognize the seriousness of this situation. Satan will surely attack us and we must fight him the best way we can. We must be in constant prayer."

"But what about Robert and his wife and their problem?" asked Mildred. "Do you think Satan could have caused that?"

"Whether the devil could have caused the situation or not, we can't say. But he will certainly use it to try to hinder the work and make us discouraged. We have to be alert to his tricks and surround ourselves with prayer. We have to resist him. That's what the Bible says, 'Resist the devil, and he will flee from you' (James 4:7). And, I had better get a letter off to George right away to alert our prayer warriors."

We continued our devotions, praying for Robert and his wife and then for ourselves, that we would not be discouraged but would, by the grace of God, stay with the infant church.

After Robert left, I wrote out my messages and Bible studies word for word. I sent them down to Dolores in El Callao by one of the truck drivers. She corrected them and sent them back to me. In order to increase my vocabulary and give me more fluency, I read the messages exactly as Dolores corrected them. Later on, with practice, I could read them without appearing to do so. Then, much later, I could preach with fewer notes.

The very day that Robert left, as soon as our household chores were out of the way, we began to visit the church members in their homes. We made many mistakes with the language but nobody laughed at us, at least not to our face. They were delighted with our visits. We understood less than half of what the people said, but we tried to control the subject matter of our conversations so that we could use words which we had in our limited vocabulary. Little by little we could understand more as the Spanish sounds became more familiar.

There were quite a few of the members and their children present the first Wednesday night we conducted a service alone. The Bible study went well. The people, and especially the two deacons, were very helpful in correcting mispronunciations and supplying some words needed to better explain the teaching. I had just finished the Bible study and was mentioning some of the things that they should remember as we went to prayer, when Angel Alvarado appeared. He remained standing just inside the side entrance, behind the last bench.

We had met Angel in El Callao. He preached several times at the open-air meetings conducted by the church. Some years ago he had heard the Gospel, believed and received Christ as his Savior. Having studied for the priesthood, he was well educated. But, he always used such big words and such flowery language that we new missionaries could never understand him.

Angel had understood the Gospel truths so well and had such capabilities that the Mission hired him as a full-time evangelist. For about eight years he had been used greatly in winning many people to the Lord. In the towns where our mission worked—San Félix, Upata, El Palmar and Tumeremo—many believers loved him as their spiritual father.

We did not know that Angel was in the area. Usually Mr. Hausser directed Angel's activities, assigning him to help the missionaries in special meetings and to engage in personal evangelism in the homes. I thought it strange that he would come unannounced, but assumed that Mr. Hausser had sent him to help us in Robert's absence.

I greeted Angel, bidding him welcome, and invited him to take a seat, but he remained standing. I continued to enumerate the prayer requests. The brethren knew, of course, the reasons for Robert's departure on that Monday morning. I reminded them of the hard trip it would be, first to Ciudad Bolivar, then through El Tigre in the eastern oil fields to Puerto La Cruz on the coast, and the need to make it in less than three days. I asked special prayer for Robert's continued safety and especially for the next day, Thursday, when he would be taking the Pan American plane out of Puerto La Cruz.

The brethren were nodding their heads, indicating that they would remember, when Angel interrupted. "I have received a message giving me information about Don Roberto."

"How could that be, Angel? Roberto just left here Monday morning. He couldn't possibly have gotten to Puerto La Cruz until this afternoon. How could you have received a message from him so soon?"

Angel smiled, "I didn't say that I received a message **from** him, but **about** him."

I was about to speak again, but I had to think of the Spanish words I wanted to say. As I hesitated, Angel quickly took advantage. He came forward and stood at my side. Angel spoke, enunciating every word slowly. This time he wanted me to understand.

"Don Roberto went swimming in the Caribbean Sea this afternoon. You see, he arrived in Puerto La Cruz this morning about 11:00 o'clock. The driver of the truck dropped him off at the Pan American ticket office. The clerk told him that he had bad news for him, that his seat on the plane had been taken by a government official."

This happened often during the war years when many government officials and military men used commercial flights. Angel was telling us that Robert had been "bumped."

Angel paused, looking over the small congregation. He was pleased at the effect he was having on the uneducated country folk. They were holding on to his every word with open-mouthed wonderment. I tried to speak but I was so surprised that I just couldn't think of the Spanish words fast enough, so Angel continued.

"Don Roberto was saddened even more when the clerk told him that there would not be another opportunity for him to go until the end of the month. There was nothing that he could do about it, so taking his suitcase, he walked down the street toward the Mission Home. He had lunch with the missionaries and, in the afternoon, went to the beach for a swim."

By this time, I had recovered from the initial surprise of hearing Angel's "revelations." I prayed for wisdom to handle the situation properly and for the right words to do so.

"Brother Angel, listen to me, please," I said slowly, "and give me time to think of the words I need. And when you answer me, please use simple words so that I can understand. Tell us when and how you received this message."

Angel threw back his shoulders, stood up straight, and said, "In dreams and visions, in my hammock this afternoon. I had chills and tremblings as God spoke to me."

He paused to give the brethren time to marvel. It also gave me a few moments to think.

"No, Angel, that was not God. God does not speak to man in that manner today. If anyone spoke to you, it was the devil."

There was a united gasp from the people at my words. They were shocked at me, who dared to say such a thing about their beloved Angel. I thought, "How can I have a confrontation with this man with my limited Spanish?" Another silent prayer went up to heaven, "Lord, help me. Only you can put the correct words in my mouth."

Then began a discussion. Angel ignored my plea for him to use simple language. However, I was understanding almost every word. Not only that, but the Lord brought to my memory words which I did not use fluently until years later, words which I had studied but which had not as yet become a part of my vocabulary. During the discussion, the two deacons started to leave by the patio door. I called them back, telling them that this was their problem as much as it was mine. Carlos and Eugenio came back and sat down on the last bench.

The end of the discussion came when I again told Angel that he was being used by the devil. Turning to the congregation, I told them, "Time will prove that this man is being used by Satan. God did not speak to him as he claims. When we receive Don Roberto's letter, we will know what happened. We have prayed for his safety and that nothing will hinder him from arriving at his wife's home in good time. I have faith in the Lord. He will answer our prayers."

I closed the meeting with a short prayer and dismissed the congregation. I then spoke kindly to Angel and invited him to come by the next day to talk about this problem and have prayer together. Angel never did come back to talk to us. Instead, he visited among the brethren in their homes. He began to prophesy about the future, telling them of events that were supposed to happen to them because of the war. He lived off the goodness of the brethren, some of them so poor they could hardly support themselves and their children, let alone another grown person.

A few days after the confrontation with Angel, a letter came from Mr. Hausser. He had sent it by mail because he feared that if he sent it by some truck driver it might be opened and its contents made public. Mr. Hausser had discovered that Angel was into spiritism, and instructed us that, if Angel showed up, we should not allow him to preach in the church. His financial support had been cut off, so probably he would be leaving our area.

Of course, we already knew that Angel was involved in something occult, reverting to and taking advantage of many of the superstitions prevalent among the uneducated people. But we were anxiously waiting for the letter from Robert that we could show to the brethren as proof of Angel's error. Finally the letter came, over a week later. **It was postmarked in Brownsville, Texas**. We literally tore open the envelope as we sat down to read.

"Dear Ed and Mildred: Greetings in the name of Jesus. What a fast and wonderful trip! That truck was a new one and the driver was expert on those terrible roads. We arrived in Puerto La Cruz on Wednesday morning before noon. I had the driver drop me off at the Pan American office where I presented my ticket and reservation. But, what a shock to hear the clerk tell me that I had been bumped by a government official with priority. To make it worse, there was no other passage available until the end of the month. Oh, boy... was I ever **down**."

I stopped reading. "Oh, dear," exclaimed Mildred, "Angel was right."

I started to read again. "There wasn't a thing I could do about it. I picked up my suitcase and started down the street toward the Mission House. It's only about two blocks away, you know. As I was leaving the office, a man brushed past me nearly knocking me down. I had only walked about 100 feet when I heard the airline clerk calling my name. He waved for me to return. When I entered the office again, he said, 'You are in luck, this man just cancelled. You can leave tomorrow morning as scheduled.' Of course, I answered with a 'praise the Lord; God does answer prayer.' I gave them both my testimony and told them why I was so anxious to leave. They were very much impressed, and to say the least, I was rejoicing. How fast one's feelings can change, Ed and Mildred, from great sadness to almost overwhelming wonderful joy.

"Well, I went to the Mission House. Our friends rejoiced with me when I told them what had happened. I had lunch with them and then went to the beach and had a dip in the ocean. I'm glad you insisted that I take my swim trunks with me. Wednesday night I went with the missionaries to the prayer meeting in Puerto. The next day I was on the Atlantic Clipper, flying to Caracas and then on to Maracaibo. Here, late in the afternoon, I found the offices of *La Estrella de la Mañana*. If you haven't seen this magazine yet, it is THE evangelical magazine of Venezuela. I met brother Asdrubal Ríos who showed me around the print shop and the bookstore. He took me to supper and had me give my testimony in their church that night.

"I am now writing this letter on the plane to Brownsville, Texas, and will mail it from there at the airport. You should have it in a week or two. I know you have been praying for me and are anxious to know how things went. God bless you. Thanks for your prayers. Greet the brethren. Yours in Christ, (signed) Bob."

We were silent for a while, then almost together, we exclaimed, "Oh, no!"

"Now what am I going to tell the brethren? Mildred, it looks like Angel was right."

"No. Wait a minute, Ed. Angel was only partly right. Robert did get home as planned."

"Yes, that's right. But, how do we explain the contradiction? It must have been the devil who sent Angel the message. But if so, why didn't Satan tell Angel the whole story? Oh, wow, the devil really goofed this time."

The next day at the dinner table, we were again discussing the incident. "You know, Mildred, I've been thinking much about all this. It has reminded me again of what Mother Bachman told us and the advice she gave us. But I never thought we would see the evidence of Satan's work so soon after getting to the field. I guess the devil thought that we would be easy prey. We really are invading his territory."

"I agree, Ed. And I don't understand either why Satan didn't reveal to Angel about that cancellation and that Robert got off on his flight as scheduled. There must be an explanation."

"That's got me puzzled too, Mildred.... Maybe we'll understand it some day. Anyhow, the Lord has given us the victory for now. But we still have to deal with Angel before the Tumeremo church even though he has been dismissed by Mr. Hausser as the Mission evangelist."

"Oh, I forgot to tell you, Ed, that when you were downtown this morning, Esther came by to bring me some flowers. She told me that Angel has been making a fool of himself. He told Felipe that he was going to die with that sickness that has plagued him for so long, and the next day Felipe was out working in his garden. Do you remember Doña Clara's neighbor who was so sick? Well, Angel went to her house with some of the brethren to pray for her. He told her family that the Lord told him that if he would lay his hands on her she would get better. They buried her late yesterday afternoon."

"That's too bad. It seems that the devil has overstepped himself this time. But look at what he has really done. He is destroying the wonderful testimony that Angel has had. I wonder how he ever got involved in spiritism. He seemed to know the Bible so well."

At the Sunday morning service, I read Robert's letter to the congregation and then gave a Bible study on spiritism the best way I could. There wasn't time for Dolores to check it.

Angel continued to prophesy and each day came up with something new. Soon the people realized the truth and, although they loved him as their spiritual father, they began to reject him. When he saw that he had worn out his welcome, he packed up and left for parts unknown.

Some months later we heard that Angel had stopped off in the town of Guasipati where a veteran missionary friend of ours tried to help him. He professed to repent and for a brief time stayed there with the missionary. He was heard of next out on the coast where he appeared in a church service, desperately sick, trembling and talking crazily. The believers took him to a hospital where he was admitted to the psychiatric ward. He seemed to quickly recover and was released in the care of the missionaries. Again he seemed to have ended his escapade into spiritism and was given a call to pastor a small church on the coast. He did well for a time, but then suddenly retired from the ministry to do secular work. No one knew where he was for many years. Then, when we were again working in Venezuela, some thirty years after the Tumeremo incident, we heard that Angel was living somewhere in our territory. Later, we heard that he had died, apparently still under some kind of demonic influence.

It was some six months after my confrontation with Angel that I received a number of booklets written by Dr. Shaddach, of Ashtabula, Ohio, recommended by the Sunday School Times. The one on spiritism and demonism gave us a possible answer to why the devil revealed to Angel only a certain part of what had happened to Robert.

Dr. Shaddach suggested that Satan, because of his very nature, cannot do anything that will bring glory to God. Then we understood, that in the case of Angel, the devil revealed to him the bad things that were happening to Robert. The trip to Puerto La Cruz, his swim in the ocean, were only incidental. Satan could not reveal to

Angel the fact of the subsequent cancellation, that Robert did get on the plane and was on his way to join his wife. This would have brought glory to God and blessings to His people who were praying. Satan, because of his hatred toward God, and his inherent quality of evil, could not reveal the good part of Robert's journey home and thus had to double-cross his own servant.

We rejoiced and thanked the Lord for giving us this experience early in our missionary service. It caused us to accept the truth that indeed we were involved in a SPIRITUAL WARFARE. The incident with Angel—"a fallen angel"—made us more alert to the fact that we were wrestling "not against flesh and blood, but against principalities, against powers, against the rulers of the darkness of this world, against spiritual wickedness in high places."

We realized anew the need to act upon the advice: "Wherefore take unto you the whole armour of God, that ye may be able to withstand in the evil day, and having done all, to stand" (Ephesians 6:13). And the advice: "Submit yourselves therefore to God. Resist the devil, and he will flee from you" (James 4:7).

Chapter 12

Frontier Missionary Life Continues

The Conversion of Carlos Hernández

"For there is one God, and one mediator between God and men, the man Christ Jesus." (I Timothy 2:5)

"Ed... **Ed**... **ED!**"

The second "Ed" was a little louder, and the third, a yell. Mildred stood in the doorway of the improvised carpenter's shop. I was making so much noise that I did not hear her calling. I was ripping a board down the middle of its thickness to make two thin panels for a wardrobe. There were no sawmills in our area to do this hard hot job for me.

"It is 10:30; your deacons will be here soon. You had better get cleaned up."

"Right you are, Hon." I removed the sweatband from my forehead and wiped my face with the hand towel that dangled from my belt. We had no regular electric service, consequently, no power tools, no electric fans, and no refrigeration. Just a tiny whisper of hot air creeped in through the barred windows of my carpenter's shop from the sun-bathed sparkling packed white sand of the street. At night, a weak DC current was provided by the local light plant allowing us only two dim light bulbs in the house for about three or four hours.

Our little church in Tumeremo had celebrated the Lord's Supper the day before. Now, on Monday morning, the deacons and I were to meet for an informal discussion of the spiritual condition of the church and its members and spend some time in prayer. In order to give the deacons time to do their chores on their farms, the meeting was held at 11:00 A.M.

I usually dedicated Monday mornings to carpentry work, but on that day I cut it short. After a quick shower, and with fresh clothes on, I was waiting for deacons Carlos and Eugenio to arrive. They were a little late; well, not really, for time is relative in Hispanic

America, depending upon the situation. They arrived about ten after eleven, which wasn't bad at all.

Walking past the carpentry shop, they saw the frame of the wardrobe I was working on. "How did you learn to make furniture?" asked Eugenio. "Are all missionaries carpenters?"

"No," I replied, "but they ought to be, especially if the Lord calls them to minister in frontier towns like Tumeremo. Being able to do some cabinet making saves us money. Then too, it gives me the exercise I need to keep me physically fit."

We sat down on the crudely made native chairs, the seat part of which is burro skin leather. The texture and different colors of the hair make for interesting designs.

"The answer to your question, Eugenio, is another proof of how the Lord works in our lives. One of my professors in Bible college used to say, 'Whom the Lord calls, He enables.'"

"I believe that," agreed Eugenio. "When I was saved, I knew that I should testify to my relatives and friends, but I was frightened. I have always been rather timid to speak to people, but as I prayed about it, the Lord took away my fears and gave me words to witness."

"Well, in my case" I explained "the Lord began to prepare me for the mission field long before I was saved. When I was about to enroll in high school, the Great Depression was still going on. Lower and middle class families could not afford to send their children to colleges or universities. Therefore, it made sense to choose the Vocational Course which introduced me to such trades as mechanical drawing, carpentry and masonry, which would enable me to earn a living.

"The Lord knew what training I would need on the mission field and helped us make the right decision. Many times in my life the Lord has guided me in this manner. The Bible also tells us that, as believers, there are no accidents in our lives. Praise the Lord for the assurance that Romans 8:28 gives us. '*And we know that all things work together for good to them... who are the called according to his purpose.*' That means **ALL** things, good or bad."

Then the deacons and I got down to the business at hand. We discussed the spiritual condition and needs of the church and people. We took turns praising the Lord for His goodness and then prayed for the specific needs of our people. When our prayers ended, I reached for my mandolin to accompany us as we sang a couple of choruses to end the meeting.

"Did you know, pastor, that Carlos also plays the mandolin?" asked Eugenio.

"You do? You never told me that, Carlos, Here, play something for us." I offered him the mandolin. But Carlos pulled his hands away as if he were afraid that it would burn him.

"No, Pastor Eduardo, I cannot."

"But, why not? If you play the mandolin, I think I can find another one and we can play together in the services."

"Never... never. I promised the Lord that I would never touch a mandolin again. Please, please never ask me again."

Then, with a polite "*Con su permiso* [with your permission]," Carlos picked up his Bible, and stood up. I had already learned this custom of standing to indicate that the subject is closed and the visit is ended. The host must then acquiesce and stand also. Eugenio joined Carlos and, as they turned toward the door, I heard Carlos whisper "I wish that you hadn't told the pastor."

At the door, they both turned to say, "Adiós, pastor. *Hasta miércoles* [Good-bye, pastor, until Wednesday]." I was shocked with the firmness and seriousness of Carlos' voice. I thought, "There has to be a story behind this."

Some days later, out visiting, Mildred and I stopped at Eugenio's house. After some conversation, I brought up the incident. "Carlos must have a real good reason for his decision never to touch a mandolin again."

"He sure has. I don't agree with him, but then we must follow the dictates of our own conscience. As we left your home that day, Carlos made me promise never to tell you why. I will honor his wishes. Maybe some day, when he knows you better, he will tell you his story."

Walking home, I remarked to Mildred, "I'm sure Carlos' story would make good telling and bring glory to God. When he gives his testimony he always speaks in generalities about his past life and the wonderful change the Lord has made, but never any details."

Almost a year passed by before I knew the whole story. I gleaned part of it from the believers in Tumeremo, and part from the members of the El Callao church. Then later, when he knew me better, Carlos did fill in the gaps. It takes a little time for us missionaries to understand the different culture of the people and for the people to understand us. When this happens, and we have proved to them that we love them, they begin to open up to us.

Carlos was raised on a farm just outside of Tumeremo. His education was limited to the three R's—reading, 'riting and 'rithmatic. He had a natural ability for farming and, while still in his late teens, acquired a piece of farm land along the main road which led to El Callao.

In his early twenties he married beautiful Nicomedes and they settled down to raise a family in the little house he had built. With wise management, Carlos and his growing family were able to live comfortably. He became a respected member of the farming community as well as in the town of Tumeremo. He also became known in El Callao where he often went to sell produce from his farm. He was always pleasant, with a smile and cheery word for everyone.

Then tragedy struck. His first son, whom he loved dearly, fell sick and, in spite of all they could do, died before they could get him to the hospital in El Callao. This was a tremendous blow to Carlos, so heavy that he lost control of his well-ordered life. Carlos, who only occasionally took a social drink, began to drink heavily, and once started he could not stop.

Things went from bad to worse until he was roaming the country roads and streets of Tumeremo with a group of cronies who lived just to drink the bubbly country corn liquor. He would go home in a drunken stupor to sleep it off. In the morning he would do a few chores until the thirst got the better of him and then be off again to find his drinking friends. Fortunately, relatives who lived on nearby farms helped to keep the farm going. But with their own work to do, they barely kept it from becoming completely run down. At least Nicomedes and the children had a roof over their heads and enough to eat.

Carlos would play his mandolin and his buddies would put on some comical skits with immoral implications and be rewarded with free drinks. But one night an argument started and turned into a free-for-all brawl. Trying to save his precious mandolin instead of himself, Carlos was hit over the left eye with a broken bottle. The injury was so

Carlos Hernández, alcoholic

serious that, without proper medical attention, he lost the eye. It was some time before the infection in the eyeless socket healed, but before long Carlos was back satisfying his habit again and playing his mandolin from bar to bar. Now he was known to everyone as *Tuerto Carlos* (one-eyed Carlos).

At age sixteen, Carolina, oldest daughter of Carlos and Nicomedes, was to be married to a fine young Venezuelan in El Callao, Teófilo Griffin, a prosperous goldsmith. El Callao was the commercial center of the several gold mines being exploited in the area. The solid gold "nugget" jewelry of El Callao was famous the world over.

Carlos sobered up enough to go to El Callao to give away his daughter. Teófilo paid all the expenses including the cost of transportation for the family to and from the wedding. There was a big fiesta and Carlos charmed everyone with his wit and mandolin playing.

One morning a few years later, Carlos was awakened by the noise of people talking in front of the house. Getting out of his hammock, Carlos splashed some water over his face and reached for the cup of coffee Nicomedes had ready for him. Going out to the front yard, he saw some of his relatives standing together under the shade of the mango tree. Fear gripped Carlos' heart when he saw his brother from El Callao talking excitedly to the others. He heard such expressions as *qué vergüenza* and *qué barbaridad* [what a shame—what a terrible thing].

Carlos gripped his brother's arm. "What is it, what has happened? Is it Carolina or one of the children?"

"Yes, it is your daughter Carolina," answered the brother.

"What has happened to her? Is she sick? Is she dead? Tell me quickly," screamed Carlos.

"Sit down, brother, and you will hear what has happened to your daughter and that accursed husband of hers." The brother angrily pushed Carlos into a chair with such force that Carlos thought that he was to blame for whatever had happened.

"Your daughter and your son-in-law have had a spell put on them by those gringo Protestant missionaries."

"Spell? Gringo Protestant missionaries? What are you talking about?" Carlos shouted back at his brother.

"What am I talking about? I'll tell you what! You know, when that first Yankee Protestant missionary came to El Callao, he and his family could not speak Spanish. So when he preached, only those 'English' people got 'converted,' as they put it."

"Well," remarked another of Carlos' brothers, "that's not such a tragedy. Many of them are already Protestants and belong to that Anglican church there in El Callao."

"Yeah, but that's all changed. Let me explain. After a few years he went to the United States, and when he returned he brought with him about six more gringo missionaries and their families. Now they are learning to speak Spanish and have started a Baptist church. They are putting a spell on everybody. The *padre* [priest] is furious and threatens all kinds of action. He says he is going to run the gringo missionaries out of town.

"Well, a few weeks ago the Baptist church had what they called an evangelistic campaign. To our family's shame, your son-in-law and your daughter went forward and said that they too would become Protestants. Now they are telling everybody that they have gotten saved, whatever that means."

Now, Carlos understood the concern of the family, but refused to believe it. "I don't believe it, my Carolina would not forsake our mother religion. I know that Teófilo comes from a Protestant family, and might join them, but not my Carolina," Carlos argued.

"Oh, but she has. She has abandoned our blessed mother Mary and her church. I did not come up right away to tell you for I wanted to make sure. Yesterday, I went to see them and they confessed to me that they had forsaken our religion. They even tried to get me to look in that devil book called the Bible that our priest has forbidden us to read."

Carlos now exclaimed, "*¡Qué escándolo!* [What a scandal!] This is a terrible shock. I can't be sure about Teófilo, but I know my daughter Carolina has always been a faithful follower of the Virgin. It must all be Teófilo's doing, he must have convinced her to abandon the Virgin and follow the gringo *americanos*. *El diablo* [devil] must have blinded her.

"Well, we'll see about this." Calling to his wife, Carlos asked, "Nico, are my good clothes clean? I am going to El Callao. I will pull them right out of that gringo's religion."

"How will you go, Carlos?" asked one of the relatives. "We are between crops and have no money to pay for your passage."

"Don't worry about that," spoke up the brother from El Callao. "No problem, Carlos. You can go with me. My boss gave me two days off and loaned me his pickup."

In the late afternoon, Carlos arrived at his son-in-law's goldsmith shop. It was the dry season, so they had made the trip in only four hours. During the trip Carlos became more and more agitated as he thought of the shame his daughter had brought into the family. They had always been faithful to the "Mother Church." Now one of his own had abandoned her.

Mad as a wet hen, Carlos rushed into the shop, past the other employees, to where Teófilo was working. His face livid with rage, he banged his fist on the work bench, and shouted into his son-in-law's face, "You apostate, you... you blasphemer... what have you done to my daughter? The both of you will burn in hell, and... and...." So excited and upset, Carlos' voice was high-pitched and shrill. His mouth still opened, but not a sound came out.

Teófilo was taken by surprise but, since he had become a believer in Christ, he was even more calm and collected than before. Unruffled, he stood up and put his arm around Carlos' shoulder and gently led him from the shop into his office.

"Dad, come sit down and tell me what this is all about." Teófilo looked down on his father-in-law. His six-foot-two-inch height made Carlos, at five foot six inches, look very small.

Carlos was shaking like a leaf in a hurricane, and he was scared. He did not know why. He had never been frightened by any man no matter how big and ferocious he might be. Maybe he needed a drink. In his excitement he had forgotten his habit. His mind was concentrating on how he was going to convince, threaten, cajole... try anything to drive his daughter and her husband out of this heresy and get them back to the "right way" and the "true church."

Calmed down by the quiet manner of his son-in-law, Carlos spoke, "I hear that you have abandoned the blessed Virgin and have believed the false teachings of the cursed Protestants. You have abandoned the faith and have taken my Carolina with you. For shame! I wonder that the 'Mother of God' does not punish you in some horrible way."

Teófilo, now seated in front of his father-in-law, reached out and took one of Carlos' hands in his. "I'm sorry to have caused you so much grief for I love you as if you were my own father. Carolina and I planned to go to Tumeremo next week to visit you and Nicomedes and tell you about the wonderful experience that we have had."

"What difference does it make? Today, next week, whenever? You have denied the religion of our fathers," shouted Carlos as he pulled his hand away. "Where is Carolina? I want to see my daughter."

"Very well. We now live in the big house across the street. Come, Carolina will have my tea ready. She also baked some corn cakes this afternoon."

The two men started to cross the packed yellow-clay street, littered with protruding rocks and loose stones. Carlos tripped over one of the rocks and would have fallen except that Teófilo caught his arm to steady him. Even then the younger man had to help Carlos up the high curb. It was then that Carlos realized how weak he was. All that he had eaten was that little breakfast, a piece of cassava bread, a piece of cheese, and a cup of coffee.

In the house, as Carolina rushed to embrace her father, he asked, "What has this man done to you, *mi amor* [my love]? He must have had a spell put upon you to make you deny the faith of your father and mother, of your grandmother and all our ancestors."

There was a pause while Carlos caught his breath. Then he continued, "Well, we'll get this straightened out pronto. I've come to take you out of that gringo missionary's religion and get you back under the care of the Virgin—she will forgive you... Where are the babies? Get them and come. Your uncle is waiting in the pickup to take us back to Tumeremo."

"Now, *papito, cálmate* [little daddy, calm down]. First of all, nobody has put a spell on me. To the contrary, a spell has been taken away. The blindness has been lifted from my eyes. Here, papa, come sit down. Drink some of this tea. Eat a piece of this cornbread."

Carlos could not resist the tender sweetness of his daughter. As he sat down at the table, he questioned, "Since when did you start drinking tea?... I'd rather have coffee."

Carolina turned to the kerosene stove where some water was heating, took the pot and poured the boiling water into the *colador*, the native coffee-maker. In a matter of a few seconds, Carolina placed a cup half-full of the strong black coffee on the table, filled it with warm milk, and stirred in two heaping teaspoons of sugar. Along side the *café con leche*, she placed the dish with the cornbread to which she added several slices of white country cheese and some native jellied grapefruit rind. While Carlos ate hungrily, Carolina sat down beside him, put her arm over his shoulder, and quietly spoke to him.

"Daddy," she again assured him, "nobody has put a spell on us. The blessed truth is that nobody can, now that we have Jesus living in our hearts. We are not afraid of the *brujos* [witch doctors] anymore and their spells. Jesus won't allow them to hurt us. He will keep us safe forever, and when we die, He will take us to heaven to be with Him forever."

Carlos looked at his daughter with amazement. Could this be his daughter, his quiet little daughter, who spoke with such assurance? There was also some fear showing in his eyes. How could she even mention the witch doctors without crossing herself?

"Carolina, don't talk like that. I beg of you, pray to the Virgin and ask her to help you. You must trust in her power for she is the 'Mother of God'... *Por favor, mi querida hijita* [please, my dear little daughter], forget this Jesus business."

Teófilo sat off to the side quietly listening. He wisely refrained from speaking. He was pleased to hear his wife talk with such assurance. Up until then he was not too sure of her new-found faith since most of the preaching had been done in English. Of course, he had translated everything for her and he had purchased a Bible in Spanish for her from the missionaries.

As Carolina talked, Carlos became more tranquil and he was not trembling anymore. The coffee, bread and cheese, plus Carolina's calm spirit and soft voice worked magic.

"Daddy, please listen. We don't understand it all yet, but we have a wonderful peace in our heart ever since we accepted Jesus as our one and only Savior." Emphasizing the words **ONE** and **ONLY**. "We never had such peace when we worshipped Mary.

"And, Daddy, the 'gringo missionaries' as you called them, only preach from the Bible. We saw it with our own eyes in the Holy Scriptures, that it is a message from God and we believed it. Our priests have kept this good book from us. Daddy, it is not the 'devil's book' as they tell us. They just want to scare us for they don't want us to know the truth."

"Now wait a minute, Carolina. How do YOU know all this? You don't read English. Teófilo had to tell you, and how do you know that he has not deceived you?"

"No, Daddy," she quietly assured him, "Teófilo did not tell me any lies. The missionaries did preach mostly in English because they are just learning Spanish. And, yes, Teófilo did interpret the messages for me. But, Teófilo bought me a Spanish Bible and I have read it for myself. See, Daddy, here it is." She picked up her Bible from the end of the table.

Carlos shied away from the Book as if afraid that it might infect him with some terrible disease if he touched it. He looked at his daughter again in amazement. He could hardly believe his ears. His little daughter, timid Carolina, talked with such assurance and such firmness.

"Daddy, you will stay with us for a few days and we'll have much more time to talk."

Carlos couldn't understand it. He had come down from Tumeremo to fight for his faith and to pull his daughter and her husband out of the gringo's religion. Now he wasn't so sure. Why did he feel so different? He felt almost as though God was talking to him through the words of his Carolina. Carlos shook his head as if to shake off the effect of what he was hearing. Maybe a little drink would help. He mentioned this to his daughter.

"No, Daddy, we don't have strong drink in the house anymore. Our lives are completely changed. Jesus took away all those bad things which harm people." She looked sadly at her father as she remembered his habit.

"Jesus will do it for you too, Daddy. He will forgive your sins and change your life. He will make you a good daddy again like you were before our brother Carlitos died."

Carlos' eyes filled with tears as the memories he had tried to drink away surged up again in his mind. His head dropped onto his folded arms and he began to sob.

Teófilo then came over to him and, placing his large hands on Carlos' shoulders, spoke to him kindly, "Stay with us, Dad. Get a good night's sleep and we'll talk all about it mañana."

Carlos nodded agreement and Carolina led her father to a small room off the patio. It was simply furnished with a chest of drawers, a small table upon which was a basin and pitcher of water, a chair, and a comfortable hammock strung diagonally across the room. On the table, Carolina placed a small thermos of black coffee in case he should awake and crave a drink.

"Sleep well, Daddy, I'll pray for you," she promised as she kissed him on the forehead.

Carlos lay awake for several hours trying to get his thoughts in order. He just couldn't understand it all. What could have happened to Carolina and Teófilo? And how could it be that he himself now felt so calm? What would his brother and the rest of the family think? Well, tomorrow he would have it out with Teófilo. Finally, Carlos dropped off to sleep,

Teófilo had some difficulty convincing the brother waiting in the pickup outside that Carlos was going to remain with them for a few days. But, after a few heated words from the brother, he decided that the big fellow was telling him the truth.

The next day, Teófilo went to his shop, greeted the employees, gave out the various jobs for the day, and then, as his custom was, returned to the house for breakfast. Carlos was at the table sipping his coffee. Carolina had prepared breakfast; a warm dish of *pistraque* [ground, toasted white corn, prepared like cream of wheat, eaten with milk and sprinkled with brown sugar], and the usual slices of bread and butter, white cheese and very sweet *café con leche*.

After their meal, Teófilo with Bible in hand, began the conversation. He found Carlos quite passive and, though inquisitive, not disposed to argue as he had been the night before. Evidently the Holy Spirit had prepared his heart. He listened attentively as Teófilo explained the way of salvation. Teófilo himself was still a babe in Christ, but he had had an inquiring mind and from his youth, had studied the Bible. His relatives, immigrants from the English-speaking islands of the West Indies, were of the Anglican faith with some Wesleyan doctrine mixed in. So when he heard the messages of the first really evangelical missionary to come to El Callao, and through the work of the Holy Spirit, he understood the truths that he had always wondered about. Teófilo then made public his profession of faith in Christ as Savior.

Thus it was that Teófilo readily found the texts necessary to convince Carlos of his lost condition, his need to repent of his sins and to accept Christ as his Savior. Carlos had difficulty at first because of his belief that the Roman Catholic "saints" could intercede for him as he recited the rosary and prayed to Mary. Carlos had no difficulty with the sin question, he knew that he was a sinner. He had for some time been weary of his drunkenness. He felt remorse for the way he had treated his wife and children. With tears, he acknowledged this before God.

Finally, Teófilo showed him I Timothy 2:5, "For there is one God, and one mediator between God and men, the man Christ Jesus." This convinced Carlos that the saints could not intercede for him. After reading John 14:6, "Jesus saith unto him, I am the way, the truth, and the life; no man cometh unto the Father, but by me," Carlos understood that there was no other way to God except through Christ.

At last Carlos said, "I want to be saved too. Teófilo, help me to pray."

"First of all, *querido suegro* [dear father-in-law], you must mean it with all your heart."

"I do—I do—I truly want to be saved."

Teófilo then led Carlos in praying the prayer of the repentant sinner, "God be merciful to me a sinner, and save me, for Jesus' sake."

What rejoicing there was in the Griffin home that day! Carolina was overjoyed. "Thank you, Lord Jesus, you have saved my Daddy."

Yes, Carlos had received Christ as his **only and sufficient** Savior!

Chapter 13

A Powerful Witness

"Therefore being justified by faith, we have peace with God through our Lord Jesus Christ." (Romans 5:1)

Carlos spent two weeks in El Callao, meeting with the little group, learning simple Gospel choruses and studying with them from his new Spanish Bible which Teófilo gave him. At first, Carlos wondered if he would be able to persevere, he had been such a slave to alcohol. To his surprise, the Lord took away even the desire for liquor. It was a great miracle. Then, one day, Carlos came out of his room with his Bible open.

"Carolina, I have found the reason."

"The reason for what?" questioned Carolina.

"The reason why I have no further desire for rum or my old life. Here it is right here." He had his finger on II Corinthians 5:17, the visible proof that a person has been born again.

"Carolina, I am a new creature in Christ. The Lord has made a complete change in me. I now want to live my life for Christ. I have a peace in my heart that I never felt before. I just know that everything is going to be better for my family and me from now on."

The next day Carlos was to go back home to Tumeremo. At breakfast, Carolina told him, "You must tell Mamá all about what has happened to you. You must tell everyone, even your old friends, that you are a true Christian now. We will be praying for you that you will be strong and not fall. Trust the Lord, He will keep you from falling. I asked the Lord this morning for a verse to give you as you go home. Here it is, Daddy, let me mark it in your Bible."

She opened it to Jude 24 and 25. "Now unto him that is able to keep you from falling, and to present you faultless before the presence of his glory with exceeding joy, to the only wise God our Savior, be glory and majesty, dominion and power, both now and ever. Amen."

Just then Teófilo came in. "Brother Carlos, good morning." He emphasized the word "brother" as he spoke.

Carlos looked at Teófilo and questioned, "Brother? You are my son-in-law, not brother."

"Yes, brother. You see Carlos, now that you are born again, you are not only my *suegro* [father-in-law], you are also my brother in Christ. We are now family, not only by law, but by the grace of God. We are God's children, and thus, brothers," explained Teófilo.

Teófilo added, "You had better get ready; young Alberto Peña is at the gas station on the corner getting his truck ready. He says that as soon as he finishes his coffee, he will leave."

Teófilo had barely gotten this out of his mouth when a truck horn sounded outside. Carlos gathered his things together and Teófilo grasped his hand.

"God bless you, Dad. Peña has a box for you already on the truck. It has some food stuff in it for you and the family that Carolina got ready yesterday. It also has some material for Nicomedes to make some dresses for the girls and for herself."

A kiss from Carolina and from the two grandchildren and Carlos climbed into the truck's cabin. With a *Vaya con Dios* from Teófilo, the truck started down the street, headed out of town toward Nacupay, crossed the Yurary River and turned east toward Tumeremo.

It was about 2:30 in the afternoon when Peña pulled into a shady spot on the road where a narrow lane wound through the banana grove up to the house. The family heard the truck coming and then stop. They guessed that it might be Carlos. They wondered in what condition he would be arriving. Nicomedes stood in the doorway of their typical mud country house with its grass roof. Smoke was circling up from the outside kitchen where one of the girls was heating water, it would soon be time for their afternoon coffee.

Nicomedes shaded her eyes from the glare of the sun. She spoke to the young man who had come to stand at her side. "No, that's not Carlos."

"Sure it is, Mamá. Carolina must have fitted him out with new slacks and shirt. The sombrero is new also."

"But look how straight he walks, and so spry too. No, Manuel, it is not Carlos."

Soon Carlos came out of the shade of the banana plants. Now they could see him plainly. "It is papá, Mamá. How healthy and happy he looks, and he is sober too."

Carlos approached the house, smiling broadly, the spaces between his lost teeth showing dark under his full mustache. Manuel stepped out to meet his father. They embraced and, as they turned toward the house, Nicomedes heard her husband say, "There is a cardboard box down by the road, please go fetch it, my son."

Then he stood before her, the first time in years that he had not come home drunk. Setting down the small bundle of dried salt meat he had brought from El Callao, and the white cotton bag in which he carried his Bible and some Gospel tracts, he extended his arms to embrace his wife. He kissed her and then led her to a bench on the shady side of the house. She did not know what to make of it. It reminded her of the romantic Carlos she had married.

Pulling up a chair, Carlos sat down in front of her. Four pairs of eyes in vertical order peered around the corner of the kitchen: Maria, age four, Pedro six, Rafael nine, and Raquel eleven. There were six living children, including Manuel, age sixteen, and Carolina, now married, age twenty-two. Carlitos, their first boy, would have been nineteen, had he lived. Carlos took Nicomedes' hands in his and, looking intently into her eyes, quietly spoke.

Mi querida [my dear], I have much to tell you. God has spoken to me about my past life and I have nothing but sorrow in my heart for the way I have treated you and the children these past years since Carlitos died. I want to ask your pardon. Can you forgive me?"

"Of course, Carlos; how could I not forgive the man I have loved all these years, and especially the one who now seems more like the gentle and loving man I married."

Carlos raised his wife's hands to his lips, hands browned and work-worn from toiling in the fields. He looked up into Nicomedes' face again, tears coursing down his cheeks. She wiped away his tears and gently kissed him on the forehead.

"Carlos, what has made this change in you? You seem like a new man."

"*Sí, mi amor* [yes, my love], I am a new man. I have been born again. God has forgiven me of all the bad things I've ever done and I now have Jesus living in my heart."

In astonishment Nicomedes drew back and pulled her hands out of his. Mouth agape, eyes full of wonder, she raised one of her hands in protest. Finally she found words and gasped, "You... you have become an evangelical? How could you forsake our Virgin Mother?"

Carlos answered her calmly, assuring her that something wonderful had happened to him, not bad. Then, begging her to listen, he related to her the events of the past two weeks.

"Nicomedes, I could not resist God's call for me to repent of my sins. I just had to *entregarme* [surrender myself] to the blessed Lord Jesus. I accepted Him as my one and only Savior and received Him into my heart. He has made me a new man. He has taken away all my old desire for rum. Now I want to serve God and I want to become once again a good father to my children and the kind of a husband to you that I was during the first years of our marriage."

As Carlos talked, Nicomedes could not help but admit in her heart that whatever had happened, it had to be something miraculous to bring about such a change in her husband.

"I do not understand it, Carlos, but if it is a new faith that has done this for you, it must be of God. But what will the padre in Tumeremo say?"

"What can he say? He never tried to help me when I needed him. In fact, he participated in all our fiestas and often joined us in the cantina. Besides, we are a free people and we can worship God as we like. Free, yes free, my dear wife, free from the devil and free to live for Christ. Look at this, Nicomedes, what Teófilo showed me in the Bible."

Taking his Bible from the sack, Carlos opened it to one of the already dog-eared pages. He and Nicomedes were two of the few country people in those days who could read and write. They insisted that their children also get an education, meager as it was in the frontier areas.

Carlos read from John 8:32. "And ye shall know the truth, and the truth shall make you free." Dropping his finger down to verse 36, he read, "If the Son therefore shall make you free, ye shall be free indeed." Carlos explained that he had learned that the "Son" was Jesus Christ and that the "truth" was the Bible, and then added: "No longer will the traditions of the Catholic church and our superstitions have control over our lives."

At daylight the next day, Nicomedes was in her kitchen getting the fire started and preparing the morning coffee. Carlos strolled around the farm, making mental note of what he must do first. The farm was really run down in spite of the efforts of the relatives. Back at the house, he called the children to come have breakfast with him. They thought it very strange, so different from their usual way, which was to eat whenever they felt like it.

Carlos explained to Nicomedes and the children that, as a true Christian, he had a new love for his family and wanted them to be with him as often as possible. At least at breakfast they would be together and he would lead them in Bible reading and prayer. He had learned to do this from Teófilo and Carolina and the other new believers in El Callao.

After devotions that first morning home, Carlos and Manuel began their day's work. They cut several bunches of bananas, picked two hundred ripe oranges, and dug up about 25 pounds of sweet yucca roots. The next day, at daybreak, this produce was loaded on their burro, and on another one borrowed from his cousin, to take them into town to sell. These items would make a down payment on some garden tools he needed, such as machetes, hoes, and an axe.

On the way there and back, Carlos was greeted by several of his old drinking cronies who hardly recognized him, clean-shaven, mustache trimmed, clean clothes and all. They could not understand why he didn't even stop to say hello. The truth was that Carlos still had a fear of yielding to temptation, and wanted to be stronger before witnessing to them.

Back home again, they ate a hearty meal of native stew, seasoned with the dried salt meat. The sun was high in the heavens and, as was their custom, they went to their hammocks. Carlos slung his under the shade of the mango trees. He swung lazily, making a little breeze in an effort to cool himself. He thought about the events of the last two weeks which had brought about such a change in his life and had given him a new beginning. Yes, a new beginning, for was he not born again? He could not imagine himself more happy and contented.

By 2:30 he was out in the garden, hoeing between the bean plants, pulling the weeds and mounding the soil around the little hills from which the squash vines were snaking and twining about each other across the furrows. By 5:00 o'clock he had finished that task and was ready for his pouring shower.

Manuel and Raquel had their chores and one of them was to carry water up to the house from the lagoon at the bottom of the hill. They did this early in the morning, depositing the water into two 50 gallon drums and several five-gallon tins. This was an important chore, for the water was vital to cleanliness as well as for cooking purposes. These country folk never bothered to boil or filter the water as the city or town people had to do. It seems that they had built up an immunity to any disease germs the water might contain.

After his *cafe con leche*, a piece of dry cassaba bread and cheese, Carlos was sitting in a straight home-made chair leaned back against the mud wall of the house, reading his Bible. He was memorizing some verses from the Psalms which he had already come to love. Little Maria and Pedro came to him, saying, "Papá, we have brought your mandolin. Please play something for us. Maybe a song you learned while you were with Carolina."

A chill of fear ran up and down Carlos' spine. His reaction, both mental and physical, was rather violent. He felt sick to his stomach. Visions of his past life in the streets and bars flashed through his mind. He sprang to his feet, grabbed the mandolin violently from poor little frightened Maria's hands. Maria and Pedro ran to their mother's side where she was pounding the shells off the dried corn that she would later grind into flour.

Carlos was trembling. To him the mandolin had become the symbol of his past. His head lifted toward the heavens, he exclaimed, "Dios mio; Dios mio, do not allow me to fail you."

The sensations that Carlos felt were confusing. He felt a strong temptation to play one of the barroom songs and return to the old life. At the same time he felt a strong loathing of himself for having such feelings. But his spontaneous prayer was answered and the feelings left him as quickly as they had come. The Lord calmed his troubled heart and mind. He dropped to his knees beside the chair, lay the mandolin on the ground, bowed his head low in his hands, and prayed to his Savior: "Thank you, Lord Jesus; all I want is for you to be Lord of my life."

When Carlos came to know me better, he told me the story. He told how he had begged the Lord to forgive him for his violent reaction. He prayed that the Lord would tell him what to do with his mandolin. As he prayed, he felt that he should destroy the instrument, which would always be a reminder of his past sins which he wanted to forget.

You must understand that Carlos was the first believer in the area. If I had been there I would have tried to show him how his mandolin could be converted also and be used to play hymns and choruses honoring to the Lord. But Carlos destroyed his mandolin that very night. When we talked about it, Carlos assured me that, when I played my mandolin in the services, he was not offended in the least. However, he still felt that he should keep the vow he had made that night to never play a mandolin again.

During Carlos' first week at home, their relatives came to see him, wanting to know how he had fared on his trip to El Callao. He gave them his testimony about his new found faith in Christ. While they did not like what they were hearing, they did not have much to say. Carlos was the senior male of the family, and as such, according to custom, was the *cacique* [chief] of the clan, whose word was to be honored and obeyed.

It was late in the afternoon of his second Saturday home that his big test came. Five of his old friends appeared on the farm, coming up to the front patio as always.

"Carlos, old buddy, we have missed you and have come to celebrate Pedro's saint day with you. Look here, we have two bottles of Aguardiante." Paco spoke as he held aloft the two bottles of corn liquor. "You, Carlos, will have the honor of breaking the seal on the first bottle."

Carlos greeted his old friends with a smile, embracing them each in turn as custom dictated. As he caught the odor of rum on their breaths, he experienced again the chill of fear running up and down his spine. The smile quickly disappeared from his face, changing to an expression of sorrow and pity. He spoke seriously and firmly to them.

"No, my friends, I cannot go with you any more. God has come into my soul and has put my life back on to the right way."

Pedro spoke up, "I cannot believe what I am hearing. The police told us when we passed the *alcabala* [check-point] on the way out here that you have gotten religion. So what, Carlos? You have always accompanied us before and you still were faithful to the Virgin. I don't see how a change in your religion can keep you from enjoying a fiesta with your friends."

"No, Pedro, I cannot," interrupted Carlos. "I have not gotten religion; not the old one or a new one. What has happened to me...."

That was as far as Carlos got. Pedro shouted out, this time very angrily. "Do you mean to tell me that you will not take a drink with me, Pedro? Am I not your best friend?"

Carlos extended his hand, placing it on Pedro's shoulder. "Pedro, yes, you **were** my best friend," emphasis placed on the "were." "You are still my friend. But I have a new Friend now who is closer to me than a brother. His name is Jesus."

"Jesus?... Jesus?... I know of no Jesus around here," exclaimed Pedro, still shouting.

Paco spoke up, "There is a Jesus on a farm out toward El Dorado, but he is a rich rancher. He cannot be Carlos' new friend."

Carlos held up his hand to silence his friends who were now all talking at once. "Let me explain, my friends. The Jesus of whom I speak is Jesus the Son of God."

Understanding at last came to Pedro. "Oh, **that** Jesus. You mean the little baby in the Virgin's arms. How can this be? You are talking nonsense, Carlos. A little baby cannot help you. Anyhow, he is just part of the statue in the town church."

Carlos patiently explained, "He whom you call—and I once did also—'the baby Jesus', is the true Son of God who came to earth to die for our sins on the cross of Calvary. He is no longer a baby. He died and rose again. Now He is in heaven at God the Father's right hand where He prays for us. The Bible tells us that all who will receive Him into their heart will be forgiven of their sins and one day go to heaven. No, my friends, I do not have a new religion. I have Jesus Christ in my heart since I accepted Him as my own personal Savior. I can no longer go with you to drink and sing and dance like I used to. My Savior would not want me to do it, nor do I have the desire to do it."

While Carlos and Pedro were exchanging words, one of the men had asked Nicomedes for several of the small gourds which every country family used for drinking. He came up to Carlos and Pedro, opened one of the bottles of rum and poured some into two of the gourds, offering them to the two men. Pedro quickly took the cue.

"Carlos," he said, "you cannot refuse to take at least one little drink with me who has been your best friend for many years, especially on this my saint's day." (According to their custom, to refuse to drink with them would be a great discourtesy and an insult.)

As he spoke, Pedro offered one of the gourds to Carlos. Carlos hesitated for a moment, then reached out and took it from his old friend's hand. The cheer coming from the men sent a chill into Nicomedes' heart as she watched, but the cheer died on their lips, turning to a gasp as Carlos tipped the gourd and let the rum run out onto the ground. Five astonished men, cried out almost in unison, "No!... No!... I can't believe it!"

Carlos, saved,
Powerful witness and soul winner

These were violent men and at the slightest provocation would start a fight. There is no telling what might have happened, humanly speaking, for the situation was explosive. But two large men appeared from behind the outdoor kitchen where they had been listening. They came into the patio and stood just behind Carlos. Nicomedes' brother had heard the men talking as they passed by his house which bordered on the road, and suspected that there might be trouble. So, he had come up the back way, around the lagoon, to Carlos' cousin's house and together they came up through the plaintain grove that divided their properties. Whether or not their appearance was a deterrent to some violent action we do now know, but it gave Carlos the opportunity to further witness to the men.

He briefly related the events which led to his conversion. He spoke of the joy and satisfaction he now had as a believer in Christ. It was a wonderful and practical testimony and the men were convinced that something had indeed happened to enable Carlos to refuse a drink.

The incident served as genuine proof to the family that Carlos was indeed a new creature in Christ. The two relatives who had witnessed the confrontation assured Carlos that they would stand behind him even though they did not agree with him. Some time later they accepted Christ as their Savior. Nicomedes, also witnessing Carlos' resistance to the temptation to drink again, that very night asked Carlos to help her receive Christ as her Savior. The two older children came to Christ some time later during one of their family devotion times.

Chapter 14

The Morales-Martínez Family Story

"...Believe on the Lord Jesus Christ, and thou shalt be saved, and thy house." (Acts 16:31)

"Mamá!... papá... Sara... Paquito... run quickly!... hide..., Isidro is coming up the hill," shouted little Jorge as he ran panting around the corner of the vegetable garden and across the little clearing toward the house.

Ana Morales looked out from the door of her house, and shaded her eyes against the reddening rays of the setting sun, now low in the sky over the field of ripening corn. She could barely see a man's head popping up above the yellow stalks and disappearing again. Yes, it was her oldest son Isidro staggering up the footpath along the edge of the field. As he straightened up, his head would come into view, then, losing his balance, his head would disappear again.

"Come Sara, come Jorgito. Your father is out in back." So saying, Ana picked up little Samuel, caught up her large towel and several pieces of heavy cloth. They would need some protection from the cool night mist, depending upon how long it would take Isidro to fall into his usual drunken slumber.

Ana passed through the back door of the house out into the patio. Her husband, Gerónimo Martínez, was sitting astride a native wooden chair. He had the flat side of his machete held tightly between one leg and the seat of the chair, the usual position when a farmer file-sharpened his machete. He was getting this versatile farm tool ready for tomorrow when he would continue clearing off the lower field. Ana called to her husband.

"Gerónimo, come right away. Isidro is coming home, drunk again. Tell Paco."

Without waiting for her companion's response, Ana and the children hurried across the patio into the banana grove. Gerónimo quickly stored his machete and file on a rock under the raised floor of the house, along with the garden hoe. Grabbing his straw hat, he ran into the grove after Ana. Just in time, for Isidro was already staggering across the clearing in front of the house. As Gerónimo caught up with Ana, he explained about Paco, their second son.

"Paco is in town; he got caught by the *policía* and has to clean up the office of the *Comandante* and the magistrate's courtroom. He will not be home until late."

"Why isn't he more careful when he is in town with his friends? Were they caught too?"

"No, Ana, just Paco. The others got away."

Going quickly through the banana grove, they reached the small *trapiche*, just inside their neighbor's property. This was a small sugar mill under an open pavilion covered with palm leaves where Don Matías, their neighbor, squeezed out the juice from the sugar cane and cooked it down to make hard cones of the crude brown sugar called *papilón*.

Ana settled the small children down on some dried palm leaves and covered them with the cloths she had brought with her. Jorgito gathered up some cane chaff and made his own bed over against the pile of fire wood. Ana and Gerónimo sat on low stools. It was already quite dark and the children were soon asleep. Night comes quickly in the tropics, almost no twilight at all. It's as if some giant shade were pulled down across the sky. Ana and Gerónimo sat there talking softly so as not to awaken the children.

"It is very cool and damp tonight," commented Ana as she pulled her towel around her shoulders. "At least we have cover if it should rain."

"Yes," agreed Gerónimo. I'm sorry I did not stop to get my jacket."

Several hours passed by. Ana had dozed off, her head resting against the cane crusher. Then she was awakened by a touch on her arm.

"I have been up to the house. Isidro is fast asleep on the floor of the kitchen. I locked the door and window, just in case. Come, we can go home now."

So saying, Gerónimo picked up Sara and shook Jorgito awake. Ana gathered up little Samuel and, followed by half-asleep Jorgito, they picked their way through the banana grove, the silvery rays of the almost full moon showing them the path. It was almost midnight. Soon they were all sound asleep, swinging in their hammocks, assured from experience that they were safe from their son. Isidro would sleep until late in the morning. He would awaken with a "big head." His bleary eyes would search the faces of his mother and father, fearing to see marks of the beating he may have given them when he arrived home the night before.

Isidro would not remember anything of what might have happened after he left the bar in town. He would be relieved to see that he had not harmed his family which he did love very dearly. He would be repentant and would swear never to drink again. It was a vain resolution. The cheap liquor Isidro drank turned this young man, still very close to his Indian ancestry, into a ferocious, violently angry bully, ready to beat up anyone he may encounter, just as the "fire water" did to his Indian brothers on the North American continent. When they would see this happening, his friends would slowly disappear, getting away from his flailing arms, and Isidro would stagger home to take out his anger on his family.

One day, shortly after the incident just related, the Mission's evangelist, Angel, arrived in Tumeremo. This was long before he had fallen into spiritism. He stayed in Don Carlos' home and each day would go to town to visit the homes of whoever would listen to him explain the message of salvation through faith in the living Christ.

Don Carlos invited his farmer neighbors to meetings held under the great mango trees. Angel was a gifted preacher and very knowledgeable about the state religion, having studied for the priesthood before his conversion to Christ. As a result of this "campaign," several others of Carlos' and Nicomedes relatives and neighbors were saved. The believers banded together and, with the help of the missionaries in El Callao, were baptized and a local church was organized.

Then the miracle for which Ana and Gerónimo were hoping came about. Both Ana and Gerónimo had accepted Christ as Savior during the meetings on Carlos' farm.

One day, without thinking, Isidro walked down the street where the police station was located. There was a need that day for some strong muscles to move furniture around the municipal offices. Isidro was "commissioned" to this work as well as the usual clean-up jobs.

That day, Angel, the evangelist, came into town to get a permit to hold an open-air meeting in the town's Plaza. As he was coming out of the Comandante's office, he recognized Isidro. Receiving a nod of consent from the officer, Angel began to speak to the young man. The Comandante was heard to say to his secretary, "If the evangelist converts THAT wild Indian, I myself might be persuaded to become a believer."

Well... God's ways are wonders to behold and will always assure Him of the glory. Isidro opened his heart to the witness of the Holy Spirit as Angel read the Word to him, and received Christ as His "one and only" Savior. No one would believe it, but time proved that indeed a miracle had occurred. From that moment on Isidro never drank another drop of liquor.

Not long after that, missionaries Robert Fletcher and his wife were sent to Tumeremo. The house they rented also served as a meeting place for the little local congregation. Carlos and Eugenio were the first deacons. Ana and Gerónimo attended but could not be members yet.

A year later, Mildred and I were alone in Tumeremo. About three months after that confrontation with Angel, Isidro's younger brother, Paco, sent word requesting us to visit him in his parents' home. Paco could not come himself because the last time the police had put him to work, he had run away and, if they caught him again, it would go hard with him.

During the interview with Paco I learned one more truth I needed to know when dealing with Hispanic Americans. Paco had been in trouble a few times, not seriously, but enough to make him realize that he needed help. He had resisted the urging of his parents to accept Christ as Savior. But, watching his brother, he became convinced that Christ might be the answer to his problems. "If Christ could change Isidro into a decent citizen, He certainly might help me, Paco, who never did anything as bad as Isidro had done," he said, self-righteously.

"All right, then, Paco, do you admit that you are a sinner?"

"A sinner?" indignantly asked Paco. "I, a sinner? Oh no!... Oh, I have some problems that I think Christ could help me solve. But I am not a **sinner**."

I was surprised to hear Paco deny that so emphatically. It was the first time in my ministry that I was asked to help a person come to Christ who denied being a sinner.

"However small your problems may be, Paco, those problems are a result of sin. We are all sinners, Paco... Look what it says right here in the Bible." I showed him Romans 3:23.

"Let's read it together. 'For all have sinned, and come short of the glory of God.' See, it says ALL have sinned; that means you and me." Paco had been sent to the little one-room school at the cross-road halfway into town and so could read the text for himself.

"I see what it says, but it has to be wrong. I am not a sinner. I have not killed anyone, I have never been with a woman, I have never taken money or anything from a person so as to make him poor. No sir, I am not a sinner."

"But, Paco, my friend, to commit sin doesn't mean just to do those big and serious ones that you have named. Sin is any act or thought that is against the will of God. Even a little white lie is sin. Why, Paco, it says in the Bible that if you know that you should do something good and you don't do it, you have sinned." I showed him James 4:17 and let him read it. Paco was puzzled. He admitted, "I didn't know THAT was sin."

As we continued to talk, I learned that the people did not consider those little things sin. Those little "white lies," often said to save oneself out of a difficult situation, or said so as not to offend someone, were called *mentiras piadosas*, meaning "compassionate lies." According to many people, it was not sin to take a few coins, pocket some trinket in a big store, or lie. Sin was murder, adultery, and robbing great sums of money.

I discovered that this belief resulted from listing sin in two classes: mortal sins and venial sins. Mortal sins were the more serious ones, that needed to be atoned for. Venial sins were small and unimportant, forgiven after reciting a little prayer or repeating the rosary.

After more conversation and reading of the Bible, Paco seemed to understand that indeed he was a sinner, though I had reservations about any real repentance. Reviewing again the verses which show the need of accepting Christ as Savior as a definite act of faith, Paco bowed his head and prayed. I sincerely hoped that he really meant business.

Yes, Mildred and I, like all first term missionaries, had much to learn about the people and their culture. In the States we used to tell people to come to Christ "**just as you are**." We found such an argument, without detailed explanation, to be invalid in Venezuela. We discovered this one afternoon as we came home from visiting in the country.

Nearing town, we stopped to give out some Gospel tracts to a number of women seated by the side of the road. The women had bundles of clothes beside them. They had just come up from the lagoon where they had done their weekly wash. As yet no water was piped into the homes and very few could afford to build tanks in which to store rain water.

Two of the younger women seemed interested in the tracts so we stopped to chat with them. From the Bible, we showed them verses about the Lord and His salvation.

"I think the Gospel is beautiful," declared one of the women. "Sometimes I wish I could surrender myself to the Gospel."

"Well, if you really believe that the Gospel is true, why don't you surrender? Christ will save you; your sins will be forgiven and you will have everlasting life."

"I can't," replied the young lady.

"And why not? If you believe in your heart, what is there to stop you?"

With an expression on her face which seemed to say, "Are you blind? Can't you see?" She held up her hand with a cigarette between her fingers, its smoke curling into my face.

"Besides smoking, I like to sing and dance, and I love the drinks which the men treat me to. I just love the fiestas too much to give them up."

"But," we assured her, "you don't have to give up anything, smoking or whatever, to accept Christ as your Savior. He wants you to come to Him just as you are."

I was about to explain this more fully, but the young lady's attitude had changed completely. She said rather disdainfully, "You must think I was born yesterday if you expect me to believe that. I know better."

"But..." I started to speak again.

"Don't 'but' me. I won't be fooled by your trickery. I know some of your believers and everyone of them gave up smoking, drinking, the fiesta... everything."

So saying, she turned her back, lit up another cigarette and started to talk to one of the other women. We wanted to explain what we meant. We didn't want to give up that easily. But just then the truck for which they were waiting arrived. The women climbed in, with their washing, and were immediately on their way south out of

Tumeremo. The women would be left off at their respective homes, a service for which they paid a few pennies.

"Well," I remarked to Mildred as we and Eddie continued our walk into town, "I never expected that reaction. That's the last time I'll ever use **that** argument."

"I guess that is one of the reasons they use the expression, '*entregarse* [surrender yourself] to the Gospel,'" suggested Mildred. "It is true that all of our people gave up their vices as soon as they were saved. I can't think of any of them that do have a problem, can you?... I guess being "saved" to our neighbors means also giving up the world's vices."

"I guess so. But I am sure that our people don't think that they are saved because they gave up their vices. They testify to believing they are saved by the grace of God, through faith in Christ and not by their works. The fact that our people do give up their vices and worldly pleasures is a proof that they are saved. I guess the lost think that giving up their vices is a means of getting saved. They don't seem to understand that believers give up their vices because they are saved and want to please their Savior."

Mildred took me by the hand and gave it a little squeeze." We still have much to learn, Ed. But the Lord has helped us so far, and He will continue to do so. I just know He will continue to teach us," she encouraged.

Chapter 15

More
New Learning Experiences
Loneliness Overcome - Our First Weddings

"And every one that hath forsaken houses, or brethren, or sisters, or father, or mother, or wife, or children, or lands, for my name's sake, shall receive an hundredfold, and shall inherit everlasting life." *(Matthew 19:29)*

When Bob Fletcher left to join his wife in the States, Mr. Hausser said that we could move back to El Callao, if we wished. But we felt that the Lord had brought us to Tumeremo for a purpose, so we decided to stick it out until He told us to leave. We were glad that we did.

Admittedly, we felt very much alone. We experienced some new and different emotional conflicts. For almost a year we had no personal contact with our co-workers. We had no one to talk to who understood English, no one of our cultural background who would understand our needs, no one to whom we could unburden our concerns or go to seek counsel. Of course, there were the letters going back and forth, but these dealt mostly with questions and answers about the language. A young missionary, Bob Rodgers, did come to vacation with us for a few weeks. Eddie appreciated this diversion, Bob played games and took bicycle rides with him.

Mildred and I were kept busy—very busy. The toughest part of our work was the ministry of visitation. Most of the believers lived way out in the country. We did not have a car, so we walked many miles over either dusty or muddy trails, depending upon the weather. As we dragged ourselves home after one of those visits out to Carlos and Gerónimo's farm, or to Celestino's little *finca* [farm] in the other direction, we often encouraged ourselves with such remarks as: "I was reading in the health book that walking is the best exercise." It would help to brace up our spirits, but it did not take away the aches and stiffness from our legs.

In town, Mildred began a number of home Bible clubs for the children. It was difficult for her at first but the children themselves would help her find the words she needed to explain the lesson. She had the same language problems that I had. As time went on, however, Spanish words and expressions came more easily and, praise God, we did not need to spend as much time in preparation of lessons or messages.

Our greatest joy came from seeing how the Lord was blessing the work. That year we saw the believers growing in Bible knowledge and others coming to salvation in Christ. The love and fellowship of our Venezuelan brethren in Christ filled the void in our hearts and **conquered our loneliness**. We were much encouraged and became very happy with our life in the frontier town of Tumeremo. It proved to be a great learning experience.

We found the Lord's promises to be true, especially that one where He assured His disciples that: "And everyone that hath forsaken... brethren, or sisters, or father, or mother,... or lands, for my name's sake, shall receive an hundredfold...."

********** ********** **********

Isidro and Carmen - Our First Marriage

"Marriage is honorable in all, and the bed undefiled...."
(Hebrews 13:4a)

"...a man... joined unto his wife,... shall be one flesh."
(Ephesians 5:31)

One Sunday morning I arose extra early to go over my message for the worship service. My notes from El Callao, along with some letters from the States, had arrived by truck late the night before. I was inking in the corrections which Dolores had made for me, when there was a knock on the patio door. It was Isidro Morales accompanied by Carmen Rosa.

"Come in... come in... To what do I owe this pleasure?"

Isidro and Carmen exchanged glances, each waiting for the other to speak. Finally it was Carmen who explained, "Isidro and I want to get married."

"Hey, that's great! You are both saved and baptized as well as faithful members of our little church. Carmen, were you ever married?"

"No, pastor Eduardo, I have never been married. My little boy and girl were born before the Lord saved me, during the time that I worked as a housegirl on the Condado *Hacienda* [ranch]."

"I thought as much, Carmen. I just wanted to be sure. Isidro will make a good father for little Carmencita and Luisito. When would you like to have the ceremony?"

"Well, pastor, we don't know exactly what we have to do," explained Isidro. "Will you please make the arrangements for us with the *alcalde* [mayor]? Then, as soon as all the legal papers are ready, we will be married."

The following week, I visited the City Hall, actually three rooms in a small building shared by the National Guard and the Police Department. This was the first marriage I would perform and I needed to know the procedure. It was the secretary of the City Council who really ran the government of Tumeremo and it was he who recorded all the information about marriages and other civil business. He even directed the judge's schedule.

The information had to be written in longhand in the archives, which was done by a lesser secretary, usually a retired school teacher. I already knew that, according to Venezuelan law, all marriages had to be performed by a judge. The fees were nominal, making it easier for the poor. After the civil ceremony, the marriage could be "blessed" in the couple's church.

I was surprised at the cordiality of the secretary, a very polite and educated man, apparently from *categoría* [high society]. I gave him all the information necessary; the names of Carmen's two children, names of the couple's parents, residence, etc. The two children would be listed as "recognized" by Isidro, and he would then become their legal father by adoption.

When I gave the full names of Isidro and Carmen, I had to repeat Carmen's last name, Rosa. The secretary dropped his pen, picked it up again and nervously began to straighten up the papers on his desk. Gaining his composure, he looked at me with a rather sober expression.

"Well, well... so little Carmen Rosa is getting married. Is this Isidro Morales a good man? Will he treat her and the children well?"

"Oh, yes," I assured him. "His life is completely changed since he accepted Christ as his personal Savior. Are you acquainted with Carmen?"

"Just casually," the secretary answered. "She is from an old family of ranchers, original settlers in these parts. Their descendants didn't know how to manage their finances. The family is now very poor. I did hear recently that Carmen and her father had changed their religion."

I had had several dealings with the secretary, mostly about our I.D. cards, but, because he was always so busy, I never had been able to talk to him personally. Now I took the opportunity to talk to him about Christ and His gospel, giving him a short account of Isidro's testimony. The secretary mentioned that his aunt was an evangelical and attended a church in Caracas. She had sent him a Bible which he read occasionally for its literary content.

I asked him if he had ever considered the claims of Christ upon his soul. He admitted that he had, but gave up thinking about it for the sake of his political future. The secretary had just recently married into another prominent political family and could not jeopardize his future advancement in the government by showing interest in "the religion of the lower class people."

The following Sunday morning, after service, I informed Isidro and Carmen of the date for the marriage. "Lord willing, we will do it two weeks from yesterday."

I told them about the conversation with the city secretary and the opportunity I had to speak to him about the Lord. Carmen listened with bowed head and then, almost in a whisper, admitted, "He... he is the father of Carmencita and Luisito. I thought that I might have to name the real father of my children, so, when Isidro asked me to marry him, I told him about it."

"That explains his interest in the kind of a man Isidro is. He is apparently anxious about them even though he does not publicly recognize them as his."

"No, and I don't want him to. I have learned a lot these past few years. I was bitter at first, but since the Lord saved me, I don't want to hurt anyone," declared Carmen.

"I understand, *hermana* [sister] Carmen, and you don't have to say anything more."

"But I want to tell you. As my pastor, I want you to know how it happened, then nobody can make up any stories about me later on. I was very young when I went to work at his parent's hacienda. Though I yielded to him, I never had any illusions that he would marry me. I knew also that, because of his family, he would never come forth and recognize the children as his. He did secretly pay twice for the midwife and now and then the children receive gifts from an unknown source. I never let him touch me again after I accepted Christ as my Savior and when he knew I meant business, he quit chasing me."

"Well, we'll keep this secret to ourselves. The children will come to love and respect Isidro as their father. Maybe, when they are grown men and women, their true father will make himself known to them. We'll commit the whole matter into the Lord's hands, shall we?" We bowed our heads and I prayed that the Lord's will would be done.

The following week, Mildred and I went to visit Gerónimo Martínez and Ana Morales out on their little farm. The purpose of the visit was to try once again to convince them to get married. An added argument was the upcoming wedding of their son Isidro. They had been believers for a few years and now their only argument was that they did not have money enough to buy new clothes for a wedding. Ana would need a new dress and shoes. Gerónimo would need new slacks, a shirt and shoes.

Most of the poor farmers never saw any cash from one year to the next. They contracted their entire crop of corn or other produce to a storekeeper in town. In turn, the storekeeper would supply them with whatever they needed through the year, keeping an account which would be balanced out when they brought in the harvest. It was a very inequitable way of doing business. They paid top price for what they bought but received the bottom wholesale price for their farm products. More often than not they had to buy back their own corn at retail price.

Now that they were believers, the finances of our members were getting better. Don Carlos, now a successful farmer, was much help to them, showing them how to farm more efficiently, to conserve their time and energies, and how to "bargain" when they made the contract. The Lord sent rain when it was needed, and gave them an abundance of crops. This year, with the *platanos* [cooking bananas] producing well, they would have a surplus.

But, at the moment, there was no cash flow to buy new clothes. This problem was quickly solved when we offered to loan them enough money to buy what they needed. We went home that day feeling good with our mission accomplished. I again visited the city secretary to arrange the marriage of Isidro's parents. The secretary was pleased, saying, "The government in Caracas has a campaign going on to try to get all unwed people married." Then, jokingly,

"They might give you a medal for your good work here in Tumeremo."

The wedding of Isidro's parents was to take place the week after the wedding of Isidro and Carmen. But, Isidro and Carmen requested that the wedding dates be reversed, so that Gerónimo and Ana would be married a week before them.

"Pastor Eduardo," Isidro explained, "when my father and mother marry, my name will no longer be Isidro Morales, it will be Isidro Martínez. My father will officially recognize all his children and their last name of Morales will also be changed in the records to Martínez. I am happy my parents will marry and I want to be married with my father's name, Martínez."

"I understand, Isidro, and I will see what I can do tomorrow when the offices open. I hope we will have no problem changing the dates. The schedule is full of weddings, but in your case, nothing needs to be added or changed, so it will depend upon the secretary's helpers, if they can get all the information about your parents handwritten into the archives on time."

On Monday, after I explained the reasons to the secretary, the dates were changed. He was very understanding and cooperative. So, on the Saturday scheduled, Gerónimo Martínez and Ana Morales were married in the presence of their children, Isidro, Jorgito, Sara and Samuelito. Paco, already in military service, was represented in proxy by his cousin. The two deacons of the church, Carlos and Eugenio, as well as we missionaries were the witnesses.

The following Saturday, Isidro, now Martínez, and Carmen Rosa were married. During the ceremony, Isidro officially adopted little Carmencita and Luisito. The secretary, smiling broadly, insisted upon being the first witness to sign the marriage and adoption papers. The religious ceremony was held in our church for both couples. Then the reception took place in the large patio of our house, after which, Isidro and Carmen were escorted out the south road to the ranch where Isidro had been working. Isidro had been permitted to build a small house on a fertile corner of the ranch property where he would also have his own little farm.

What a testimony Isidro was in the town of Tumeremo. First of all to the power of the Gospel of Christ to save and change lives. Most everyone, especially the police, knew the young man of Indian descent, who turned into a wild brute when under the influence of liquor. The people could hardly believe that it was the same man who now quietly testified to the power of Christ in his life.

And now Isidro had taken Carmen to be his wife, and little Carmencita and Luisito to be his adopted children. This marriage gave a tremendous testimony to the difference the Gospel also makes in a society prone to libertinism. It is all to the glory of our God, the Creator of the family, when a man, in obedience to the divine commandment, commits himself until death to be united in one flesh, as he leaves his father and mother and cleaves to his wife.

Chapter 16

Our First Baptism

"Then they that gladly received his word were baptized; and... were added unto them [the church] *...and they continued steadfastly in the apostles' doctrine and fellowship, and in breaking of bread, and in prayers."*

(Acts 2:41,42)

For several weeks, I had taught some Bible lessons on Christian living and church membership to our believers waiting baptism. Then one Sunday morning each one gave his testimony. There were seven: Gerónimo and Ana Martínez, two of deacon Eugenio's older boys, and three ladies who had recently been saved. The baptism was planned for that afternoon.

Tumeremo was suffering a dry spell. In the hot tropics this is a serious situation. With midday temperatures of over 100 degrees, the vegetation turns yellow and dries up. The water in the lagoon on the edge of town was too low to have the baptism service there. It was full of wild hyacinths and the shore edge was so muddy from the cattle tromping in it that the women could no longer wash their clothes there.

Isidro told us about a large lagoon out the south road toward the town of El Dorado. Evidently this lagoon was fed by underground springs for there was water enough for a baptism. But, this meant a hike of about six miles there and six miles back again. There were no cars to rent in Tumeremo. There wasn't even a truck available; most were gone from town, either on a trip, or were loaded, ready to leave at dawn on Monday. So, we prepared to walk.

After the morning service, the believers who lived in the country out in the other direction, such as brothers Carlos and Gerónimo, prepared a meal in the patio of the Mission house. About 1:30, the hike began, the ladies carrying umbrellas to protect themselves from the rays of the hot sun, the men with their broad brim straw or felt hats. The candidates, dressed in work clothes for their baptism, carried a change of clothing in cotton bags.

As our group trudged along the road, people asked the reason for the hike. A real Christian believer's baptism was a curiosity in that area, all that the people knew about was the infant sprinkling of their state church. So, out of curiosity, and with nothing else to do on a Sunday afternoon, quite a few joined the march. I was glad for the opportunity to preach the Gospel to the many unsaved who joined us.

In spite of the hot tiring hike, we all felt rejuvenated when we came up over a rise in the road and a clear view of the lagoon burst on our sight, an oasis in a semi-desert area. As we approached, we could see a clean sandy beach. The water looked clear, clean and cool. To the left side of the lagoon, several yards back from the water, stood four giant mango trees, their lower branches almost touching the ground from the weight of ripened fruit. With a shout we rushed, with one accord, to pick a mango. Tearing the skin off with our teeth, we bit off pieces of the yellow juicy pulp, not caring if some of the juice ran down and dripped off our chins.

After a little time of rest, we held the service. The people were very attentive as the testimonies were given and I spoke briefly about the way of salvation. There was evidence of much interest as our people gave out tracts and talked personally with all who would listen.

When the baptism of the candidates was over, they and I changed to dry clothes. There were clumps of bushes scattered along the beach side of the lagoon several yards up from the water. These became our dressing rooms, the men at one end and the women at the other.

As we gathered together for the hike home, someone suddenly shouted, "*Baba... baba*," pointing to the other side of the lagoon where there were overhanging trees and bushes. "Baba" (pronounced "bahbah") is the name given in Colombia and Venezuela to a certain kind of cayman or alligator which has a short tail like the tail fin of an airplane. It is smaller than most alligators. The largest we saw in the lagoon was about eight feet long.

As we turned to look, we counted about a dozen pairs of eyes and foreheads just above the water level. Their eyes shone red as they slowly moved out of the shade of the overhanging bushes into the sunlight. They began to move toward where I had baptized.

"Alligators!," I yelled, waking up to the fact that we had been in the water with them. Then, more calmly, "Where in the world did they come from? We're too far interior. How did they get way up here? I know that there are big ones in the Orinoco River Delta, but way up here?"

Don Carlos was smiling broadly at my expression of surprise and disbelief. "Brother pastor," he began to explain, "the *baba* have been in this area for a long time. They probably originated in the low marsh lands between the Orinoco River Delta and Guyana. Many years ago we had much more rain than we have now and the small tributaries of the Cuyuni River used to fill up like big rivers and sometimes created small lakes. The *baba* could have come up from there."

"I never knew there were alligators so small, and with such a funny tail," Mildred remarked as we watched several *baba* leave the water and climb onto some mounds of sand.

"Yes, the *baba* are small compared to the alligators in the Orinoco. But don't think that because they are small they are not dangerous," warned Carlos.

"That's right," added deacon Eugenio. "I found out how extremely vicious they are once when some of my cows wandered this way. The *baba* did not bother my cows, but they sure came after me. I had to dismount from my horse to tie some ropes on the cows to lead them back toward my farm. I didn't realize that I was so close to one and it put a big slash in my boot. My horse was so nervous I could hardly mount up, she nearly threw me."

"Well," remarked Mildred, "this is an experience to write home about. Just think. The Lord kept them away all the time we were having the baptism."

"Yes," I agreed. "If I had known they were here, I think I would have been too nervous to enter that water."

By this time, we were walking down the road back toward home. Suddenly I stopped in my tracks. "Hey, wait a minute, you two men knew they were here all the time, didn't you?"

Both deacons were laughing heartily. It was a good joke on the pastor. "Well," explained Carlos, "there was no other place where we could baptize, and since we believed the service should be held, we asked the Lord to keep them away, and the Lord answered our prayers."

Eugenio added his word of assurance. "¡Sí! brother pastor, you were never in any danger. We were watching and would have warned you if we had noted any movement."

"Well, I guess what I didn't know, didn't hurt me," I admitted. "Anyhow, all's well that ends well. Praise the Lord for this good day. Now we had better keep moving or it will be dark before we get back to town."

That night the little congregation celebrated the Lord's Supper and gave the "right hand of fellowship" to those who had been baptized, welcoming them into the church membership. The service was barely over when Mildred and I were in our beds. We were exhausted from the busy day and especially from that long hike to the lagoon and back in the blazing hot sun.

********** ********** **********

The days passed quickly and soon we were approaching Christmas time. Mildred threw herself into the work of preparing recitations and little dramas for the children and young people. It was very difficult for this was the first time she had to do this work in Spanish. She also improvised with whatever material she had at hand and made decorations for our living quarters and the meeting room. It took a lot of her time, but with the daily home-schooling of our son Eddie, it helped to keep her mind comparatively free from our Christmas-time homesickness, a malady which attacks young missionaries, their first term away from home.

The little chapel was filled on the Sunday morning that the Christmas program was given. Mildred sat down in front where she could prompt the children with their recitations and Scripture verses. I stood in one of the two large double doorways which opened onto the streets. As I watched over the heads of the congregation, I sensed a presence behind me. Turning, I was surprised to see the city secretary, stretching his neck to see inside. Stepping out, I addressed the official.

"*Buenos días, señor, y Felíz Navidad* [Good day, sir and Merry Christmas]. Why don't you step inside where you can see better. Here is a chair by the door. You are most welcome."

"Thank you, Reverendo, but I cannot stay. I was on an errand in this neighborhood, and as I passed by I heard the children singing. I am expecting a car to pick me up very shortly to take me to Ciudad Bolivar. I have received an appointment to be secretary to the Governor."

"Congratulations! It will be Caracas next, I wager."

I was going to say more, but the secretary held up his hand to request silence. He whispered, "I want to hear what those children are going to say."

The secretary moved closer to the doorway. I looked over his shoulder and saw that it was little Carmencita. Her hand held that of her still smaller brother, Luisito, as she and he climbed onto the platform and began to recite together a little poem, *Mañana Es La Navidad* [Tomorrow is Christmas]. Then the other children joined them in singing the poem.

I realized then why the "errand" had brought the secretary past the mission house that morning. He was leaving the area, having made progress in his political-civil service career and would probably not be back in Tumeremo for who knows how long. Somehow he had learned about this Christmas program and wanted to see his little daughter and son before leaving.

As the little girl and her brother finished the recitation and were receiving applause, the only emotion that I could detect from the secretary was a deep but subdued sigh. As he turned away from the doorway, he would have gone on without saying a word. But I walked with him down the street and spoke quietly.

"Mr. Secretary, I know your secret and, may I assure you, I will keep it."

Startled, the secretary stopped, and looked at me. Then he simply said, "Gracias, Reverendo, I appreciate that.... I guess Carmen told you."

"Yes, she felt that, as her pastor, I should know just in case any unusual thing might happen to the children."

"God forbid," he exclaimed. "But I will be in touch to let you know where I am."

"Forgive me, Mr. Secretary, but I would like to ask you a question. If you think I am out of line in asking it, please tell me."

Receiving a nod of assent, I went on. "As you know, I am new in your culture. I see many similar cases to that of Carmencita and her brother, as well as many other variations of the same. Tell me, is this a common occurrence?"

"Yes, it is, Reverendo. But, just between you and me, I loved Carmen, and left to the ideals of impetuous youth, I would have married her. But class difference is very strong here. There is too much Indian blood in Carmen's family. I would have destroyed my career. My family convinced me of that." His words went trailing off as he stared into space, remembering.

"You will get used to it, Reverendo. It is a way of life here with commonlaw marriages. Most wealthy men, and some not too wealthy, have their concubines, one legal wife and as many others on the side as they can afford. Personally, I don't like it, it is not right. My evangelical aunt has had much influence upon me, but, who am I to fight the customs?"

Just then a limousine came down the street and pulled up at the curb. "Here is my car, Reverendo. If you remember, please say a prayer for me *de vez en cuando* [once in a while].

With the typical shrug of the shoulders, and a wave of the hand, he slid into the seat beside the driver and was off on his way to a greater political career. I never saw nor heard from the secretary again. I stood for a moment, thinking. "Yes, I have much to learn."

Chapter 17

Mildred's Illness

Return to El Callao

"Yea, though I walk through the valley of the shadow of death, I will fear no evil, for thou art with me; thy rod and thy staff they comfort me." (Psalm 23:4)

Christmas in Tumeremo, with its extra activities, was history. The following week we just relaxed and did some reading. We wrote letters home, which we could now do shedding only a tear or two. A year and four months had gone by since we arrived in Venezuela. It was time to review our life and work in Tumeremo, and make plans for the New Year.

The next week we went to El Callao to attend our annual Field Council meeting. All the missionary couples had come from their stations with their children. What a great time it was just to be together and enjoy each other's fellowship. Because of the bad roads in the interior of Venezuela, most of us did not see another co-worker except at these yearly meetings. It was the first time we had seen any of them since the year before when we moved to Tumeremo.

Baptist Mid-Missions functions through its Field Councils and the missionaries meet together annually to plan the work of the various stations. During the sessions this year, there was a lengthy discussion about getting a Bible Institute started. Field President Sylvan Hausser had argued, "World War II will probably continue for a number of years. Missionaries are leaving for necessary furloughs and, as you already know, will not be able to return for the duration. Soon there will not be any missionaries to direct the work. A school must be started without delay to train Venezuelans to pastor their own churches."

The vote was unanimous in favor of immediately establishing a Bible Institute. It came as a big surprise to me when the missionaries voted to make me the director. I protested.

"Oh, come on, now. You can't mean it! Why Mildred and I have been on the field only a little over a year. We are still stumbling over the language. I think you should name someone else. Besides, Mildred and I love our home and our work in Tumeremo and want to stay there."

"Well," Mr. Hausser replied, "We don't want to force you into anything that you don't believe to be the Lord's will. As far as your qualifications are concerned, we know that your grades were excellent in Bible college. Yes, you will need help with the language, but Dolores can continue to correct your work. Even though the need is urgent, we would not be able to start classes until September. So take a little time and pray about it. If you decide in favor of it, you will have several months to get things ready."

After the meetings were over, we returned to Tumeremo. We did pray about the request of our fellow missionaries, but only half heartedly. We were happy in the work of our first missionary assignment and fully convinced that it was the Lord's will to continue in Tumeremo.

Upon arriving in Venezuela, our first priority had been to learn Spanish. The second was to learn the culture of the people so that we could better help them in spiritual matters. When we moved to the frontier town of Tumeremo, we discovered that we also had to learn to cope with the scarcity of many of the necessary things of life, especially water and nutritious foods. We had brought with us from the States as much as possible of our household goods and clothing to last us until furlough. We could not take food with us, of course, so we had to learn to "live off the land," that is, learn to eat, and if possible like, the native-grown foods.

Meat was scarce and there were no fresh green vegetables. There was a variety of starchy roots eaten like potatoes, many different kinds of beans, and the protein-rich pigeon pea. We did praise the Lord for the delicious and healthful tropical fruits, bananas, plantains, papaya, mangos, oranges and passion fruit for juice, and the guava and wild grapefruit for jellies.

Both Mildred and I had been raised in Philadelphia and knew nothing about farming. But, in spite of our lack of agricultural knowledge, we went to work to try to provide some of the table items not available, but needed to help us maintain our health. The first problem we tackled was the scarcity of chickens and eggs.

Brother Celestino had a small farm not too far out from Tumeremo, but made most of his livelihood making charcoal and selling it to the town people as fuel for their *anafres* [small charcoal cookstoves]. He helped me encircle the mission property with chicken wire, and build a roosting house for the hens we were buying from our neighbors. We cleaned the back patio of undergrowth and prepared a corner near the house for a vegetable garden. The soil was sandy, very much like that of south New Jersey. With the help of some natural fertilizer, a good crop of beefsteak tomatoes was produced. Our neighbors had never seen any so large and red.

Before very long, we had about 30 laying hens and were getting all the eggs we needed. We set some eggs and in time we had all the friers and stewers we could eat. We even began to send eggs down to our missionaries in El Callao.

**Celestino and wife,
Farmer and charcoal maker**

To help maintain our health, we strictly obeyed the rules for tropical living: midday rest followed by a cool shower, never put our bare feet on the ground because many parasites, including the hook-worm, enter the body through bare feet. We had been taught that "cleanliness is next to godliness." We became almost fanatical about it. But we believed that, if we did our part, the Lord would keep us healthy and free of the common community diseases. However, in spite of all our precautions, Mildred took seriously ill.

We had been in Tumeremo just about a year. It was February 18. I went into our bedroom after my afternoon shower. Mildred was still in her hammock. While using beds for sleeping at night, we each had our hammock for resting in the afternoon. It was cooler that way. "Hey, sleepy-head, did you forget that we wanted to visit sister Mercedes this afternoon? She is going to give you some little gardenia plants to place in our patio."

"No, Hon; I didn't forget, I just feel tired. I may have *calentura* [low-grade fever]."

"You do feel warm," I agreed as I felt her forehead. "Do you ache anywhere?"

"A little."

"Well, you just swing there until you feel like getting your shower. I'll take the bike and go to the post office. We just might have gotten some mail today."

Back from the post office, I looked in on Mildred. She had moved from the hammock to the bed. She mustn't feel any better, I thought. Going into the kitchen, I squeezed some lemons and made up a glass of lemonade for her.

"Don't you feel any better, Hon?"

"Not much. But how good this tastes, and so cool. Where did you get the ice?"

"The little store down on the corner just got a kerosene refrigerator with a freezer on top. As I came by the store I saw a lady coming out with a dish of ice cubes. I went in and bought a tray. Thought you would like a real cold drink. The lemonade will be good for you."

"I had a little chill, while you were gone, so decided to get under the covers. I'm aching more and I think my temperature has gone up."

While taking her temperature, I felt her pulse. It was a little fast. She also felt warmer. "You do have a temperature. It's 103."

I gave her a couple of tablets of Cortal, a kind of aspirin, but much stronger. Each one of us had taken quinine in prophylactic doses ever since coming to Venezuela. The area south of Upata through El Callao, especially along the Yurari River, was known for its malaria. So I upped Mildred's dosage of quinine, just in case.

The next few days were confusing as to what Mildred's problem might be. She lived on lemon and orange juice. Her temperature went up and down and her body still ached. She would feel better and get up, and then in an hour or so, be back in bed, aching all over again.

There were no private doctors in Tumeremo, nor was there at that time a hospital. When people got sick, they doctored themselves with home remedies, herb concoctions, or went to the witch doctors. The believers, of course, did not use these *curanderos* [healers]. If their sickness continued, they would be taken to El Callao.

Deacon Eugenio told me about the National Guard doctor, stationed with the unit in Tumeremo. But, he was out on bivouac and not expected back for two more days. The doctor lived in his own private house not far from ours, so I checked with his housekeeper each day.

Saturday afternoon the doctor did return home, but in no condition to see patients. He was almost dead drunk and had to be helped into the house and put to bed. When I got there the next morning at 8:00 A.M., I was ushered onto the veranda where the doctor was sipping his coffee. Quickly explaining why, I begged him to come to the house to see my wife. Being the official doctor of the National Guard, he had no obligation to see private patients, but he agreed.

Sunday School was in progress when the doctor arrived. The believers had had prayer especially for Mildred. She had tried to get up and dress for she loved to play the portable organ for the singing. Mildred had learned to play so as to have music in the services. But this morning, she couldn't make it.

After a cursory examination, the doctor pronounced, "Definitely malaria. Has she been taking quinine?"

"Yes, a prophylactic dose of 5 grains a day, like the rest of us. We doubled the dose when her fever and chills came on."

"Well, triple that. Give her 30 grains for three days. Plenty of fruit juice. Cool sponge bath twice a day. Give warm enemas with a teaspoon of boric acid once a day. This is the remedy we used with good results in Africa, when I served with the Foreign Legion."

This explained the doctor's French accent. Later conversation informed me that as a young man, after graduation from medical school in Paris, he served his term of military service with the French Foreign Legion. Then he immigrated to Venezuela, but before he could practice medicine in Caracas or any of the coastal cities, he had two years in the interior of the country. He would soon be finished with that and then he would enjoy the "good life" in the Capital.

We did as the doctor instructed, but Mildred grew worse. Her fever continued with the temperature at 104 degrees. She couldn't keep anything in her stomach. It was now ten days since she first fell ill. I was scared, but it was no use going to the doctor again; besides, I heard that he had taken a vacation and had gone to stay with his girl friend out in the country.

That night Mildred's sleep was restless, fitful and disturbingly nightmarish. I sat up with her, periodically applying cool wet cloths to her forehead. An answer to my questions should come tomorrow from our Field Council president. Should I take Mildred to El Callao, or should I plan to take her further out, maybe even to the States? I had sent a letter to El Callao a few days before with Luis Peña, our friendly truck driver.

Sure enough, Peña himself arrived about 10:00 A.M. Upon Mr. Hausser's urging, he had left El Callao a little before dawn. The trails were dry, so he had made good time. Peña's truck was in good condition, not large, but did have a wide comfortable cabin. Mr. Hausser's letter read, "Bring Mildred down to El Callao. We have three doctors here now. Surely one of them will know how to treat her. Get ready right away. Peña will wait for you. We are praying."

We needed no urging, and a little after noon we were on our way. I supported Mildred on pillows in the cabin. Peña was most solicitous. Peña's helper and Eddie road on top of the load of *bálata*, [blocks of crude rubber a foot or more square]. Peña had hurriedly loaded these on his truck at the warehouse in town while I got Mildred dressed and a few clothes packed for the three of us. It was a great fun trip for Eddie, but an anxious one for Mildred and me.

Peña drove carefully in consideration of his sick passenger, but made good time. A little after 5:00 P.M. we arrived in front of the mission home in El Callao. Soon Mildred was made as comfortable as possible in bed in one of the spare rooms.

"We have a new doctor in town," Mr. Hausser informed me. "He is a young Venezuelan of French descent, Dr. Nouel. He is a great diagnostician even though young. He gets his patients well on the way to recovery as no one has ever done before in this old town. I have already alerted him of your coming and have sent our houseboy to ask him to come right away."

Eddie and I hardly had time to eat a quick supper the cook had prepared in anticipation of our coming, when Dr. Nouel came in. I followed as Mr. Hausser ushered him into the sick room. Dr. Nouel was thorough in his examination.

"It looks like a very acute attack of tercio malaria, but I don't understand why the temperature maintains itself so high. It is now 104.5 degrees. You say that in the last few days it has not gone down in the morning?"

"Right, and she has chills almost continually and nothing stays in her stomach."

"Tercio malaria should be intermittent and she should have had some relief, at least every other day. Well, we'll know for sure after I make the blood tests of this specimen." He put the vial in his case and left for his office down on Main Street.

Mr. Hausser told us, "Dr. Nouel is a young doctor, not too long out of internship. He studied in the States and took his internship there after graduating from medical school in Valencia. You should see the latest lab equipment he has. He does his own testing—won't trust anyone else. His family is rich and set him up here until he fulfills his required two years, then he'll probably move to Caracas. But, you know, he told me that he likes it here where he has more opportunity to see all kinds of medical problems before the specialists in the big cities get them as patients."

About 10:30, as we were getting ready for bed. We heard a knock on the door which had already been locked and barred for the night. It was Dr. Nouel. He had to come in person for there were no telephones as yet in the interior towns. We had not expected him until morning.

Dr. Nouel explained to Mr. Hausser and me. "It is not malaria, definitely not. I am afraid your wife has something more complicated. She will sleep all night with the tablets I have given her. But in the morning, you must get specimens of her urine and her stool. Have them ready for me. I will be here about 8:00 A.M. to get them and to take more blood. She must not eat anything until I say so. She may have some strained orange juice, nothing else."

Mildred spent a quiet night as the doctor said she would. Though awfully worried, I did get some sleep. Eddie slept on the closed veranda, swinging in his hammock.

The next day, Dr. Nouel got his specimens and in a few hours was back at the mission house. His first question was, "Did this lady have all her shots before she left the States?"

"Yes, of course, we all did; new vaccinations, three typhoid shots a week apart. We even had yellow fever shots." I assured him.

"Well, my lab tests say that she has a very severe case of typhoid fever. We must start treatment right away. She must not be moved. We must take every precaution that the typhoid does not spread to other members of the household. It is a good thing that you all have protection. When did she have the shots?"

"Why it was the month before we sailed. That would be in August 1941."

"Almost eighteen months ago. Her immunization should have lasted longer than that," affirmed Dr. Nouel. "She must be very susceptible. Did she have bad reactions from the shots?"

"Yes, she spent a day in bed after each one."

Dr. Nouel gave very strict orders that his instructions be followed to the letter. Mildred must have nothing to eat except a very weak broth and strained orange juice. She must be confined to her room. I must be the only one to enter her room to serve her and attend to her wants. I must be the only one to wash her dishes and drinking cups. They must be washed with strong soap and then rinsed with scalding hot water. Everything must be thoroughly sterilized.

"What about medicine?" I asked.

Dr. Nouel shook his head. "Here we have a problem. First of all, stop all medication, no more quinine, nothing. Unfortunately the medicine she should have for the typhoid is not available here in the interior. Strange to say it, but typhoid is almost unknown here. I have sent an urgent telegram to the distributor in Caracas. The medicine is concocted in Cuba where they have a lot of typhoid, at least, they did have in times past. I hope they have some in Caracas, but if they do not, they have my instructions that a message be sent by Pan American Clipper to get some back to Caracas by return plane. But we shall hope that this will not be necessary.

"Here is a prescription for a medicine they do have in the *farmacia* [drug store] on the corner. I must be honest with you. This medicine will help to keep your wife from getting any worse, but it will not cure her. Give it to her according to the instructions on the bottle."

"On the bottle?" I asked. "Is it a patent medicine? If so, why the prescription?"

"Yes, it comes already made up from the pharmaceutical company as do most all medicines we prescribe here in Venezuela. We cannot trust the pharmacists to make up our prescriptions as ordered. Some substitute other drugs if they are out of the one we prescribe. We doctors have to know all the manufactured drugs available and prescribe accordingly.

"By the way," Dr. Nouel added, a serious expression on his face, "you evangelicals believe in the power of prayer, do you not?"

"We sure do." This from both Mr. Hausser and me.

"For the next couple of days, until this medicine I prescribe starts to do its work, your prayers for Doña Mildred might make a big difference in her recovery. If there is any change in her condition, let me know right away. The druggist will let me know as soon as the vials arrive and we'll get the injections started immediately."

The next week was a trying time, especially for Mildred with her physical trial, and for both of us mentally, as we waited for the injections to arrive. I went to the *farmacia* every day, just in case the medicine should come in and they would delay in advising the doctor. On the strict diet of weak broth and strained orange juice, I could see Mildred getting thinner by the day. Eventually she lost twenty pounds and, from the continuous high fever, lost all of her hair.

Since we were saved, we have made it a practice to have daily family devotions. We would read the Scriptures, pray for family and friends, and commit ourselves to the Lord for His direction through the day. We marvelled how often the text for the day would fit the need, or it would help us find the solution to a problem that had been eluding us.

About a week after Dr. Nouel had diagnosed her illness, Mildred, very disheartened, was crying when I came into the room. I comforted her and she felt better. Then we settled down for our Bible reading and prayer. The Scripture referred to for that day in the devotional book was Hebrews 11:8-16. The key text was Romans 8:18, "...the sufferings of this present time are not worthy to be compared with the glory which shall be revealed in us."

When I finished the reading, I tried to say something encouraging, but unthinkingly I remarked: "How wonderful to have these precious promises of a better life to come, without sickness and problems, in heaven with the Lord."

Mildred began to sob again. "Oh, Ed, I don't think I am going to get better."

A chill gripped my heart. Silently I protested, "Oh no, Lord. Please, no. I just couldn't go on without her." Then aloud, "Don't talk like that, Hon. I'm sure you will get well."

"No, Ed, the Scripture you just read fits my condition. The Lord gave it to me to prepare me for dying and going to be with Him, I just know it. You must have been thinking that too when you spoke about being in heaven with the Lord where there is no more sickness."

"Now, Mildred, you mustn't even think such a thing, let alone say it. I am sure the injections will come soon and you will start to feel different. The medicine you are taking is helping you to hold your own. Let's commit ourselves once again unto the Lord. We must trust Him. Remember our life verses, Psalm 37:3-7. 'Trust in the Lord... Rest in the Lord....' Now is the time to REST—to have patience—He has a purpose in allowing you to suffer this way."

After prayer, Mildred felt some relief from her fears, but as time went on and the medicine did not come, she passed through more times of discouragement. She would try to pretty herself up. She would comb her hair and large clumps of it would come out in the comb. I felt helpless and frustrated to find words to comfort her. I needed such words myself, for I too felt discouraged, and I was scared! Maybe Mildred was going to leave me, maybe the Lord was going to take her home. Maybe the verses were meant to prepare us. I hated such thoughts and I fought to clear them from my mind.

When good health continues and there are no setbacks, missionaries working in backward areas without doctors, usually don't even think about serious sickness nor how to plan for it. In our case, Mildred was awfully sick and the medicine she needed was a thousand miles away, and the nearest air travel contact three days away over rough and sometimes impassable roads.

What could we do? Human means had failed. Only the Lord could help. As Dr. Nouel had said, "You know how to pray... do it." So, we prayed, committing ourselves day by day into the Lord's hands. And we found Him sufficient.

I suppose that every child of God at sometime in his life is faced with the possibility that this illness "may be my last and I am not going to get better, I am going to die." These are times when our faith is tested. We don't understand why. For a time we are confused. But then, as we spend time in the Word of God, our questions are answered and our fears are dispelled. At last we understand that our Good Shepherd is still caring for us. The dark valley of death through which He is leading us, is only the **shadow** of death. Jesus comforts us as He makes known His presence with us. Then He helps us to completely **surrender to His will**, whether for life or for death. This experience of Mildred's, though difficult at the time, was good for her and for me, and, when it was all over, we thanked Him for it.

But, it was all of ten days before the injections arrived. They did have to come all the way from Cuba. Dr. Nouel started the series of injections. It was like magic. Mildred began to improve immediately. But, it wasn't magic, it was the Lord. For some reason the Lord chose to try our patience and faith, and then bring about the healing through the prescribed medicine. All together it was five weeks almost to the day when Mildred awoke one morning and said "You know, Ed, I feel so much better that I know I am healed."

Dr. Nouel had explained that Mildred's condition had been complicated and made worse by the treatment prescribed by the doctor in Tumeremo. While such a treatment had good results in malarial cases, it served to make things worse in her case where the infection was settled in the bowels, and where any kind of irritation should be scrupulously avoided.

"Why did the Lord permit this to happen?" Mildred and I asked ourselves over and over again as we sat together in her room, reading the Bible and devotional books and praying. Our co-workers were allowed just a word of greeting and encouragement from the doorway.

Why? And again, why? In addition to teaching us patience through tribulation, He would show us His purpose in this sickness in bringing us down to El Callao. The Lord knew that we would rebel at any idea of leaving Tumeremo, our work. We had come to love our brothers and sisters in the Lord. Our ministry in Tumeremo had been going well, souls had been saved, the believers were being built up in the Lord. Why was it necessary to move us to El Callao? Very shortly now, we would understand.

We continued to pray during Mildred's convalescence. "Lord, show us your will for us." We reminded ourselves again of our life verses: "Trust... Delight... Commit thy way unto the Lord... Rest in the Lord, and wait patiently for him...."

We rehearsed the events of Mildred's illness and praised the Lord again for bringing her through that "valley of the shadow of death." We thanked Him for **restoring our souls** after both Mildred's and mine had been so **troubled**. We rejoiced in the assurance that our Good Shepherd **was leading us** "in the paths of righteousness for His name's sake."

Finally, Dr. Nouel gave us the "all clear," Mildred was removed from isolation. He said there was no further danger of infection to others. The next day, Mr. Hausser called us into his office. He wanted to tell us that it was still the opinion of our fellowworkers that we should take the lead in getting the Bible institute started.

"You have just gone through a very trying time and probably nothing has been further from your mind. But, the situation remains the same and we all believe that we must act right away and that you have the organizational skills to set up its curriculum and get the work started. We missionaries stationed in El Callao will help with teaching classes.

"So, Ed and Mildred, please pray about it again. We are hoping that the Lord will lead you to accept the assignment. This may be the reason why the Lord brought you to El Callao again. It would be a great result from the terrible trial that you two have just gone through."

We returned to our room to talk it over. This time we would try to pray more objectively. We were silent for several minutes, each with his own thoughts. Finally: "Mildred, there is no doubt that what Mr. Hausser said makes sense. We should be training our young people for full time service in our churches. Yet, I hate to leave Tumeremo. I've come to love that work and the believers, and I believe that they love us also."

"I know, Ed, and in spite of the difficulties, I also love the people, my work with the children, the Bible Clubs and the Sunday School. But, I guess we ought to try to put our own feelings to one side and think about the need of the whole field and give it priority."

We spent the next few days praying. As we talked, we carefully considered all the pros and cons we could think of. We continually thanked and praised the Lord for healing Mildred. But, she was still very weak and thin and her dresses just hung on her. However, her motivation was getting stronger day by day. We still felt drawn to the work in Tumeremo, but the priority argument finally won out. Each day brought stronger feelings that we should accept the assignment. We finally did. Then, as if to give heavenly approval of the new work we were to do, everything began to fall into place. Mildred's recovery became more rapid and, with hardly any searching, we found a comfortable house to rent right on Main Street on the edge of town.

Then, early one day, Luis Peña took Eddie and me up to Tumeremo. Mildred was not yet strong enough to travel. Peña and his helper assisted us in packing our furniture, clothes, tools and other miscellaneous items, and loaded them on the truck to move them to El Callao. We even crated the chickens in slat boxes. Brother Celestino who had lived in the Mission house and had taken care of things in our absence, helped also.

Early the next day, many of the believers came to ask about Mildred and to help us finish packing. Carlos came in from the country and I explained to him and Eugenio, the reasons for our move. They were sorry, but understanding the need for a training school for pastors, they and our people were willing to let us go. Our packing finished, they all gathered around Eddie and me to pray. A few tears were shed as we exchanged our good-bye hugs.

We left Tumeremo late in the afternoon. This trip to El Callao was uneventful except for running out of gas and having to spend the night sleeping out on the prairie. A little after daybreak, a large truck came through. Peña borrowed some fuel and we were on our way again.

Soon I had our things arranged in the rented house. Some of the brethren of the El Callao church had previously helped me get the place cleaned up, holes plastered over and the walls painted. We fenced in the rear patio with the chicken wire that had been around the property in Tumeremo, and the chickens were comfortably housed in a covered enclosure already there. The large galvanized water storage tanks hauled from Tumeremo and rather battered from the trip, were repaired and set up ready for the first rain. About a week later, Mildred felt strong enough to make the move and to start transforming the house into a home. A girl from El Palmar came to help Mildred with the housework.

Thus began another episode in our missionary life. We would be preparing workers to take their rightful places in their churches. Our goal was to teach these upcoming leaders in such a way that they, in turn, "would be able to teach others also."

The Lord had a second reason for bringing us back to El Callao which we will tell you about in future chapters. Suffice it to say for now that, the **enemy of our souls wanted** to use Mildred's illness **to destroy** our missionary life and service, **but God used it for good!**

IV
Move to El Callao

Chapter 18

A Bible Institute Planned

As soon as we were settled in our house in El Callao, I got busy holding meetings with my co-workers to decide on the subject matter most needed in the curriculum for the Bible Institute. Then the various subjects were divided among us missionary teachers.

Again we rejoiced in how fast the Lord worked in a few short months to supply all our material needs, including the school's buildings. We obtained a property about a quarter of a mile outside El Callao on the road to El Perú. To the house already there, we added several rooms for Mr. and Mrs. Hausser and the girl students. The Hausser's, besides teaching a class or two, would supervise the physical care and welfare of the students. A plain building was built to be used as a dormitory for the boy students, a storeroom and one classroom.

Dolores would maintain the house in town next to Teófilo's, which would also provide a place where visiting missionaries could stay. Mildred and I planned to build our own house on the property within the next year. Meanwhile we stayed in the rented house in El Callao.

********** ********** **********

The Angel Morandy Story

"I will go before thee, and make the crooked places straight: I will break in pieces the gates of brass, and cut in sunder the bars of iron." (Isaiah 45:2)

Toward the end of May, the work to get the property ready for the Bible Institute was almost complete. The finishing touches would be put on by some of the men of the church who had been helping. It was then decided that Mr. Hausser and I should make a trip to the Orinoco River Delta region. The purpose of the trip was to hold evangelistic meetings and to check on prospective students for the Bible Institute. Missionary Ruth Hege had eight young people in the church in Tucupita who desired to prepare for the Lord's service.

Angel Morandy was one of the prospective students. His father was violently opposed to his son's new faith and attendance at the Evangelical Baptist Church. Though not a wealthy family, because of his profession as a *Maestro de Carpintería* [master carpenter], a maker of fine furniture, they were considered *alta categoría* [high society]. To have one of its members embrace the Gospel and leave the mother church was an unbearable disgrace.

On several occasions Angel's father came into the church, took hold of Angel's ear, and pulled him out into the street. It was very embarrassing for a boy of seventeen. One time, Mr. Morandy tore his Bible to shreds. Another time he threw the Bible into the cook-stove fire. Angel's mother, while a devotee of the state religion, was sympathetic toward her son "who could do no wrong," a typical Hispanic American mother's attitude toward her first-born son.

Once, Angel was sent to stay with relatives in the town of Urucoa. His father thought that by separating him from his friends and his church, he would soon forget his new religion. But Angel so witnessed for the Lord there in that town that a few young people got saved. His relatives were so embarrassed that they sent Angel back home.

"Is that the Bible you rescued from the fire?" I asked Angel during the interview we had with him. "Miss Ruth told us about it."

"Yes. My father was so angry that he stomped away and did not see me pull it out and throw it into a bucket of water. See, some of the edges are charred and the pages are wrinkled."

"Well, Angel, we are satisfied with your testimony of salvation and call to the ministry," Mr. Hausser assured him. "We are happy to welcome you as a student in our Bible Institute. But, there is one essential condition; we must get the approval of your father."

"I know, and that is what has me worried. He will never give it."

"Well, we'll make it a matter of prayer and Pastor Eduardo and I will visit your father to talk with him about it."

The day after our interview with Angel, we were hardly out of our hammocks when Angel knocked on the door. Even as Mr. Hausser was opening the door, Angel started to speak.

"The Lord gave me a promise last night," Angel blurted. "I have faith that things will work out for me to go to the Bible Institute."

He was talking so fast and with such excitement that we could barely understand him.

"Whoa... back up... take a breath. We haven't had our coffee yet," urged Mr. Hausser.

In the *sala* [parlor], the housekeeper served us coffee and several slices of toast and some white native cheese, the typical Venezuelan "eye opener." The real breakfast came some time later.

Angel was just bursting to tell us something. "Last night after prayer meeting, my father was waiting for me when I tried to sneak into my room. I thought he was going to beat me, though he never has, you know. But, *gua*! [Wow], he sure chewed me out. Made me feel like I, his son, had betrayed him. He called me unfaithful and a traitor to the Virgin. He has always wanted me to follow in his footsteps and be a carpenter like him. When I kept telling him that I didn't want to be a carpenter, he agreed to send me to the university so maybe I could be a lawyer or a doctor or have some other profession.

"This morning I got up before dawn. I sneaked out of the house, got my Bible from where I had hidden it, and went down to the *caño* [little branch river] to read and pray. Sitting there on a rock, I asked the Lord to give me some sign, maybe some verse with a promise.

"Well, I was separating some of the pages that were stuck together, when my eyes fell on some verses in Isaiah 45:2." Angel opened his battered Bible and read the words, "I will go before thee, and make the crooked places straight: I will break in pieces the gates of brass, and cut in sunder the bars of iron."

"And that is just how I feel," explained Angel, "like I am in prison behind gates of brass and bars of iron. My father's heart is as hard as iron. He won't listen to the Gospel. But, now I believe that the Lord is going to soften my dad's heart. At least, I take these verses as a promise from the Lord that my father will give me permission to go to Bible school."

We were impressed with Angel's sincerity and faith in the Lord. Angel was jubilant. Mr. Hausser placed a hand on Angel's shoulder. "I too believe that the Lord will work it out for you, my boy. The

Lord is faithful, He will have His will in our lives if we just submit to Him and trust. Let's pray together and commit this matter into the hands of our Sovereign God."

After prayer, Mr. Hausser advised Angel, "I would keep a low profile for a few days. Try not to antagonize your father. We will pay him a visit and see what the Lord will do."

Missionary Diplomacy

According to Matthew 10:16b, Jesus advised His disciples: "...be ye therefore wise as serpents, and harmless as doves."

We let several days go by. Then one day in the middle of the morning, when Angel's father would be working in his shop, we visited him. We found Mr. Morandy working on a fine piece of furniture, a combination chest of drawers and clothes closet. He was quite cool toward us, but Hispanic American culture demanded that he at least treat us with courtesy and civility.

We expressed our admiration for the excellent work he was doing and for his fine set of carpentry tools, all neatly stored on shelves or hanging from clips on the clean white-washed walls. He began to warm up as we discussed the use of the different tools as well as the tooling and finishing of the hard woods available in Venezuela.

Addressing Mr. Morandy, I asked, "Did you know that Pastor Hausser, in addition to being a minister of the Gospel, is also a master carpenter like yourself? He is teaching me how to put to practical use the wood-working theories which I learned in vocational school in the States. Believe me, it is quite different here in Venezuela where one has to work without the advantage of electric power tools. I admire you for your exactness in the work. You are probably a perfectionist, as is Mr. Hausser."

His raised eyebrows reflected a new interest and a change of attitude. Then began an animated exchange of opinions between the two men. Mr. Hausser had perfected a special way to sharpen the chisels used on the wood-turning lathe. He showed Mr. Morandy his secret and demonstrated it on a piece already in the lathe. In the absence of electricity, both the stone grinder for sharpening the tools and the wood-lathe were hand-powered by the young boy who helped keep the shop clean and who, when a bit older, would become an apprentice.

Needless to say, the ice was broken and the prejudice against us evangelical missionaries began to melt away. Mr. Morandy called the house girl to prepare coffee and soon we were seated casually in the shop sipping the delicious *café con leche*. The conversation continued and soon Mr. Morandy was listening to a simple presentation of Gospel truths.

Mr. Morandy resisted the Gospel and his need for accepting Christ as his Savior. It was quite evident that his unwillingness to consider the claims of the Gospel was based upon the cultural and social effect it would have upon his relationship with family and friends, and especially upon his customers. He did not want to think of the spiritual aspects.

Finally, Angel's father gave permission for his son to go to the Bible Institute. The permission was granted after he understood that the students, in addition to their studies, would be given some vocational training so that they would be able to become self-supporting. Plans were being made to farm the Bible Institute property so that the boys could work to help pay for their board. They would also be taught the art of carpentry. The girls would be taught home economics: sewing, cooking, baking, and child care.

Needless to say, Angel was overjoyed and strengthened in his faith as were the other young people of the Tucupita church, especially those who would be his fellow students.

Classes began in September. Angel was an excellent student and soon gave evidence of leadership qualities. He was always in the forefront of the extracurricular activities. He took part in the street meetings in town, taught a Sunday School class and spoke quite frequently in the youth meetings.

Note:

When we had to close our school after two years, Angel and three other students were transferred to a Bible Institute on the coast. During Angel's stay there, he became a very effective preacher and traveled several times as such with the Institute choir and Gospel team. On one occasion, while preaching in a church in a town in northern Venezuela, his mother, visiting relatives there, attended the service. And then, Angel's cup of joy ran over. When, he gave the invitation, his mother came forward to accept Christ as her Savior.

After graduation, Angel worked as a secretary in a business firm to pay off some debts he had incurred. Then he accepted the call to serve as pastor of our church in San Félix, a fishing village and commercial center on the Orinoco River. Under his ministry the church grew in numbers, the auditorium was enlarged and more Sunday School rooms were added.

While ministering in San Félix, Angel married Teolinda, a fellow graduate of the Bible Institute. Their first daughter was born in San Félix. Several years later he accepted a call to pastor a Baptist church in Caracas, capital of Venezuela. In 1970 we had the joy of visiting him and his beautiful family when we went through Caracas on our way interior to our field.

As the years went by, Angel's father mellowed considerably. Later he moved his family to Caracas, seeking better health conditions. Eventually he too received Christ as his Savior.

That text in Isaiah 45:2 had become Angel's "life text." He never ceased to testify of how the Lord had continually **gone before him**, guided him along paths that sometimes seemed too crooked to see where he was going, **straightened out those places**, and when necessary, **broke in pieces** the gates of brass and the bars of iron, which spiritually **symbolized those things that sometimes opposed the ministry**.

Angel Morandy and family, 17 years later

Chapter 19

Rogelio Mata of La Horqueta

"If we confess our sins, he is faithful and just to forgive us our sins, and to cleanse us from all unrighteousness."
(I John 1:9)

While visiting in Tucupita, Mr. Hausser and I made several trips into the Orinoco River Delta region accompanied by the young people who were planning on going to our El Callao Bible Institute.

The Orinoco River empties into the Atlantic Ocean four times as much water as does any other river of its size in the world. Through the centuries, the soil carried down from the upper regions has been deposited at the mouth of the river. The accumulation of this soil has divided the river into many smaller ones called *caños*. These *caños* intertwine with each other, forming a crazy-quilt land pattern. The river itself forms two main channels that empty into the ocean, a large channel on the south, up which some ocean-going vessels can sail. Tucupita, the capital of the State, is located on the smaller north channel.

At the juncture of two small *caños* is a tiny farming village called La Horqueta, pronounced "or kay tah." An *horqueta* is a "y" shaped crutch used to support a branch heavily laden with fruit to keep it from breaking and the fruit from resting on the ground. The *caño* divided itself in two, forming a "y." So, the town located there was named La Horqueta.

We spent four days there and quite a group of young people, along with a few adults, were won to the Lord. One young man, Rogelio, gave immediate signs of leadership. We left him in charge of the group. We gave them some Bibles and hymn books and they promised to hold regular Bible reading and prayer sessions. They had learned several hymns and choruses taught to them by our young companions. They also promised to keep in touch with the believers in Tucupita when they went there to sell the products from their gardens and orchards.

Later that year the Orinoco River flooded. About 150 miles up river from Tucupita lies the city of Ciudad Bolivar, capital of our State, where the river narrows considerably as it runs between two hills. There the river rose sixty feet above normal. The city would have suffered terribly except that it is built on one of the hills. The reader can imagine the flood conditions down in the delta region just at sea level. The government sent in launches, dugout canoes, row boats, anything they could commandeer, to rescue the people. Many lost everything they had for they could take nothing with them except the clothes on their backs. Cows, pigs, and chickens had to fend for themselves, only their pet dogs were allowed to be rescued with them.

The Tucupita church, located on higher ground, was used as a refuge for many of the dislocated people. Ruth Hege and the brethren of the church ministered sacrificially to their physical needs and used the opportunity to minister spiritually to them as well. There was much sickness as latrines and sewers ran over. Many of the people were unloaded on the mainland and then transferred by truck up into the northern plains where rich oil fields are located. It was into this area where Rogelio and his family were taken.

Rogelio found work in the oil fields. He earned more money in a week than he had seen in his whole lifetime. In La Horqueta life had been uncomplicated, there was little need for money as most business was done by trading. But, along with the financial prosperity realized through the oil companies, came gambling, dance halls, drunkenness and an immoral life style.

Rogelio, as a very young believer, was not able to resist the temptation and fell into serious sin. However, being a true child of God, he could not continue that way for very long. First came remorse. He was miserable. He became convinced that, since he had betrayed the Lord, the Lord had rejected him and he was lost forever. He knew of no one among his friends where he was working who could help him with his spiritual problem.

He gave up his job and returned to the delta region. The river had gone down, and many of his family had already returned to begin life again in the region they loved best. He thought, "Perhaps I can find the missionaries who led me to the Lord and they will be able to help me."

Arriving back in Tucupita, Rogelio sought an interview with Ruth Hege.

"Señorita Ruth, tell me, am I eternally lost?" Rogelio asked her after briefly relating to her how he had turned his back upon the Lord.

"I think that you can find the answer yourself, Rogelio," replied Ruth. "Tell me, when you accepted Christ as your Savior, did you do it with all your heart?"

"Yes... yes... I did, I know I did," Rogelio affirmed.

"Well then," continued Ruth, "was there a verse in the Bible you learned during the time the group was with you in La Horqueta?"

Rogelio reached into his pocket and took out a battered booklet; it was a copy of the Gospel of John. He opened it as he said, "Pastor Eduardo marked a verse when he gave me this book; it's here near the beginning. I did learn it, but lately I haven't reviewed it like I should."

Rogelio showed Ruth the verse; it was John 5:24. "That's a good verse, Rogelio. Read it to me carefully."

Rogelio read, "Verily, verily, I say unto you, He that heareth my word, and believeth on him that sent me, hath everlasting life, and shall not come into condemnation, but is passed from death unto life."

"Now, Rogelio, you said that you believed in God's Word, and you have accepted Christ as your Savior. Read it again. Because you believed, what does it say that you have?"

He looked at the verse, reading it in a half whisper. "It says that I have everlasting life."

"Right. If you have a new life that is everlasting, can it ever end?"

Rogelio's brow creased as he tried to reason through this idea. Slowly a smile formed on his face. "I see it now. If the new life God gave me is everlasting, it can't end, can it?"

But then the frown returned again. "But, Señorita, what about my sin? I am so ashamed of what I have done and for having forsaken the Lord."

"The Bible also tells you what you can do with your sin, Rogelio. Toward the back of the Bible we find the first letter of the Apostle John. In the first chapter, in verse nine we read... here, read it for yourself." She showed him the place in her Bible.

Rogelio took the Bible and read where Ruth pointed. "If we confess our sins, he is faithful and just to forgive us our sins, and to cleanse us from all unrighteousness."

"You see, Rogelio, for God to forgive your sin, you have to do something. What is it?"

"I have to confess my sin."

"That's right. Who does the Bible say will forgive you of your sin?"

"God."

"So, to whom do you have to confess your sin, Rogelio?"

"To God, Señorita. To God."

"Wouldn't you like to do it?"

"Yes, I do. Can I do it right here? Or do I have to go to church?" Rogelio was not long out of the State church and he was thinking about the confessional.

"You can do it anywhere, Rogelio. As soon as you know you have done something that does not please God, you should confess it right away. And you don't have to say it out loud. I don't have to hear it, only God has to hear it."

Rogelio bowed his head. Ruth could see his lips moving. She also saw a couple of tears drop onto the open Bible. Then Rogelio raised his head. Though his cheeks were moist, his face was almost split open with one of the widest smiles the missionary had ever seen.

"God has forgiven me, I know He has, I can feel it right here," as he touched his chest. "Oh, what a relief... I feel so good!"

"Praise the Lord, Rogelio... Now, let me show you something else, right there where you have the Bible still open. Read those two verses," as her finger pointed to verses 7 and 8.

Rogelio read: "But if we walk in the light, as he is in the light, we have fellowship one with another, and the blood of Jesus Christ his Son cleanseth us from all sin. If we say that we have no sin, we deceive ourselves, and the truth is not in us."

Rogelio then asked, "What does that mean?"

"This explains what happened to you and tells you what you can do about it," Ruth Hege explained. "When you received Christ as your Savior your sins were forgiven and you received a new life which is forever. When you sinned, you did not lose your salvation, so you do not need to be saved all over again. What you lost was fellowship with the Lord. You felt like you were lost, but you were not.

"Now, Rogelio, according to the verse you read before, what does it say that **you** have to do about your sin, and what does it say that **God** does?"

Rogelio thought for a few seconds, then said, "I have to confess my sin to God. Then God will forgive me and take me back into fellowship again."

"Right! Now you're getting it... Just one thing more, Rogelio. You have already learned that you do not confess your sin to man, but to God. But, if you have offended someone because of your sin, you should also make things right with that person.

"Now the verses which you just read says that sin will always be with you. You don't **want** to sin, but you will. You will have to trust the Lord to help you, **but you have to do your part also**. Do you understand what **your part** is to help you avoid sinning? Read verse 7 again."

Rogelio, with some hesitation, acknowledged, "I have to walk in the light as He is in the light. But, what does that mean, Señorita? What is the light that I have to walk in?"

"There are many verses which explain this, but in the book of the Psalms (119:105), King David, referring to God's word, the Bible, wrote, "Thy word is a lamp unto my feet, and a light unto my path." God's Word is **light**. You should study the Bible, and try to live in obedience to what it tells you. **This is walking in the light**. Can you understand this, Rogelio?"

"I think I do, Señorita. Pray for me that I will understand more and more and live for the Lord. I want to please Him and be faithful and not fall again.

Ruth Hege and Tucupita Church, 1943

Thanking the missionary, Rogelio left to go to the home of relatives. He decided to remain in Tucupita to attend the church services, and learn more about the Bible and how to live the Christian life. He enjoyed especially the fellowship with the young people. He went with them visiting house-to-house, and his enthusiastic testimony helped to win a number of people to the Lord. He found some work to help support himself in order to stay several months. During this time, Rogelio felt the Lord's call to the ministry. He had so impressed the brethren of the church that they offered to support him if he wanted to go to the Bible Institute.

"I do want to go to the Bible Institute," replied Rogelio, "but I have been praying about something I think the Lord wants me to do first." Going on to explain, he said, "As you know, my family and neighbors are now back in La Horqueta. I feel ashamed that they saw me fall into sin while working in the oil fields. They had heard me testify so assuredly of my faith in Christ, and the power of the Gospel to save. But then I fell.

"Do you remember, Señorita Ruth, the day you helped me come back to the Lord? You told me that I did not have to confess my sin to man. But, if I might have offended someone, then I should make things right with that person. Well, I know that the Lord, has forgiven me for forsaking Him. But what about my family and friends? They must be offended with me.

"For this reason I feel that I should return home to La Horqueta and live among them for a time to show them that although I fell, the Lord did not let me stay down but lifted me up again. I want them to see that the Lord **can save** and can **keep** those who put their trust in Him. I want them to see that the eternal life I have in Christ is really forever."

So Rogelio went back to La Horqueta to live with his parents. He began his "ministry" there by having his morning devotions out under the almond tree in the front patio by the road where everyone could see, and also hear him. He would read a portion of the Bible out loud and then sing a few choruses all by himself. This went on for a few days during which time his changed life and his calm, quiet spirit began to impress his parents and immediate neighbors.

Soon his mother and father and younger sisters were sitting with him. It wasn't very long before Rogelio was able to lead both his parents and one sister to accept Christ as Savior. Later on several of his neighbors came to Christ. Within two months there was a group of some forty people, almost the entire little community, early in the morning before going to work, meeting daily with Rogelio. He had lengthened the devotional period to include more singing as he taught them the songs he had learned in Tucupita. He also interspersed the songs with a number of homespun exhortations to illustrate the Biblical truths they were learning.

On Sundays, those who were saved traveled to Tucupita in their motorized dugout canoes to attend the church services. As time went on, they were baptized and became members.

Rogelio, finally satisfied that the Lord had been vindicated and honored, informed the brethren that he was ready to go to the Bible institute. By that time, our institute, for lack of personnel, had been closed, so Rogelio was sent to the Bible institute in the coastal mountains.

Sudents - Rogelio Mata, Tomás Caravajal, Esteban John

In due time, Rogelio graduated, married Clara, another graduate, and began his life of service to the Lord. Rogelio pastored a number of churches, and served as a part-time professor at the Bible Institute from which he graduated. One of his favorite verses was the words of the apostle Paul in II Timothy 1:12, "...I know whom I have believed, and am persuaded that he is able to keep that which I have committed unto him against that day."

Truly the Lord is able, to **save**, to **keep,** and to **satisfy**, all who put their trust in Him.

Chapter 20

The Story of Don Pedro of Urucoa

"...Take heed, and beware of covetousness; for a man's life consisteth not in the abundance of the things which he possesseth." *(Luke 12:15)*

"But seek ye first the kingdom of God, and his righteousness...." (Matthew 6:33)

While we were still in the Orinoco River Delta region, a family of believers living in Urucoa urged us to hold evangelistic meetings there. This was an opportunity we could not ignore. We would also be able to interview a prospective student for the Bible Institute.

Urucoa is a town on the mainland, but still a part of the Orinoco River Delta region, located on one of the small rivers that run into the big river on the north side. It took a whole day to make the trip by rented *curiara*. This motorized dugout canoe with built-up sides was partially roofed over. In spite of the little shade under the roof, it was a hot, sweaty trip. I was going to be refined and say "perspiring," but it was much, much more than that.

Yet, in spite of the scorching sun and oppressive heat, it was a beautiful trip, especially as we passed from the main river into the *caños* with their thick foliage on both sides. The trees sometimes bumped their heads together over the water, forming a canopy of shade. At times it seemed as though we were going through a misty green tunnel. In the dim light, the water around our boat took on all sorts of mysterious black shadows and reflections.

All kinds of birds were flying about, chirping or singing their songs and displaying their beautiful feathers as their wings were spread wide in flight. There were green parrots and their little brothers and sisters, the *periquitos* [little parrots], with their yellow-striped wings. There were the large macaws, both the blue-yellow ones as well as the red-greens, and the ever present canary flashing golden yellow streaks across the caño.

The blossoms of many varieties of flowering plants and trees exhibited all the hues of the rainbow. But the only animal life in those *caños* was a crocodile or two lurking under the low bushes or sunning itself on a muddy river bank. Occasionally we would come to a clearing where someone ventured to live. Beautiful flowers would almost always be seen growing close to the mud walls of a crudely built hut. A banana grove with papaya trees planted here and there served as a background. Invariably a couple of cows would be grazing nearby.

However, after several hours of this, the trip could have gotten quite boring, but for the group of young people accompanying us. They kept up a continual chatter, played Bible guessing games, and competed to see how rapidly a Scripture verse could be learned verbatim.

Just after sundown our party arrived at Urucoa. Obdulio and Angel, were sent to find the family of believers who was to have prepared a place for us to stay. In a short time, the boys returned accompanied by the believer, Mr. Contreras, and another man. The latter introduced himself as Don Pedro who was allowing our group to stay in a new house he had built as a gift to his oldest daughter, soon to be married.

What a relief we missionaries felt as we entered the house and were greeted by the smell of fresh cement instead of the usual musty smell of dirt walls and floor. Instead of a grass roof, this house had a galvanized one and cement floors. There wasn't much furniture; just a couple of boxes, a few native chairs and one crude table. Our suitcases could be supported on the boxes and there were hooks in the walls from which we could sling our hammocks.

Outside the side door, Don Pedro had placed several 50 gallon drums and had them filled with water from the river. He also loaned us two gasoline pressure lamps for light. Don Pedro assured us, "*Está en su casa* [this is your house—make yourselves at home], be comfortable. If there is anything that you need, just ask. When you hold your meetings, I will be here to keep order. Good night, and may God and the Virgin keep watch over you."

After he had gone, I remarked to Mr. Contreras, "Don Pedro is so nice and accommodating I thought that he was a believer until he committed us to God and the Virgin."

"No, he is not," replied Contreras. "Don Pedro is very *simpático* [nice], but a believer? Definitely not. In fact, he is very worldly."

"He must be well-off financially," suggested Mr. Hausser.

"That he is. Don Pedro is the pharmacist here in Urucoa. He is also *político* [a politician]. He has the only drugstore in the area, and he practically runs this town. He has great influence also in Caracas. He is a favorite among the *jefes* [chief leaders] there."

"Well, we must definitely pray for him. Such a man would be good for the Gospel work in this area," commented Mr. Hausser.

"Don't count on it," was the pessimistic answer. "This town is very hard and he is the hardest of all. He is generous, good to the poor, but he has no interest in spiritual things."

"Then why is he so courteous and kind to us who have come to preach the Gospel?"

"That is a mystery to us also, Don Eduardo. We mentioned that we needed a place for you to stay, and you could have knocked us over with a feather when he offered us this house."

"Well, some people, even educated ones, are superstitious. Maybe Don Pedro thinks that we will put some kind of a blessing on this house and will bring good luck to his daughter and husband when they move in," commented Mr. Hausser.

We had a short prayer meeting to thank the Lord for a safe trip. Then, as soon as our hammocks were hung, we were in them, swinging ourselves to sleep. We men and the boys were in the large front room and the girls in two smaller ones off to the side.

We were all awake early, anxious to get out into the streets. Unfortunately the rainy season began to move in and we had difficulty doing our evangelistic work. We split up into two teams, and, between showers, visited in the homes, leaving Gospel tracts and invitations to the night meetings. Tropical showers don't last long, but the rain comes down in *chorros* [torrents], and if caught in it, in seconds you are soaked to the skin. But, in spite of this hindrance, we witnessed to quite a few, several of whom later made a profession of faith in Christ.

We had planned meetings at night on different street corners of the town, using the gasoline lanterns for light. But, because of the rain, the public meeting had to be held in the large living room of the house. Hammocks were taken down and stashed away out of sight. We borrowed a few chairs from friendly neighbors, but the majority who came, had to stand. Consequently the meetings were not very well attended. Most of those who did come were young people. Don Pedro was there to keep order, as he had promised. And, he was indeed needed, for several of the young men would get to acting up and making noise. Just a look from Don Pedro and a snap of his fingers was sufficient. They quickly quieted down.

While in Urucoa, we met and had our interview with Juan Contreras and his parents. Seventeen-year-old Juan, was a little fellow, chubby, with an ever present cheery smile. Juan's mother and father had been born-again believers for several years and all their children loved the Lord. They were delighted that Juan would be studying with us for the Lord's work.

The last night that we were there, the big room was filled with young people and several adults. Halfway through the service, the rain came down in torrents. With no ceiling, the noise of the rain hitting the tin roof, made it impossible to continue. It also made it impossible for the people to leave. We had a captive audience, so we missionaries and our young folk from Tucupita began to talk personally with the people, talking up close so as to be heard.

For some reason, Don Pedro was attracted to me and followed me around, listening as I spoke of the Lord and of His claim upon the lives of the people. Maybe the man was fascinated, as many were, to hear the funny accent of this young Yankee missionary. Anyhow, Don Pedro listened attentively as I spoke to a young fellow who seemed more serious than the rest. I noticed that he had listened carefully to the testimonies and messages during the services on the other nights. Now he had been standing alone, reading one of our Gospel tracts.

"Do you understand what you are reading?" I asked, shouting so as to be heard above the din coming from overhead.

"I am beginning to," was the boy's reply. He was about fifteen years old.

I then briefly explained the way of salvation, placing my Bible in the boy's hand so that he could read the verses for himself. Then I asked, "Now do you understand that you are a lost sinner and need to receive Christ as your Savior?"

"Yes, I do," was his answer.

"Then, will you, here and now, accept Jesus as your one and only Savior?"

I was thrilled to hear him say, "Yes, I will."

I led the boy in prayer, he repeating after me, a prayer of repentance and acceptance of Christ as Savior. The boy himself then thanked the Lord for saving him.

No one else was paying attention, each was busy with his own conversation. Besides, the noise prevented anyone from hearing what another was saying. So I was startled to hear hand-clapping behind me, and Don Pedro screaming in my ear, "Good! Good! I'm glad."

Then Don Pedro said, "See that girl over there, talking and flirting with the boys? Please, go talk to her, she needs the Gospel."

I was taken back and was about to question Don Pedro about his interest, but the druggist was dragging me by the arm toward where the girl was standing. He interrupted the girl and the young men, telling them to listen good to what I would show them from the Bible.

They listened obediently, but with no interest in what the Bible said about their spiritual need. The girl finally ended the Gospel presentation with, "I don't care about that nonsense. I am too young to give up my life for religion. I love to dance, go to parties, and I love the fiestas. Maybe when I am old I might be interested. Come back in about thirty or forty years."

The group returned to their chatter and laughter. Don Pedro was disgusted. He took hold of my arm again and began looking over the people as though searching for someone in particular and then started to pull me toward another small group by one of the other windows.

"Wait a minute, Don Pedro." I held back and began to direct him toward a corner where no one was standing. I needed to talk to him.

"Don Pedro, I don't understand it. The several times we have talked, you said that you have no interest in the Gospel. Now you seem anxious that these young people receive Christ as Savior. In fact, you were quite elated when young Reuben accepted Christ as his Savior, and disgusted when the girl wouldn't listen."

Don Pedro, very serious now, began to explain: "Reuben is my second youngest son. Yes, I am happy to see him embrace the Gospel. That young snip over there, is my second daughter and she really needs the Gospel. I am afraid for her." Pedro paused, shaking his head.

"Yes, of course," I agreed. "But we **all** need Christ, whether old or young."

"Well," continued Don Pedro, "I'll explain. I am afraid of the way things are going today. It is hard to control our children, they are getting more and more rebellious. They go to their parties and dances, the boys are wild and the girls don't know how to protect themselves. Some come home pregnant and bring disgrace to their families.

"In my business, as well as in my political activity, I have to make trips to Caracas. In the Capital there are a number of Protestant churches and among my friends there are some evangelicals. I have observed that in those families, the young people are obedient, they respect their parents, as well as other adults and, by and large, they live moral and decent lives. They work hard, make money and contribute good things to our society. There is only one evangelical family here that talks about the need of accepting Christ as Savior. There is need for a missionary to organize a church and get our young people straightened out, saved, like you say."

"Well, I see that we agree about the conditions of our society today. Certainly the young people need Christ, But, what about you? You need Him too."

"I? Oh no, I don't need the Gospel! I have a good profession and business. I have everything, good health and all the money I need. I have a good name in the town and with the government officials. I am a mature man, I have control over my passions, I don't need anything to help me like the young people do."

"But, Don Pedro, you are not understanding the full purpose of the Gospel message. Yes, it does change lives for good in this world, but even then, as Jesus once said, 'a man's life consisteth not in the abundance of the things which he possesseth.' The important aspect of the Gospel has to do with **eternity,** with the forgiveness of sin and **eternal life for the soul**."

We had asked around about Don Pedro and found that he was not the moral man with control over youthful passions that he claimed to be. True, according to the life style commonly practiced then, the public considered him a good family man. "So what if he has his concubines, here in Urucoa and up in Caracas, he always takes good care of his wife and children."

I refrained from speaking as Don Pedro began to compare his philosophy of life with the teaching of the Bible. He went on and on and on. Finally, I asked him, "But, what about life after death and preparing for it?"

Don Pedro had his ideas about this also and started to explain. But as he began to talk about this, and of meeting God some day, he was not as sure of himself as he thought he was. He had already mentioned that he was too intelligent to believe that a man's soul went to an intermediate place to get cleansed sufficiently to get into heaven. He also criticized the idea of paying to have prayers said for the dead.

As Don Pedro talked, he apparently began to see how foolish some of his arguments were and that he was beginning to contradict himself. He began to pause more often to think about what he was saying. His words came more slowly. He paused longer this time, looking at me with a blank stare. I wasn't sure that he was even seeing me, he was that deep in thought.

Then, "*Caramba!* [gracious!] I am beginning to understand. How could I have been so blind as to think only of making things better in this life? I see now that matters of the soul and life hereafter are more important...." A longer pause this time. Then, "Eduardo, my friend, please go through it again for me, step by step as you did for my son, Reuben."

With the Bible open in front of us, we read together the verses which showed that he, as a sinner, must repent, ask forgiveness of God and accept Jesus Christ as his Savior. We looked at verses which gave assurance of salvation. Don Pedro then bowed his head and there, in front of those remaining in the room, prayed that God would forgive him and save his soul.

The rain had almost stopped by that time so all could hear as he repeated after me the prayer of a sinner reaching out to God, asking for more understanding, and accepting Jesus Christ, God's Son as his one and only Savior. What a surprise it was to everyone. What rejoicing among the believers. Don Pedro had been born again! We had witnessed a miracle.

********** ********** **********

The next morning, by daybreak, we were up, packed and ready to leave. Mrs. Contreras, Juan's mother, had prepared a good breakfast for us. There were fried eggs sunny side up, over a dish of boiled white rice, native bread toasted over an open fire with some fruit jelly made from ripe guavas, and, of course, coffee and milk. We ate well, leaving not even a crumb, for we were not sure if we would get anything else to eat before reaching Tucupita sometime in the late afternoon or early evening.

After prayer for a safe journey and committing the believers, old and new, into the Lord's hands, we gathered our things together and started the walk down to the river where the *lancha* [launch] was waiting. Passing the corner where Don Pedro had his pharmacy, we saw him standing outside at the curb, his assistant standing by with a bowl of hot water in his hand. Don Pedro, who also did some minor surgeries, had just lanced a very large and very sore boil on the neck of an elderly man.

Seeing him so occupied, and not wishing to interrupt, we simply waved him a good-bye, with an "Adios, brother Pedro, may the Lord be with you." He acknowledged this with a quick wave of the hand.

At the river, our things were quickly stowed under the benches on the boat. As the young people began to take their places, we heard the clop-clop of someone running on the street above the steep bank. It was Don Pedro, breathing heavily as he came slipping and sliding down the muddy bank ignoring the natural steps that had been cut in the earth.

"What are you doing? Where are you going?" he shouted, gasping for breath. He was so excited that his voice was at high pitch. "I don't believe it. You are leaving us already?"

"Yes, brother Pedro," explained Mr. Hausser. "We have to get back to Tucupita and then to El Callao where we have our headquarters."

"But, you have just begun your work here, you haven't even scratched the surface. And, what about your new converts? Certainly you can't abandon them. You know they will go back into their old ways. Many of them cannot read nor write. Who will teach them! I can read the Bible and learn more about the Gospel and the true Christian life for myself. But, what about them?" He was so upset he was trembling and his face was as red as a beet.

"Calm down, brother Pedro," admonished Mr. Hausser. "The Contreras family will help them hold meetings and you too can help. From time to time, someone will come out from Tucupita to hold meetings and counsel with you. I have responsibilities back in the interior. I am sorry, truly sorry, but I cannot stay."

Don Pedro then grabbed me by the arm, his finger punched my chest and, with the voice of authority that he was so accustomed to using, demanded, "You, Eduardo, you must stay with us, you cannot go, we need you."

I was shaken up by Don Pedro's urgency. I realized the great need of those people where there was no organized evangelical church. Truly the harvest was white, but, oh, how few the workers.

As I listened to Don Pedro pleading with me, I was so choked up that I couldn't speak. Mr. Hausser came to my rescue.

"Brother Eduardo has a big job to do back in El Callao. We realize the need for more missionaries and Christian workers. That is why we are founding a Bible Institute to train Venezuelans to be missionaries to your people and to be pastors of the churches. My young co-worker here is going to head up the Institute, so he cannot stay here. I assure you that as soon as possible the Mission will arrange for someone to come here on a regular basis."

Don Pedro was crushed. Finally we were able to get our final good-byes said and to break away. Don Pedro silently climbed back up the bank and disappeared toward his drug store and the old man he had left waiting to have his treatment finished. We all stood looking after him, each one of us with our own very sober thoughts.

Finally Mr. Hausser quoted Matthew 9:37 and 38. "...The harvest truly is plenteous, but the labourers are few; Pray ye therefore the Lord of the harvest, that he will send forth labourers into his harvest." He then added, "This has been a good practical lesson for you young people."

"Before we leave, let's have a word of prayer to claim Urucoa for the Lord." Mr. Hausser prayed and then gave the signal for the boatman to push off.

For some time the young people were silent, sobered by the arguments and appeal of Don Pedro, each one determined to study hard in the Bible Institute to be able some day to return to Urucoa or go to some other place in their country where there was no Gospel witness. Soon, however, they were singing choruses again, talking about their experiences in Urucoa, and challenging each other with questions about Bible history or its teachings. We made better time that day. In the late afternoon, we arrived at Tucupita without incident.

Several years went by before organized missionary work could be done in that area. Then Steve and Martha Green began a work in the town of Barrancas on the northern branch of the Orinoco River, not far from the delta region. In time they had a church organized with their own building. Regular visits were made to Urucoa and the believers there became members of the church in Barrancas. Later, as the congregation grew, a church was organized in Urucoa. In the Lord's good time, our prayers were answered.

Chapter 21

A Bible Institute Founded

"That I may know him, and the power of his resurrection, and the fellowship of his sufferings, being made comformable unto his death." (Philippians 3:10)

The purpose of our trip to Tucupita and the delta region accomplished, Mr. Hausser and I arrived back in El Callao on June 19. In spite of the blessings I received on this trip, I was extremely glad to be home. I had suffered from several bouts of homesickness. Believe it or not, this was the first time in our almost twelve years of married life that Mildred and I were separated overnight. Mildred and I have lived our lives **together**, done everything **together**, went everywhere **together**, worked **together** as a **team**. This separation lasted thirty long days and nights, it was a new and rough experience for me, and I'm sure it was for Mildred also.

While I was away, Mildred kept busy rearranging all her teaching aids, flannel scenes and figures that had gotten mixed up in moving, and filing them in proper order. Mildred's health was completely restored, I was overjoyed to see her vivacious again and anxious to get to work with childrens' Bible clubs. It had been decided that this should be her ministry in El Callao. Through the winning of children to the Lord, contact is made with their parents who very often are also won. This work contributes greatly to the growth of the local church.

My work during the next two months was to finalize the preparations for the opening of the Bible Institute. I arranged the courses and daily work schedules, and made sure the physical plant was ready for the students. The ten students we expected began to arrive toward the end of August. These were Dolores, Angel, Obdulio, Salgado and Pedro Pablo from Tucupita; Juan from Urucoa; Francisco from El Palmar. Eloina and Esteban lived in El Callao. Melina, orphaned, had been living with the Noel family, now she came to live with us to help Mildred in our home. Melina was like an adopted daughter, we grew to love her very much,

Classes began on schedule and we all settled down to a strict daily routine. Though the student body was small, we had them organize with a president, secretary and a coordinator to help the missionaries plan the students' work program and social life. The students selected as their school theme, *"To know Christ and to make Him known,"* based on Philippians 3:10.

All went very well. Of course, there were those usual problems which occur when young people live together in a co-ed institutional environment. Counselling and prayer, along with spiritual renewal retreats, always resulted in renewed submission to the Lord's will and a deeper dedication and spirit of self-sacrifice on the part of both students and professors.

The Institute was a great blessing, not only to the students as they learned sound doctrine and Christian behavior, but also to the local church in El Callao as it provided the students with opportunities to complete their practical work assignments. Weekly street meetings were held in different neighborhoods resulting in the winning of souls. The students learned discipling as they helped to prepare the new converts for baptism and church membership. They taught Sunday School classes and took part in the activities of the Young Peoples Society.

There were some all-day evangelistic hikes on the country roads around El Callao. Many homes were reached with the Gospel message which otherwise would not have been. A great number of tracts were distributed and the students shared their testimonies with all who would listen. A number made professions of faith in Christ. Eddie and I joined them a number of times, and both he and Mildred appreciated this occasional day free from his home-school work.

In addition to my work in the Bible Institute and Mildred's busy schedule with the Bible clubs, we helped in the local church which was being pastored by our senior missionary, Mr. Hausser. We taught Sunday School classes and week-night Bible study classes.

One day, Mildred mentioned that many of the children of her clubs spoke English as well as Spanish. This reminded us of the burden we had felt during our first weeks in El Callao, a burden to reach the more than 3,000 English-speaking people plus their children for the Lord. Since we had Sunday afternoons and evenings free of responsibilities, we could use that time to satisfy that ongoing burden, at least in a limited way.

The El Callao Baptist Church had been established some twenty years earlier with converts from among the English-speaking people.

By the time we joined the work, the membership was divided almost equally between English and Spanish, with Spanish as the language in which all the services were held. Since those living in El Callao were being evangelized by the members of our Baptist church, we decided to try to reach the ones living in the outlying little villages.

The road which passes by our Bible Institute property climbs out of the El Callao valley up and over high San Luis Hill. Looking down from the top there is a panoramic view of the village of El Perú with the offices of the Perú Mining Company in the center, the hospital, the school, and clumps of rustic homes of some of the labourers. In the background, are the buildings, the machinery, and the vats of the gold refining operation. On beyond El Perú, about halfway up another high hill, lies the community of El Chile. Still further up, on a small plateau, lies the community of St. Vincent, so named because its hilly terrain reminded the first settlers of their island home in the Caribbean. These two communities are inhabited mostly by English-speaking people. In these two communities, we began to hold English services on Sundays in the late afternoon and early evenings. We continued for several months until public transportation was suspended because the roads got too bad for the old cars, and replacement parts and tires, because of the war effort, could not be obtained.

Witnesses To the Power of the Gospel of Christ - Romans 1:16

> *"Now thanks be unto God, which always causeth us to triumph in Christ, and maketh manifest the savour of his knowledge by us in every place. For we are unto God a sweet savour of Christ, in them that are saved, and in them that perish."* (II Corinthians 2:14,15)

Many evangelical Christians have the idea that only true believers can praise God and bring glory to His name. However, it has been my experience that non-believers often bless the Lord or praise Him, perhaps unknowingly or not intentionally. In this and the next chapter, we want to relate four instances in which non-believers brought glory to God through their testimony of what He had done through the power of the Gospel of Christ.

Testimonies of non-evangelicals
First Witness - Doña Collette - the Angel LeDuc story

> *"For there is one God, and one mediator between God and men, the man, Christ Jesus."*
>
> (II Timothy 2:5, my emphasis)

We were still living in the rented house on the corner of *Calle Comercial* [Commerce Street] and the road leading out of town toward Nacupay and Tumeremo. The house belonged to the Fitipaldi family who lived in a very large dwelling situated diagonally across the corner. Two French Corsican brothers had married sisters. Since coming to Venezuela, they had prospered as both ranchers and business men. They owned a large cattle and horse ranch some miles south of El Callao, situated on the plains at the edge of a mini-jungle. They also owned and operated a general merchandise store next to their house.

The two sisters were very friendly, especially outgoing Doña Collette. Often, on a very hot, humid afternoon, she would invite Mildred to sit with her on the cool, breezy veranda of her home which, facing the east, was shaded from the sun. By contrast, the merciless rays from that burning red orb in the sky fell fully on the stucco walls of our house right where our *sala* [living room] and bedroom were located. The two women would talk and sew or crochet for about an hour or so before Mildred and I would either go out on visitation or to one of the several children's Bible clubs which Mildred conducted in town. Our son Eddie usually played with Alejandro, Collette's youngest son, at the end of the spacious veranda.

Mildred and I hadn't expected any more children, but now, into our second year back in El Callao, she was pregnant. So, much of that veranda time was spent sewing, or knitting baby clothes. Doña Collette could do marvelous things with imported French linen, crocheting pretty designs. Mildred was hoping for a petite little girl. Thus it was that baby Danny, when he came along, had to swallow his pride and humbly wear all the dainty female clothes.

Doña Collette couldn't do enough for Mildred to help her prepare. In their storeroom, she found the crib which had been Alejandro's. It was a rectangular closely-woven wicker basket, large and deep, one of the many in which bottles of fine wine were imported from France. Cleaned and painted, and hung from a wooden frame, it made an excellent, safe swinging crib. Doña Collette lined it with pink and blue satin, and gave it to Mildred.

None of Doña Collette's close friends lived in the frontier gold-mining town, and since her sister had gone to France to recover from a serious illness, she was hungry for conversation. Doña Collette was a devout Catholic and let Mildred know that she did not want to ever talk about religion. But, by being alert for any opportunity, Mildred was able to speak a word now and then about salvation through faith in the living Savior, Jesus Christ.

Often Doña Collette would ask some question like: "Why did you ever come to such a God-forsaken place like El Callao?" Mildred would then relate how the Lord had led us here to teach the people the Bible and show them that the only way to have their sins forgiven was through faith in Christ and Him alone. Doña Collette would listen courteously, but at the first pause in the story, she would quickly change the subject.

But one afternoon, Mildred related a short incident which illustrated the power of God in the life of one of His children. Instead of changing the subject this time, Doña Collette, after a short pause of apparent serious reflection, said, "I must confess, Mildred, that there is some mysterious power in your religion that we do not have in ours."

Doña Collette paused in her crocheting and touched Mildred on the arm, who stopped her rocking and looked inquiringly at the older woman. The lady went on to explain.

"There is a young Frenchman in your church by the name of Angel Le Duc. Well, he is half French, his mother was Venezuelan. Angel's poor departed father, Francois Le Duc, was a dear old friend of ours from my husband's home town in Corsica. He came over with my husband and my brother-in-law to settle down here. But, he could never make a go of it here; he fell sick and died. God bless his departed soul," so saying, she crossed herself.

"Yes, we know Angel. He received Christ as his personal Savior about a year ago, Mr. Hausser baptized him. Angel has a little farm out in Nacupay along the Yuruary River. You know he is soon to marry one of our girls, who is also a member of our church."

"Exactly. I have never in my whole life seen such a miracle. The change in that young man is marvelous," affirmed Doña Collette, and, after a pause, she continued, "I have to admit that your Gospel has done for him what the Virgin and all the Saints could not."

"Tell me about him," urged Mildred. "We understand that he had a drink problem."

"Drink problem! That is putting it mildly. Poor Angel has been an incorrigible drunkard. Every penny he earned went for rum. Whenever he was sober enough, he did odd jobs for my husband. We fed him and bought him clothes. We tried not to give him very much money and offered to save some of his earnings for him, but he always demanded all he earned. We often thought of giving up on him, but for the memory of his dear departed father (Doña Collette crossed herself again), we were compelled to keep trying to help his son.

"On many a night we would be awakened from sleep by Angel singing his way home from the saloon. He would come staggering down Main Street, barely making it to this corner. Sometimes he would climb up onto our veranda, in which case there was no problem. But many times we would hear him stumble and fall, cursing loudly, right out there in the middle of the street. Believe it or not, he would stay right there where he had fallen in his drunken stupor, but my husband and I would get up and carry him into the house. We would put him to bed in the spare servant's room where he would be safe until morning. I prayed to the Virgin that she would take away the rum demon from Angel, for the love of God and Francois, his father.

"In the morning I would make him drink black coffee. I would talk to him about his father whom he had dearly loved. I would make him confess and pray to the Virgin for help. He would be very contrite, he would cry and promise not to drink again. My heart would break for him for I knew he could not keep that promise. Angel would go out to his house in Nacupay, change his clothes and come back to do some work for my husband. A few days would go by and he would be right back in the same condition, carousing again with his drunken friends.

"Then, something happened to Angel. One day he came to me to tell me that had surrendered to Christ. He was stone sober. It was a miracle. He told me how he had been feeling so sorry about his condition. It was the anniversary of his father's death. He had been drinking, but he went into your church. It was a Wednesday night and all the people there prayed for him. He told me that his mind seemed to clear up like magic, and the pastor read the Bible to him, and he believed in Christ and accepted Him as his Savior.

"Angel tried to explain to me how God had changed him and taken away his thirst for rum. He said something about being born again, but I could not understand it all. Anyhow, I could not believe that it would make any difference. But now, it has been almost a year. How different he is, so happy and so confident. You say he is going to marry?"

"Yes," replied Mildred, "he has been working his little farm with the help and counsel of Mr. Leonard, one of our members who has the big "company" farm out there. And, yes, he is going to marry Elena, daughter of one of our faithful couples."

"How can this be?" questioned Doña Collette almost to herself, I could hardly hear her. "Why could not the Virgin help him? I have burned many candles to the saints, but they did nothing. I don't believe they even tried to intercede to God for him."

"Well, I have been trying to tell you, Doña Collette, salvation can be found only in Christ. Angel has accepted Jesus as his Savior and Lord, and God has given him a new life."

Mildred reached into her sewing bag and took out her New Testament. She opened it to II Corinthians 5:17. "See what it says here, Doña Collette. You can read it for yourself."

The older lady read, "Therefore if any man be in Christ, he is a new creature; old things are passed away; behold, all things are become new."

"You see," continued Mildred, "this new life comes through faith and acceptance of Christ as Savior; not through Mary, not through any saint; salvation and the new life is in Christ; He is the only and sufficient Savior. You need no one else.

"And, Doña Collette, there is only One Intercessor in heaven that can pray for us, and that is Jesus Himself. Look here, see what it says? 'For there is one God, and one mediator between God and men, the man Christ Jesus'" Mildred showed her I Timothy 2:5.

"Jesus Christ Himself said, 'I am the way, the truth, and the life; no man cometh unto the Father, but by me' (John 14:6). Angel has a new life in Christ, free from all vice and drink that has kept him enslaved for so long a time. And dear Doña Collette, if you would only believe...."

But Doña Collette, with a rather violent shake of her head, sprang to her feet, very much agitated. Emotionally she was typically French. She literally ran into the house. Mildred did not know what to do. She could only pray that the Holy Spirit would do His work in Doña Collette's heart. She was sure that her friend was under strong conviction.

After a few minutes, Mildred gathered up her sewing and was about ready to cross over to our house, when Doña Collette returned, completely composed. "Enough of this religion talk, Mildred. Anyhow, it must be time for your children's club, is it not?"

Mildred wanted to say more, but Doña Collette once again had shut the door. Bidding good afternoon, Mildred came home where I was already waiting to walk her to the Bible club at Mrs. Norman Welch's house in town.

Note:

Doña Collette was more determined than ever to avoid talking religion, and try as she would, Mildred could never get in more than a word here and there. Doña Collette and her husband always remained very friendly and later, during our second term, helped Eddie Jr. with his French lessons, and used to send gifts up to the Institute where we were then living.

While home on furlough at the close of World War II, we were able to return some of those favors by sending "CARE" packages to Doña Collette's parents in Paris. She and her husband would send money for us to buy warm clothing to be sent to France where such things were not yet available for any amount of money. Later, when Doña Collette and husband were on their way to visit in France, we spent a day with them in New York City. It was then that Doña Collette gave Mildred a solid gold orchid pin in gratitude for the favors. After all these years, Mildred still cherishes that gold pin, but grieves at the thought that she was never able to win Doña Collette to the Lord.

Seventeen years later, Mildred and I were again back in Venezuela. We visited Doña Collette, now widowed. There were the accustomed greetings with hugs and kisses, but as we sat down for a few minutes to chat, the first words from Doña Collette were, "Now, no religion, please."

It is hard to understand, isn't it, how the human heart can be so hard and resist the "Sword of the Spirit" for so long. What can we say? Mildred could only pray and hope that the holy seed of the Word which she attempted to sow in Doña Collette's heart might some day, before it is too late, spring up in that heart to produce salvation and everlasting life.

Doña Collette and Mildred - 17 years later

In any case, that very lovely and devout **Catholic lady did give testimony to the power of the Gospel of Christ to save and change the life of an habitual drunkard, something that the Virgin and all the saints could not do!**

> *"...Praise the Lord, all ye Gentiles; and laud him, all ye people."* (Romans 15:11)

Chapter 22

The Power of the Gospel

Three More Witnesses

"For I am not ashamed of the gospel of Christ: for it is the power of God unto salvation to everyone that believeth; to the Jew first, and also to the Greek."

(Romans 1:16)

In the late spring, Mr. Hausser fell seriously ill with rheumatic fever. His doctor insisted on a prolonged time of bed-rest. This made it necessary that I suspend any activity not related to the work of the Bible Institute in order to become the missionary-pastor of the El Callao Baptist Church. The care of the congregation also took away some of the time I was devoting to the Bible Institute, but it brought me into town more often where I became better acquainted with the citizens living and working there. This gave me more opportunities to witness to them.

I also learned more about the attitude of the people toward evangelical Christians and the Gospel. Among all the new contacts that I made, there were three that stood out in a very special way. Those three non-believers gave unsolicited testimony to the power of the Gospel.

Romans 1:16 was a favorite verse of ours. We had experienced that **power** in our own lives. We have seen what the Gospel of Christ can do for those in slavery to alcohol, drugs and religious tradition. We are convinced more than ever, that the **Gospel of Christ is the power of God** to save souls for eternity and to change the temporal life of the most perverted sinner.

Through the years, we have heard many voices that **testify** to that same power, voices of believers and of non-believers, even voices of some enemies of the Gospel. In these chapters, the reader has heard the voice of Don Pedro of Urucoa, the pharmacist and politician, and the voice of Collette, our devout Catholic friend, testify to that **power**.

Now listen to the voice of Don Jorge González as he witnesses to the power of the Gospel to make and keep people honest.

Second Witness - Jorge González, the Grocery Storekeeper

"Surely the wrath of man shall praise thee...."
(Psalm 76:10a)

"Eh, Señor Schwartz... Señor Schwartz... wait a minute, I want to tell you something."

It was Señor González, the grocer. He was hurrying across the street from his store as I was opening the gate to the yard in front of the church. It was Wednesday evening and I had come early to open the church and light the gas pressure lamps to have things ready before the people arrived for Bible study and prayer meeting.

I was surprised to hear the raspy voice of González for the grocer rarely spoke to anyone except on matters of business. We made occasional purchases from him, especially when he got in a shipment of canned vegetables or fruit. We missionaries and the American workers in the mines were about the only ones who appreciated these items. I thought at first that this was the reason why González wanted to talk to me. It certainly could not be about the Gospel. We missionaries had often witnessed to him, but he was a wicked man and wanted nothing to do with Christ. He would not listen to us, nor would he accept a Gospel tract.

I paused at the gate as González got right to the point. "You have a young man in your church who is breaking your rules."

"What do you mean? What do you know about our rules?"

"Well, is it not true that the members of your church cannot drink or smoke, go to dances or fiestas, and the movies?"

I felt a bit of resentment at González's tone of voice, but trying to keep cool, I patiently explained. "It is not a question of rules that prevent our people from doing such things. It is that they do **not want to** do them. They love Christ as their Savior and want to do those things which please Him. While we do not have laws in our church, we do expect that a truly saved person will show it by not doing those things which will hurt his health, either physical or spiritual, like smoking, drinking alcoholic beverages, going to dance halls, and the like. You see, when someone accepts Christ as their Savior, he is a new person, he is born again and no longer wants to do the things he did before...."

"Okay... okay..." interrupted González, "I didn't come over here to get preached at. I just think that you should know about this guy in your church, I think he is called Pancho."

"Yes, we have a Pancho in our church. What about him?"

"Well, every night when I close up at ten or ten-thirty... you know I stay open late to catch the crowd that comes out of the *cine* [movie theater] down the street... they buy some cookies and coke. On my way home I stop by the *Cantina de la Virgin* [The Saloon of the Virgin] by the racetrack to get my nightcap before going to bed."

"So?" I queried as González paused to light a cigarette.

"So, almost every night your so-called brother Pancho is in there drinking with the men and exchanging dirty stories. I say that he is not a true brother."

I never did like to listen to gossip, even if it might be true, and besides, I thought, "What right has a man like González to criticize anyone else?"

Irritably, I asked, "Isn't this a little like the pot calling the kettle black?"

"Never mind that. I know what I am," González sneered," but your brother is supposed to be different... One night I told him that it was **wrong for him to be there** in that saloon. I asked him what his pastor would say if he knew. You know what he said?... 'What the pastor don't know, won't hurt him.'"

Mr. González paused. I considered for a moment. It could be true, but the grocer was not above lying, especially if he could hurt the church and the Gospel by doing so. To González I said, "Why are you telling me this?"

"I am telling you this **not because** I care about your church. I wouldn't give you *dos centavos* [two cents] for it or for your so-called Gospel! And I don't care a rap what you think about me, or of anyone else, for that matter. But **your brothers** are supposed to be different, aren't they? **Well, aren't they?**" he shouted, paused, and then continued shouting. I couldn't get a word in edgeways even if I tried.

"I've watched you goody, goody people. I'm just across the street, you know. I've heard you preach about what the Gospel can do, make a drunkard into a sober homebody, make a street-woman into a saint, make an honest man out of a liar. And **that** is what bugs me. That so-called brother of yours is a **liar and a hypocrite**.... that's what he is, a **hypocrite.** And what I hate more than anything else is a hypocrite. I may be called a lot of things which maybe I am, but **I ain't no hypocrite!"**

González literally spit it out. He was still almost screaming and some passers-by had stopped to see and hear what was going on. I guess they thought I was fighting with González. But with that last word, González turned his back on me and went stomping across to his store.

I turned to the men and asked, "Did you hear that?"

"Yeah, we heard. That's the way he is. Don't pay him any attention, Padre." (The Catholics often called me Father.)

"I know. But, my friends, do you realize what he was saying at the end?... For all his rough talk, he was really giving credit to the Gospel for having power to make changes in the life of any who will accept Christ as their Savior. God would do it for González, if he would let Him. And, my friends, God will do it for you too, if...."

But as I started to preach, (I couldn't let the opportunity go by), the men, smiling, gave me a wave of the hand and moved on down the street.

Well, I hated to have to do it, but under the circumstances I had to investigate. Sad to say, it was true. The brother confessed to me that he had backslidden and was drinking again. This had been his besetting vice and we all thought that he had gotten the victory. But, being weaker than he thought, he succumbed when tempted by his former cronies. He had to be disciplined by the church, but later he got complete victory and was restored to fellowship.

This incident shows how the "world" expects a born-again Christian to be different, even though they do not know why. It is a shame that so many believers will not let God, through the indwelling Holy Spirit, transform their lives to be more Christ-like. But, when they do, the world sees the "good works" of the changed life and is bound to acknowledge that there is some "mysterious power" in the evangelical faith that gives victory over enslavement to vices.

Third Witness - President of the Mining Company, Business Executive

> *"All the kings of earth shall praise thee, O Lord... Yea, they shall sing in the ways of the Lord; for great is the glory of the Lord."* (Psalm 138:4a,5)

One day I went to El Perú to pick up Mildred who had spoken at a luncheon that the wives of the officers of the mining company occasionally held. The president's wife introduced me to her husband. After some conversation about the war and the resulting economic problems, he changed the subject to one which is always more interesting to me.

"I wish that you could persuade more of the men of your church to apply for work in our company. We would be glad to hire any of them."

"Why is that?" I asked.

"Well, first of all, we can trust them to give us a good, honest day's work. In the second place, we can trust them not to steal from us. Thirdly, they are steady in coming to work. Absenteeism, goofing off on the job and stealing are three of our worst problems and cost us thousands of dollars a year. But, your men are steady and honest. Please send us more."

I couldn't have said it better if I had been trying to convince this experienced executive to hire our people. What a testimony our people have in the business, commercial and industrial world. It is all because of Christ and His Gospel, to God be the glory!

********** ********** **********

By the end of June, Mr. Hausser had partially recovered from his illness, but not enough to resume his place in the work. He finally had to surrender to the doctor's recommendation that he return to the States. With the better climate, his chances for a full recovery would be much better. In July, he and his wife, Eunice, left for the States. This meant that I would have to continue to pastor the church.

Later that year, I had a conversation with a merchant on Main Street in El Callao that further confirmed that many people believe that the Gospel of Christ greatly **influences the moral standards of everyone**, non-believers as well as believers.

> *"...behold, I will make them to come and worship before thy feet, and to know that I have loved thee."*
>
> (Revelation 3:9b)

Fourth Witness - Julio Berríos, Merchant.

I was conversing with my new friend, Don Julio Berríos, in front of his general merchandise store. He had named it "La Caraqueña" after his native city of Caracas. This is a custom in Hispanic America.

After a few remarks about current events, Don Julio asked, "Have you heard from Mr. Hausser? How is he now, and when do you expect him to return?"

Julio's General Store, La Caraqueña

"I cannot tell you when he will return to Venezuela, though one thing is sure, it will not be until the war is pretty much over."

"Why is that?" the merchant asked.

Mr. Hausser had lived and worked for the Lord in El Callao for some twenty years and was known to all the people and especially to the merchants. Don Julio's interest was not in the Gospel, it was in Mr. Hausser as a person. Don Julio was a very friendly and caring person, and was really interested in the veteran missionary's well-being.

"Mr. Hausser would like to return to Venezuela as soon as he recovers his strength, but at least for the present, he is not permitted. You see, Don Julio, missionaries, whether Catholic, Protestant, or Evangelical, are not allowed to enter Venezuela. Even though they may have lived here for many years and have established legal residence, if they leave, they cannot re-enter."

I explained why the movement of all missionaries, including the priests, was curtailed.

"Why, that is terrible," exclaimed Don Julio. "Mr. Hausser did a good work here among us. He helped our people, as all of you evangelical missionaries do. One time, when the government school was closed, he opened one in his home, especially for the poor children whose parents could not afford a private one. I know also that many times he even used his skill as a carpenter to build coffins so that poor families could bury their loved ones.

"Not only that, but his and your example of life among us, as well as that of your brothers, helps us live better lives. Even our priests have to watch themselves, or our people begin to criticize them for their immorality and for not living as clean a life as do you missionary men.

"As you know, I am Catholic... well, at least in name, I am. My wife, yes, she is a faithful one and takes the children to mass each Sunday. We give our money to the church, though more from custom than from love. But we who **think**," he said, tapping his finger to his forehead, "know that something is lacking in our religion. You people seem to have some strange power to make your followers live better lives."

"No, Don Julio, it is not we who have the power, it is the Gospel of our Lord Jesus Christ. It is Christ who has the power to save and to change lives for both time and eternity."

But Don Julio was not thinking about doctrine, for it is doubtful if he knew very much about his own religion. He had noticed the truly clean Christian life which the believers in El Callao were demonstrating—especially the missionaries. Here was another man of the world, a successful businessman, testifying to the **power of the Gospel of Christ to change lives**. I began to talk to him about his need of the Savior.

"I admit it," agreed Don Julio, "the evangelical faith must be the right one, but..." he hesitated, apparently mulling over in his mind what I was saying.

I knew that the merchant was thinking of his business and how he might lose it if he became an evangelical Christian. But there were other prosperous commercial enterprises in the area owned by evangelicals, an outstanding one being that of brother Teófilo and his goldsmith shop. To Don Julio, I responded:

"I know that you know that the Gospel of Christ is true and by accepting Him as your Savior you will be saved. The several times that we have talked you have given evidence of your belief. But you must come to God in a personal way, confess your sins to Him and receive His Son into your heart. To hesitate is dangerous. Why don't you come to Christ now?"

"I know I should, but... well, maybe some day... yes, maybe some day I will."

The conversation ended as the merchant turned to attend to a customer who entered the store. Only the Lord knows if he ever came to Christ, for shortly after that incident, he moved his business back to Caracas. The main vein of the gold mine had petered out, workers were moving away and business was declining. Some even feared that El Callao would become a ghost town as many people moved north into the area where rich iron deposits had been discovered.

However, El Callao remained a commercial center since new deposits of gold were discovered further interior in the Gran Sabana on the border with Brazil. Cattle ranches began to be established in the area around Tumeremo. The government then built new asphalt roads to make this development possible.

Chapter 23

The Bible Institute's Demise

"Jesus answered and said unto him, What I do thou knowest not now; but thou shalt know hereafter."

(John 13:7)

Several times in our personal lives and in our missionary service, ministries that seemed to be blessed of the Lord and going along well, either suddenly came to an abrupt end or the direction was radically changed. When we asked the Lord about it,... "Why is this happening, Lord?" ...no answer came, that is, none pertaining to the situation. At those times, all we seemed to hear was the voice of Jesus saying to Peter, and I paraphrase, "You don't know **now** what I am doing, but **someday** you will understand."

Maybe in the "hereafter," we'll understand why it seemed fit for the Lord to allow our Bible Institute to "die." For the present, we could only continue to do as wise King Solomon recommended in Proverbs 3:5,6, "Trust in the LORD with all thine heart; and lean not unto thine own understanding. In all thy ways acknowledge him, and he shall direct thy paths."

********** ********** **********

When Mr. and Mrs. Hausser left for the States, we moved into the big house on the Bible Institute campus and, with the help of the girl students, Mildred took charge of the meals. But Mildred was getting along in her pregnancy, and our work load needed to be shared. James and Darlene Russell were asked to come and help in the Bible Institute. They lived in the big house and took over the household chores.

We had already begun construction of what was to be our future home on the campus. We finished just one room in which we planned to store our possessions during our furlough in the States. Upon returning to the field, we would build the rest of the house. Now, we moved into that room which was large enough to be partitioned into two, a living room and a bedroom. We ate our meals in the big house with Jimmy and Darlene and the students.

The first semester of the second year of the Bible Institute flew by very quickly. With the added care of the El Callao Baptist Church, there was so much to do that we just kept going, ignoring the rapid passage of time. Suddenly, Mildred's time for delivery was upon us. Our French pharmacist friend had supplied us with all the things necessary for home delivery. "Pay for what you use; return the rest to me," he had said. I prepared all the other necessary items.

In those days, it was unthinkable to go to the municipal hospital. It had very little equipment, almost no nurses, and, for lack of housekeepers, was always dirty. They changed the bed linens every Thursday "whether needed or not." Mildred's prenatal needs were under the care of Dr. Delipiani García, who recently opened his private practice in our part of the country. He, with the help of a student nurse, would "officiate." Usually, births were handled by licensed midwives who, in many cases, had much more experience than the doctors.

On January 1, 1945, at 3:00 in the morning, our second son, Daniel Charles was born. The doctor, who was supposed to attend the birth, had gone up to El Perú to the New Year's party held by the executives of the gold-mining company. At 11:00 P.M., he had stopped by our little house on the campus hill and, after examining Mildred, predicted that the baby would not be born until 6:00 A.M. or even much later. Consequently the delivery was assisted by a student nurse, who came up from the hospital, and a somewhat nervous husband. Praise the Lord there were no complications for which there was also much rejoicing.

Dan Charles, new arrival, January 1, 1945

You should have seen the funny look on the face of the very surprised doctor when he stopped by about 5:00 A.M. on his way home with his wife from the party. When he saw the baby, all clean and lying in his swinging crib, all he could say was, "Impossible!... Impossible!"

He then turned to his wife and remarked, "These American women don't fool around. They get it done in a hurry."

The new arrival weighed in at nine pounds and measured 21 inches. Danny came into the world screaming lustily, a portent of things to come, of a strong will needing always to be loudly and clearly made known, of a life to be lived and enjoyed to its capacity, dedicated to the Lord, his profession, and his sports.

In March, a routine examination revealed that Mildred would need an operation which should be done in the States. Thus, we planned to leave right after the closing exercises of the school year. It was with real sadness that, after only two years of functioning, the Bible Institute's classes had to be suspended. With the lack of personnel, it would have been impossible to continue, the Russell's could not have carried on alone. They then moved to San Félix on the Orinoco River to pastor the young church and carry on missionary work.

We were able to transfer four of our students to the Bible Institute in Las Delicias on the coast. These students were Esteban, Melina, Eloina and Angel. In two years they graduated and became workers in the Mission churches.

Before closing the archives on the history of our Bible Institute, we would like you to join us in **praising and thanking the Lord** as we give you a brief up-date on what our students have been doing through the years. You already know about **Angel**; he has continued pastoring Baptist churches through the years. He and Teolinda have five children who live for the Lord. Their first daughter became a Christian concert pianist.

Two of our students, **Salgado and Pedro Pablo**, sorry to report, fell by the wayside and we have no present knowledge of them.

Francisco and Melina—Francisco of El Palmar, because of his lack of secular education, could not accompany the other students to Las Delicias. He had only begun to read and write after he was saved. In our Bible Institute I had to give him his examinations verbally, which he passed with flying colors. This handicap was quickly overcome. He also rapidly grew into a stable and mature Christian, committed much Scripture to memory, and was an ardent soul winner. When we left for furlough, the El Callao church called him to be their pastor. Later, we had the pleasure of marrying Francisco and Melina.

When, new deposits of gold and diamonds were discovered in the Gran Sabana near the Brazilian border, Francisco and Melina moved there to do missionary work among the many prospectors. But, because the Gran Sabana was considered Indian territory, and by law, in the hands of the State Church, Francisco and Melina were forced to leave.

Francisco and Melina Williams family

During the years that followed, Francisco successfully pastored several churches and became a respected member of the Association of Fundamental Baptist Churches and the pastor's fellowship. At present writing, he is enjoying retirement after pastoring the church of La Providencia in the San Félix area, a church which he started as a missionary.

Obdulio and Eloina—As time went on, Obdulio married Eloina and eventually took up residence in Ciudad Bolivar, the State capital, where they are active members in their church.

Juan and Dolores—Juan was not called to full-time service but worked in the Iron Mines Company, first in El Pao and later in San Félix. He continued to study by correspondence and eventually became an electrical engineer and held a responsible position in the Venezuelan company which took over from U.S. Steel when the industry was nationalized. He married Dolores and both have ever since been very active members of the San Félix church. He became interim pastor during the year that their pastor, Ramón Ramírez, took further studies in Costa Rica. They never had children but raised an adopted boy and girl. Today, Juan is retired, but Dolores still has her business in San Félix. She travels regularly to the States to purchase merchandise to sell in her store. They have a beautiful home in the suburbs. They honor the Lord with their substance and He has blessed them in a wonderful way.

Juan and Dolores Contreras family

Esteban John—Esteban served for several years as supply pastor in the churches, but did not feel called to continue in a full-time ministry. Having been trained in wood-working and construction, he eventually became the superintendent in charge of maintenance of all the homes and offices of the former United States Steel Company in Puerto Ordaz, twin city to San Félix. He married Aquila, a girl from our Upata church, and has raised and educated five lovely children—four girls and a boy. He is an officer in the large Puerto Ordaz church which he helped to found, and where he has preached occasionally. He is now retired but still active in the local church. Recently the church lost its pastor, so Esteban is serving as interim pastor.

Esteban and Aquila John family
(Photo taken before Esteban Jr. was born.)

In recent years, Mildred and I have visited each one of these students, except for two. All are still happily married and serving the Lord. Praise the Lord!

"...Praise the Lord, ...and laud him, all ye people."
(Romans 15:11)

Chapter 24

Miguel and Mercedes

Story of Faith and Works - Part I

"Commit thy way unto the LORD; trust also in him, and he shall bring it to pass." (Psalm 37:5)

Before leaving El Callao on that first furlough, we spent several weeks visiting the members of the church to have prayer with them, and say our "goodbyes." We also wanted to explain the circumstances for our leaving and to urge them to encourage brother Francisco who would be pastoring the church. The last family we visited was that of Miguel and Mercedes.

Our ride to their house in El Perú was a rather exciting one, but not so unusual in those days. We had flagged down one of those old wooden station wagons for our trip. As previously told, these cars were in such bad condition that it could be dangerous to travel in them, but what could one do? We just could not sit at home and twiddle our thumbs, we had the Lord's work to do. Baby Danny remained at home with his *cargadora* [literally, a carrier], a young girl who lived with us for this purpose, a kind of "nanny," if you will.

We had just gotten to the top of the first section of San Luis Hill, and had made the right angle turn to the left on a level stretch of the road, and were part way up the second section, when it happened. The car up in front of us suddenly started to come down backwards.

"Hey, watch it," I shouted. "That car's coming down the hill backwards."

"I see it, Señor, I see it," our driver shouted back. "I told my brother not to take the car out today. We hadn't finished working on the motor, and the breaks needed adjustment."

I prided myself on being a good driver, but I couldn't imagine what they were going to do. The gravel road was in fair condition, but it was narrow, ordinarily too narrow for two cars to pass at one time. There were small areas that were wider and the custom was that the cars coming down would wait in those places until the cars going up could pass. The cars going up the hill always had the right-of-way.

Mario, our driver, keeping his cool, quickly threw the gears into reverse and, using his brakes, geared his speed backward to correspond to that of the descending car until its rear bumper touched the front bumper of our car. He used his brakes to slow down his brother's car. Then, at the exact moment that we arrived back at the right-angle turn, Mario veered to the left down into the first section of the hill, letting his brother continue backward, straight into the emergency ramp, where he came to a gradual stop in the soft dirt.

Other cars, coming up the hill, stopped to see what was happening. Of course, Mario and his brother were screaming at each other, each blaming the other for the situation. In due time all became calm and Mildred and I praised the Lord for saving us from what could have been a bad accident. We took the opportunity to pass out Gospel tracts and witness to the people. In due time all the passengers from Mario's brother's car found places in the other cars, and soon we were on our way again, chugging up the rest of San Luis Hill.

As our car descended the other side of San Luis Hill we could see, over the tops of the trees, the expansive clearing of white sand deposited by the gold refining process. Arriving in El Perú, just past the company offices, the driver stopped.

"*Hasta aquí, mis amigos* [To right here, my friends] is as far as I can take you. The road up ahead is too bad for my tires," explained Mario. "Nobody knows when tires will come into the country again. We can fix the old ones to a certain point, but after that, poof... I am out of business."

"That's okay," I replied as I paid our fare. "We have to cross the sand anyway to get to the home of our friends. Will you be back here again to pick us up about four o'clock?"

"Sí, Señor," Mario assured us. "If I don't meet another loco on San Luis Hill."

Getting this assurance from Mario, Mildred, Eddie and I started walking across the hot white sand. Having been deposited in this area years ago, the sand had dried out and hardened under the scorching tropical sun. It was now a baseball field.

"Oh, that smell is awful," exclaimed Mildred. "I don't see how the people stand it. It is bad enough to have to work here, but to choose to live here? Ugh." (The acrid smell came from the new deposits of the crushed granite which had been treated by the cyanide acid used in the flotation method of recovering the gold.)

"Maybe since the men live close by so they can walk to their work, and not have to pay for transportation, they get used to the smell."

"But why don't they live in one of the company's homes for workers? Those houses up on the hill behind the offices are nice, roomy and under the shade of the trees. I'd rather live up there than under this hot sun." Mildred stopped to wipe the perspiration from her face. I too was wiping my face. "I guess that's why the Americans call this place 'Chili-Mex'. It's as hot as Mexican chili peppers. The workers ignore the heat and the smell, for by living in this shanty-town and not using the company homes with utilities, they get paid a bonus."

By this time, we had walked through the white sand field and were climbing the little hill toward the group of shacks. El Perú was not really a town but an area surrounding and including the several gold mines, and consisting of many little groups of houses that could hardly be called communities. Miguel and Mercedes lived in one of these with their six children.

Miguel was fondly called *Catire*. In English he would be called "Whitey," because of his blue eyes, fair skin and blond hair. In fact, both he and Mercedes had the features of Europeans. They were probably descendants of Spanish colonizers whose blood became mixed with that of the German and Irish soldiers of fortune who came to fight for Simón Bolivar in his war for independence, and then stayed on, married and had children.

Whitey, Mercedes and their two oldest children had been saved a little over a year and were members of our church in El Callao. They had not been down to services in several weeks. We knew Whitey had been ill and we had just heard that he had to be hospitalized.

Their home was located on the back edge of the community, and Mercedes and Whitey had been able to clear off a level spot for a garden. As we approached, Mercedes was coming from the little garden and about to go in the door of her home. When she saw us, she turned and walked toward us. We could see that she had been crying, her eyes were red and watery.

As the two women embraced, Mercedes, between her sobs, cried, "Oh, pastor and dear Mildred, God sent you today. I have needed you so." When she had calmed down somewhat, we went into the house. Mercedes sent the children out to play and then explained.

"My husband has been so sick. I knew that, but I didn't think he was so far gone. He has been fighting tuberculosis, you know. He had been going to the outpatient clinic at the company hospital, but three weeks ago they told him he would have to stay. And now he is worse than ever. I went to see him at lunch time today. We read the Word and prayed together. He wants to come home to be with me and the children. He thinks he is not going to get better and...." Here Mercedes broke down again. It was several minutes before she could go on. "He said he wanted to die at home with us by his side. Oh Lord help us... Unless our dear Savior does something, my husband is going to die."

"Oh, I'm sure the Lord is able to raise him up. Whitey was a pretty strong fellow."

"I know, I know, Pastor Eduardo, but this sickness has taken all his strength away. When I was leaving the hospital to come home, the doctor called me into his office. He told me to go get Whitey's clothes and come back this afternoon to take him home. He said that medicine can do no more for him, that he would soon die, so he might as well be home with his family to enjoy his last few days the best way he can.

"I was so overcome to hear this that I ran from the hospital straight into my little garden. I fell down on my knees and prayed to the Lord to give me wisdom... What shall I do? I cried and prayed... then I prayed and cried some more. Finally, I knew what to do. Now I have it all settled with the Lord. I am going to bring Whitey home, but he is not going to die, I am sure of it. The Lord has given me peace in my heart. I know what to do."

We listened, spellbound as Mercedes spoke with so much feeling and assurance. We were astonished at the change we saw come over her. She wasn't sobbing any more; in fact, there was a faint smile beginning to bloom on her face. We waited for her to continue.

"Out there in the garden, the Lord spoke to me. He showed me that although we have been believers in Christ for more than a year now, we haven't really witnessed to our family and neighbors like we ought. I said to the Lord, 'But you know I have no schooling and when I try to witness I just can't think of words to say. You know that, Lord.'"

Mercedes paused in thought, then continued, "Then I knew what I must do. First, I confessed our failure to the Lord, then I made a promise. I said, 'Lord, you know Whitey can talk, he will be able to witness for you. You know also that I am a farm woman. Whitey helped me, yes, but it was I who really knew how and did most of the work.

"I am a strong woman, Lord, thanks be to you. With your help, I will keep the family in food from our farm. I can also sew and will make the clothing they need. Then, Whitey can go out and preach the Gospel. He can be a witness for me and the children. They will help me too when they come from school. The older ones will, I know. Thank you, Lord, for showing me what I must do. I commit Whitey unto you, Lord, for you to make him well again. I will trust in you to bring it to pass.' That's what I told the Lord."

As Mercedes paused, I suggested, "Let's all pray together and then we'll go over to the hospital to see Whitey. You know we came up here to say our goodbyes. We are leaving for our home in the States in two weeks."

After prayer, Mercedes said, "Let me get Whitey's clothes. I will bring him home and the Lord will make him better. The doctor has done all he can, now it is up to the Lord."

At the hospital, we were surprised to see how much Whitey had failed. We thought to ourselves, "This brother will shortly be with the Lord. He is too far gone." Try as we would, we just couldn't feel as Mercedes did. No doubt about it, her faith was strong, but we couldn't believe that in this case she knew the Lord's will. Brother Whitey was in too much misery, he was so weak, and that continual cough racked his whole body. The Lord would have to take him home soon to end his suffering. Later, when we spoke to the doctor in private, he agreed.

A neighbor had come to the hospital to help Mercedes take Whitey home, so in order to catch the car at four o'clock, we excused ourselves and headed back across the flat white sand. We had had prayer with Whitey and Mercedes in the hospital before leaving his room. We had committed our sick friend and brother in Christ to God the Father for His will to be done. But, in no way did we think that we would ever see Whitey again on this earth.

Miguel and Mercedes - Story of Faith and Works - Part II

> *"Being confident of this very thing, that he which hath begun a good work in you will perform it until the day of Jesus Christ."* (Philippians 1:6)

Our first furlough went quickly. The cold winter, along with strong treatments of new drugs, got rid of my chronic malaria. Mildred had a rather serious operation, but recovered quickly. Meetings in our supporting churches went well. World War II had come to an end.

The Lord supplied all the new equipment we would need for the field, including a half-ton pickup with four-speed transmission, positive traction and heavy springs for traveling through the jungles and over the plains in Venezuela. In October of 1946, we were back on the field.

The first Lord's Day of our second missionary term, found us in church in El Callao. Pastor Francisco had difficulty starting the opening exercises of Sunday School. This was because each family as they entered the building had to come and greet us. The women embraced and kissed each other. The men bear-hugged and almost knocked the wind out of me.

Then, when we were well into opening exercises, we were interrupted by a commotion outside. A group of our members living in El Perú had managed to talk a friendly truck driver into taking them to church. Mildred and I could not believe our eyes. It just couldn't be. Mercedes and her children, dressed in their very best, and Whitey, still very thin and emaciated, but looking very much alive, were in front of the group.

We rushed out to meet them. I was the first to embrace Whitey as Mildred hugged and kissed Mercedes and then each of the children. "I can't believe it, but praise the Lord, it is you, Whitey! God bless you, brother, and may God forgive me my lack of faith."

"Yes," agreed Whitey, "it is I, not my ghost, and may He forgive me too. I never thought to see you again, Pastor Eduardo. Mercedes has put all of us to shame, she never doubted that I would get well. The Lord has healed me and each day I am getting stronger. He must yet have work for me to do in my life."

"I'm sure He has, and we'll work together to find out what it is," I assured Whitey as we walked together into the church. The services that day were indeed a blessing to all. We were rejoicing that the Lord had seen fit to take us back to our field of service and to the people we had come to love. The people also were rejoicing in our return.

One of the pieces of equipment that turned out to be such a wonderful blessing during our second term was that half-ton pickup.

First of all, it enabled us to pick up and bring to the services people who lived at a distance and had no public transportation at night. Secondly, it enabled us to visit our churches in towns where no missionary was stationed. And, thirdly, we were better able to evangelize. Several times a week we would fill the back of the pickup with as many people as it would hold and conduct open-air meetings in the public plazas of nearby communities. I built a roof over the pickup to protect the riders from the hot sun and the rain.

Whitey, Mercedes and four children

Mildred renewed her Bible clubs for the children in various sections of El Callao. Once a week we traveled to the home of Mercedes and Whitey up in Chili-Mex to have a Bible club. Since many adults came to the club it became a family meeting. After the lesson for the children, I would give a lesson for the adults. Mercedes, and especially Whitey, wanted to learn all they could and would keep us answering questions about how to win souls, about doctrine and the practical aspects of how churches are organized and function. It was a great joy to see their spiritual growth over the next three years

Their family also grew numerically and soon numbered nine. We could not imagine how Mercedes could do it, work so hard in the garden and have children too. Of course, the older girls helped in the garden when they came home from school and the younger children took charge of the babies. That day when we met Mercedes coming in from the garden, she was pregnant. When she offered her husband to the

Chili-Mex Bible study class

Lord for His work, she also offered her unborn child. She named him Nahum when he was born. A brother in the El Callao church who had a Bible dictionary gave her the name, telling her that it meant "to comfort" or "to have compassion." When Nahum was presented to the congregation at church, she testified, "The Lord had compassion on me and healed my dear husband."

Whitey, because of his delicate health, could no longer work in the mines, so had to find easier work. He had a barber friend who, wanting to help the family, had Whitey come into his shop to sweep and keep the place clean. From time to time he would show Whitey how to cut different styles and it wasn't long before he could do a complete haircut by himself. It wasn't too difficult for him because in those days only men and boys went to a barber shop. As he became more proficient, Whitey would walk into the country looking for customers. Thus he had some money with which to buy clothes and other necessities for the family. Mercedes always kept food on the table from her garden, not much variety, but nourishing and satisfying.

The Bible club continued in their home and some neighbors got saved. Then Mildred wanted to start a club up in El Chile where we had held one for a short time during the early part of our first term. We went every two weeks on Friday afternoon. Sometimes we picked up Whitey who would visit and witness in the homes of the community. Soon, Whitey became a very proficient soul winner. Again we committed them into the Lord's hands as we left on our second furlough, a little early for health reasons.

El Chile Bible club

Miguel and Mercedes - Story of Faith and Works - Part III

Well...! That second furlough was a great deal longer than we expected—seventeen years. The health problem had been resolved in a matter of two years, but the Lord meanwhile had led us to work in a new field, right in our home town of Philadelphia.

Those years passed by very rapidly. I guess it is because they were full of interesting and exciting experiences, some of which are related in future chapters. In the early part of 1967, Mildred and I found ourselves back in Venezuela for a two-month visit. I was the speaker at the annual conference of our Association of Fundamental Baptist Churches meeting in El Callao. That was a blessed week as we renewed our fellowship with the brethren, some of whom are our own children in the Lord. We held Bible conferences and evangelistic meetings in churches in other towns.

The young pastor of the church in Upata explained that because of a problem caused by a charismatic group that tried to take over the church, some members had been lost, and so I should not be disappointed with the poor attendence. The church auditorium could seat about 150 people, but as the service was about to begin, there were only about forty or so present.

As the first hymn was being sung, there was a commotion in the street outside. I was seated on the platform so I could see through the open doors. Two large stake-bodied trucks had parked outside and the people, men, women and children, jumped down to the pavement and filed into the church in a not too orderly fashion.

From the doorway, in the midst of the group still entering the church, came a shout, "Pastor Eduardo... gracias a Dios, it is you!" It was Mercedes who was running down the aisle and Whitey following close behind. Part way down there was a pause as Mercedes stopped to embrace and kiss Mildred who, upon hearing Mercedes' voice had come out from the pew where she was seated. I met them in front of the pulpit where again there were embraces and kisses. It broke up the meeting. The people stopped singing. They didn't mind. They rejoiced in witnessing a reunion of brethren in Christ who had not seen each other for such a long time. Things did get settled down and the meeting continued. Now the auditorium looked better, almost full, for the group that came in added about another forty to the congregation. They had come in the two trucks from the little village of Santa Rosa about fifteen miles away.

The next morning, we were seated in the living room of Whitey and Mercedes' home in Santa Rosa. We had driven the fifteen miles in the car loaned to us by one of our missionaries.

"Pastor Eduardo and Doña Mildred, what a joy it is to have you in our home once again! So many years have gone by we thought we would never see you again!" Mercedes declared.

"We thought that also, but we are rejoicing that the Lord did bring us back, if only for a visit. We are so happy to see you all again," Mildred assured them. Then, "My, what a nice home you have, so big, and so much ground all around."

"Yes, this is very different from the shack we lived in back in Chili-Mex," agreed Whitey. "I also praise the Lord and thank him every day for the wonderful wife the Lord has given me. Mercedes is the one who has done all the work. The Lord restored my health, but I have never been strong enough to do hard labor."

I rose from my chair and idled over to the rear door. Looking beyond the patio, I remarked, "Those fields spreading out toward those hills beyond look like good farm land."

Mercedes assured me that such was the case. "Indeed, one of those fields that slopes slightly into a shallow ravine is mine. That's where we have our garden."

Mildred joined us in the doorway. "But, Mercedes, those little ones playing in the sand... surely they are not yours."

"No, dear Mildred, the Lord did give us twelve children all told, but I have long since passed the time to have any more." Laughing, she continued, "Those are my grandchildren. I am taking care of them. It is my daughters and their husbands turn to weed the garden today."

Sitting down again, I interrupted the ladies. "We are very anxious to hear all that has happened during these seventeen years. We want to hear the whole story right from the time we left El Callao. Sit down please, and tell us, Mercedes, all about it. First, how you came to live up here in Santa Rosa. Tell us everything, then we want to see your church."

"Well," began Mercedes, "shortly after you left, the gold mining companies began to give up and leave. When the companies gave up their concessions, the government began to operate the grinders and melt the rock that individual miners brought in. But it hardly paid enough to make it worth while. Little by little the families began to leave.

"We stayed in Chili-Mex until we harvested our last vegetables from the garden, and then we left also. I'm from this area, you know, my parents had a farm on the road to Upata. My grandparents owned this property here on the main street just at the edge of Santa Rosa. They had a very small house on it, which was so run down that my relatives had no objection to us taking it over. Then as our family grew, we added quite a number of rooms and the boys... I still call them boys... the four of them keep it in good condition for us."

At that moment a fine-looking young man came into the house. "Can you guess who this is?" asked Mercedes, as the fellow came over, kissed his mom and then stood next to Whitey.

"How old are you, son?" I asked. "Almost twenty-two," was the reply."

"Then you have to be... wait a minute... let's see... we've been gone seventeen years. Adding four years of our second term makes twenty-one. You have to be Nahum, right?"

"Yes, this is Nahum, and he has become my right-hand-man," proudly boasted Whitey. "Mercedes dedicated him to the Lord and His service before he was born. It was the same day she claimed my healing by faith and dedicated me to the Lord.

"Nahum finished high school and joined me in my ministry. We taught all our children the Word from the time they were little and dedicated them to the Lord. Nahum is the only one who has responded to the Lord's call. He is now enrolled in the Bible Institute on the coast."

"So, please go on with the history, Mercedes, I'm anxious to hear everything," Mildred urged.

"Well, when we moved up here we first had to fix up this house and clean the land. A friend on the town council spoke for us so that we could get the small farm, the two acres over yonder. The ground is very fertile and soon we began to reap pigeon peas and some garden vegetables like squash, melons, tomatoes and beans. Plantains came later, but the mango trees and avocados were already here." Mercedes paused for breath, then began again.

"You remember how Whitey learned to cut hair in a shop back in Chili-Mex. Here in Santa Rosa, Whitey found lots of work, the nearest barber was in Upata. Everyone he met heard his testimony, while he cut their hair, talked to them in the street or on the country roads. Well, praise the Lord, little by little souls were saved and we invited them to our house for services.

"After we had a good group, Whitey went to Upata and asked the missionaries there to come and baptize the converts and help organize us into a church... Soon we outgrew our living room. The people gave money for material, the men did the construction, the women cooked meals, and soon we had our first chapel. Now you will see a regular cement-block building with a tower and bell. The work hasn't been easy, for this is a very Catholic town.

"But you know, the people here respect our Gospel. We try to live like genuine Christians should. We always remember the verse we learned in Bible club back in Chili-Mex. 'Therefore if any man be in Christ, he is a new creature: old things are passed away; behold, all things are become new.' And we want to prove it by our lives."

"But, what do you mean when you say that the people respect your Gospel?"

"Well, they always treat us well. We have had no problems, no persecution," Whitey replied. "And they listen well when I tell them that Jesus is the only way of salvation."

"Not only that," Mercedes took up the story again, "but, believe it or not, the town council even asked Whitey to accept the position of mayor."

"They asked him? Didn't the people vote?... How is that?"

"Well, you might remember that here in Venezuela the mayors of the little towns are appointed by the governor of the district and usually they are recommended by the town fathers. We considered it a great honor, not for ourselves, but for the Lord, for them to ask an evangelical to be their mayor. Whitey accepted, but he only served for about a year and a half."

"That's right, for I soon found out that even in a small town, politics can be dirty. I discovered that some officials were using our reputation as evangelicals to make some shady deals look good. So, before my testimony could be compromised, I resigned. Anyhow, it was beginning to take too much time from my witnessing, especially out in the country roads."

"I didn't like it from the start," admitted Mercedes. "I had dedicated my Whitey to the Lord's service and I wouldn't like anything that might hinder him from that."

"By this time," continued Mercedes, "the United States Steel Company began to take the iron ore out of those big mountains west of the Caroní River. They built a small town called Ciudad Piar, for their employees, about a three-hour drive up a new road from Puerto Ordaz.

"In one of our prayer meetings, the Lord seemed to tell us that Whitey should go up there. One of our deacons had studied with the missionaries in Upata and was preaching in our church on occasions, so he could pastor our church. In Ciudad Piar, Whitey found a room to rent in a small inn run by a Christian family. He rented a stall in the public market where he cut hair. He testified for the Lord and one by one, people got saved.

"Whitey would be there for a couple of weeks and then come back home to be with us in our Sunday church services, get his clothes washed and ironed, then return to Ciudad Piar. As the group grew they got permission from the steel company to hold services in a large dining room no longer in use. More souls were saved. On one of his trips home, Whitey went to Upata and asked the missionaries to come and baptize the believers and help them organize a church.

"In a few more years they were able to call a Bible Institute graduate as pastor. They couldn't put up a building for themselves because all of the property for miles around belonged to the steel company and only two church buildings were permitted on the property, one for Catholics and one for Protestants. The latter had to be interdenominational. Both were paid for by the company. Our church, of course, was organized as the Evangelical Baptist Church.

"But see how wonderfully the Lord worked for us. The members of the interdenominational congregation were all foreign employees and officials of the company. Services were held in English and the pastor was North American. After several years the company began to eliminate the foreigners and to hire only Venezuelans or other Latin Americans. Pretty soon there were no members left in what they called the American Church, so the company turned that large beautiful chapel, Sunday School rooms, recreational hall, and the equipment, including the organ, the Sunday School tables and chairs, everything, over to the Evangelical Baptist Church. Praise the Lord for His goodness and preservation of His testimony in Ciudad Piar!"

"What a wonderful story," Mildred and I exclaimed together.

"But that is not the end," continued Mercedes. "The Lord had some more work for Whitey to do. With the development of the iron industry, refining plants were being built along the Orinoco River from San Félix to Ciudad Bolivar, and the government decided to go ahead with their plans to build a hydro-electric plant on the Caroní River. Of course, they had to build houses for the employees and, before long, there was another town for Whitey to evangelize.

"Yes, he started all over again up in Guri, the name they gave to the town. The Lord brought about the same results. People got saved and soon there were enough believers to be baptized and to form another Baptist church."

"How wonderful. God has certainly used your Whitey. Think of it, three churches started through the work of one consecrated believer in less than seventeen years."

"It wasn't me," Whitey modestly denied. "The Lord did it. You know I have had no formal training. All I did was give my testimony. The Lord saved the souls and the missionaries came and gave them lessons and then got the churches organized. The only teaching I have had is that which I received back in Chili-Mex in your Bible clubs."

"All that may be true, Whitey," I admitted, "but you were faithful in witnessing and you did show the people how they could be saved."

"Well, yes, that is one thing I know how to do. God saved me twice, once when I received Jesus as my Savior and Lord, and again when He healed me when I was dying. He gave me a new life to live for Him. All I did was tell the people what the Lord had done for me and that He would do it for them too. Of course, up in Guri, I had some help to get a church started. Quite a number of the families that came to live there already were believers and they were happy to help. So almost right away we had good meetings that attracted others."

Mercedes had sent two of the older girls into the kitchen to prepare a little lunch, then, while Whitey was talking, she went in to put the finishing touches to it. Now from the doorway Mercedes spoke. "We have a lunch ready for you to eat before you go back to Upata. Shall we have prayer first? Please, Pastor Eduardo, lead us in thanking the Lord for the food."

"Not just a prayer for the food; this story that we have just heard calls for a prayer time of thanksgiving for what the Lord has done through you and Whitey. First, let's sing some of the old choruses we used to sing back in the old Bible club days. Do you remember them?"

"Do we ever! We sing them all the time."

So we sang and sang and sang, praising the Lord until we were hoarse, then a round of prayer. We sat down to a simple lunch. How good the *sancocho* [stew] tasted. Everything except the small pieces of meat came from Mercedes' garden-farm, yellow squash, sweet yucca, onions and sweet potatoes. For dessert there was jellied grapefruit rind and slices of papaya in deep syrup. All this was topped off with a delicious cup of Venezuelan *café con leche*.

Santa Rosa Baptist Church

After the meal, we took pictures of the family and then went with Mercedes and Whitey to see their church. We met the pastor and his wife, Baptist refugees from Franco's Spain, whom the Lord led to Santa Rosa and whom our brethren helped to "get on their feet."

Back at the house, there were the goodbye embraces from Whitey and Nahum, embraces and kisses from Mercedes and the girls. As we made ready to get into our car, Mercedes asked, with tears starting to form in her eyes, "Will I ever see sister Mildred and my first pastor again?

"Well, only the Lord knows the answer to that. But we do have some tentative plans and, if the Lord wills, we may be able to come back to Venezuela again, if only for visits."

We drove back to Upata rejoicing and thanking the Lord for allowing us to see the fruit of our labors, to see how that fruit has multiplied, reproducing itself through our children in the Lord. We thought of John 15:16, the part that says: "...I have chosen you... that ye should go and bring forth fruit, and that your fruit should remain..." and Philippians 1:6, "...he which hath begun a good work in you will perform it until the day of Jesus Christ...."

ALL THE GLORY BELONGS TO GOD WHO GAVE THE INCREASE!

V
Venezuela Ministry - Part 2

Chapter 25

The Hezekiah Brown Story

"Jesus is duh onliest way to God." "I is so very proud... My bredrens has come... Praise be to God!"

"Jesus saith unto him, I am the way, the truth, and the life; no man cometh unto the Father, but by me." (John 14:6)

We had many interesting experiences during our second missionary term, some of which are related in later chapters. In this current chapter, we want to tell you about our first trip to the town of El Dorado, which bears the name of that fabulously rich gold mine, which has never been rediscovered.

It had been our desire for some time to visit El Dorado. It is located where the Yuruary River joins the Cuyuni, near the border of Guyana. We were thrilled to think that we would be the first missionaries to go that far interior.

We prepared camping equipment: hammocks, kerosene cook stove, kitchen utensils, folding organ, Bibles, Gospel tracts, etc. On this trip we were accompanied by Esteban, Eloina and Millie, Bible Institute graduates. Both Eddie and Danny went with us.

The excursion was planned in conjunction with one of our regular visits to the church in Tumeremo. We had Sunday services in Tumeremo and then, early on Monday morning, we left for El Dorado. Joining the group, was Carlos, senior deacon of our Tumeremo church, whose personal testimony was widely known in that part of Venezuela.

In our half-ton pickup, we made the 45 mile trip from Tumeremo in three hours without trouble; the government had recently thrown gravel on the bad places of the road. The scenery was beautiful and interesting. We had never seen some of the blossoming trees and bushes. At one densely forested section, we saw a family of monkeys grouped by the side of the road. We stopped to watch them as they filed nonchalantly across the road, papa leading, mama following, then three children, each holding onto the tail of the one in front.

Blue, yellow, red and green macaws filled the air with their screeches as they winged above our heads from one group of trees to another. The occasional cry of a puma, the tropical mountain lion, could be heard off in the jungle. Once a black panther standing in the road, was surprised as our pickup rounded a bend. It stared at us for just a moment and then, with a single bound, leaped off into the bushes. The small wild animals were interesting to see, but we were glad that we did not encounter a jaguar, which kills just for the love of killing.

Emeterio Idrogo was the only believer living in El Dorado. We hoped that we could either camp with him or that he would know of a place where we could stay. We also wanted him to help in a visitation program. When we arrived in town, we parked the pickup and Mildred and the girls walked one way down a street and Esteban and I went the other way, looking for Emeterio. Don Carlos stayed with the pickup to watch over the equipment. After about an hour of going up and down the streets, we gave up.

Working our way back toward where the truck was parked, we saw Mildred and the girls approaching, having just turned the corner of an intersecting street. But, they were not alone, for with them was a tall black man with graying short curly hair. A smile a mile wide cut his face in half, the proverbial ear-to-ear smile. There were just a few uneven yellow teeth, yellow but shining white in contrast with the very dark face.

"This is Mr. Hezekiah Brown," Mildred said. "He says that he is a brother."

Remembering our English-speaking friends down in El Callao, I took Mr. Brown's extended hand and said, "You mean that you belong to the Anglican Church, right?"

Countenance clouded up, smile obliterated, his face seemed to lose some of its shine. "No... No... I'se a brudder; I'se one of you," insisted Mr. Brown in his peculiar pigeon English with a creole accent. “I’se one of you. I has received Jesus Christ as my onliest Savior.”

“Well... well... that’s good,” I commented. “How did this happen?”

“Well, sir, it was most a year ago. A old lady from El Callao came up here to visit a kin in the jail ’cross duh ribber. She brung some food and clothing with her to give to duh *reclusos* [prisoners]. She name, if I rightly remembers, were Miss Francis. You know her?”

“Yes, indeed,” Mildred exclaimed. “She is a dear faithful sister in our El Callao church.”

Francis Holder, now in her late sixties, though mother of grown men, was always known fondly as “Miss Francis.” She was the mother of Teófilo Griffin whom you already have met.

“I remember when she made that trip. She took a lot of Gospel tracts with her and we gave her several copies of the New Testament in English.”

“Yes, and here duh one she give me,” as he pulled the book from his jacket pocket.

“And did Miss Francis lead you to the Lord?” asked Mildred.

“No. She try to, but I resist. You see, I’se the onliest one in dis town what speak English and when dat lady come and I see she one of my *piesan* [fellow countrywoman], like day say in Spanish, I latch on to her. It was so good to talk my home tongue again.”

“So then, when did you receive Christ as your Savior?”

“Well, Miss Francis, she give me dis New Testament. I treasure it because I has not seen a book of God since I left my beautiful island.”

“Your island? I assumed that you had come into Venezuela from Guyana.”

“No, mahn, I’se from Dominica. I come over and live in Georgetown for many year. Den I come up de ribber Cuyuni, cross over and stay to farm and sell duh produce to duh jail people. Nobody bodder me.

“Miss Francis, she pray wit me and she tell me, ‘Hezekiah, you got to receive duh Lawd or you go to duh bad place when you die. Christ die for you to save you from your sin.’ Den she make me promise to read duh good book, a little piece ever day. I sware I would, and I did. Before she go back down to El Callao she make contact with you brudder Emeterio. He already believer, you know. She tell him he got to help me find de Lawd.

"Duh trouble was dat he farm way out in duh jungle. He not come to town much. Anyhow, I read duh book from cover to cover and poke a poke (Spanish, *poco a poco* [little by little]) I see myself a great sinner. I also see dat Jesus is duh onliest way to God. I felt so sad when I read how he suffer and die for me, I feel I must do something. Then I read how duh 'postle Paul say to duh jailer how he must believe in duh Lawd Jesus Christ. I did want Him to save me too. I went to find Emeterio and he help me pray to God and I accept Christ as my Savior and Lawd. So you see, praise God, I saved. You and me," and Hezekiah pointed a bony forefinger at me, "we is brudders in Christ."

Brudder Hezekiah Brown

"Yes, indeed, praise the Lord, we are brothers, Hezekiah. Now, what about Emeterio? Where is he? We had hoped to find him to maybe stay in his house."

"Emeterio will come to town in a day or so, he harvesting some *frijoles* [beans]. He bring them in to sell. But anyway, he house not big enough for you and duh brudders and sistuhs, just one room and no patio. Now I would be joyed for you to come to my place. I is building a house on my property on Yuca Street. I got walls up and a tin roof on part of it. We can get palm branches and cober duh rest. You will have four room. Don't got no doors but we can cober one wid some ole blanket and give duh sistuhs some private. Please, come see it."

A quick inspection of the partially-built house satisfied us that it would be quite adequate as a camping place. At least we would have a roof over our heads to protect us from the hot sun and from any possible rain. There were hooks in the walls from which we could hang our hammocks. Best of all, the front was closed to the street to protect the car, and the entire property was surrounded by a cyclone fence and barbed wire.

"I is proud... so very proud," Hezekiah Brown kept repeating. "My bredren has come and day gone stay under my roof. God be praised."

"But how is it that you, a single man, are building such a big house of cement?"

"My idea is to sell after it finish and wid de money I want to go home to my beautiful island where I born. I still miss it after all dees years."

After helping us carry our equipment into the house, Hezekiah disappeared. When we first met him, he was dressed literally in rags, dirty and sooty, for, besides the small farm that he worked, Hezekiah made and sold charcoal cookstoves. By the time we were well settled in, and the three-burner kerosene stove heating up the food that we had brought with us, Mr. Brown again appeared, washed, shaved, dressed in clean slacks and a nicely pressed shirt. He always walked barefoot like most of the country people, but now he had on a pair of shoes.

While the women were preparing the meal, Esteban and Don Carlos and I visited the City Hall to obtain a permit to hold open-air meetings in the center of the town. After supper, our evangelistic program for the town of El Dorado was to begin.

It was a "joyful blessing," as Hezekiah expressed it, and a real thrill to publicly preach the Gospel of Christ in that town, visit from house to house, and talk to the people on the street. Hezekiah had sent a boy to tell Emeterio that we were there. He came the next evening and remained with our group until we left. With their help, Mildred and I and our friends were able to visit every house in town and out on the several roads that led into the jungle. Each night a public meeting was held in the open square. The first night the whole town was there, from curiosity, of course. Each night the crowd grew smaller, until on the last night the only ones who came were the several souls that had received Christ and a few of the town folk who were making further inquiry into the Gospel truths before committing themselves.

Everyone was very friendly. Their attitude was the same as that of the owner of the one and only general store. He welcomed us missionaries into his home, closed the doors of his establishment, had his woman make fresh coffee, and sat to listen as the Gospel was explained.

He said. "No doubt you saw the small chapel here in town. It is dirty and in need of repair and paint. The priest only comes here from Tumeremo once in six months to baptize the babies and bless the new marriages. They don't care about us up here in the sticks. We need religious instruction. We would welcome you to stay and teach us. Maybe we would convert."

During the heat of the day, and again at night after the street meeting, our missionary group and the new converts, along with Emeterio and Hezekiah, would meet at Hezekiah's for Bible study and prayer. It was usually during these hours that those who were interested came and made a profession of faith in Christ.

The second day, a man appeared and said, "Mr. Brown, I have just come through your field and saw your burro down. He is dead, Mr. Brown."

"Oh, no!" was Hezekiah's first exclamation. But then he said, "Well, I hates to lose my donkey, but I can't lose my happiness," he told the man. "You see, my bredrens has come at last, so what I care about a ole donkey!"

But later, Hezekiah did excuse himself to go to his farm and arrange for the proper disposal of the carcass. The donkey had fallen prey to one of the many plagues which attack the domestic animals in the interior of Venezuela where, at that time, there were no veterinarians. Today there is a program of inoculations to prevent such losses from occurring.

Indeed this was a great loss for Hezekiah for he needed the donkey to carry the wood to his charcoal kilns, and then to carry the finished charcoal into town to sell. He also needed it to haul the produce from his farm, carry water from the river and many other things he would need out on his farm. Until he had sold enough produce or charcoal to buy another donkey, Hezekiah had to carry the wood and other things on his back. But Hezekiah was too happy to allow his loss to spoil the blessings of the fellowship he was enjoying with his fellow believers.

Chapter 26

The Emelio Rivera Family

"We have to be sure we can't be lost again."

> *"My sheep hear my voice, and I know them, and they follow me. And I give unto them eternal life; and they shall never perish, neither shall any man pluck them out of my hand. My Father, which gave them me, is greater than all, and no man is able to pluck them out of my Father's hand. I and my Father are one."* (John 10:27-30)

During the morning of the third day, Carlos and Emeterio had been visiting homes along a country road. In one home, they were warmly greeted by Emelio Rivera and his wife.

"We soon discovered," explained Carlos, "that this man and his wife seemed to be already believers though they had never actually received Christ as their personal Savior. Some years past they had given up their religion with its worship of images. It seems that someone had given them a New Testament. The only one in the home who could read was their nine-year-old son, Juancito. The boy had been reading to them each day from the New Testament."

"You say that they no longer consider themselves Catholic? How did that happen?"

"Well," continued Carlos, "when the boy read the Gospel of John, they came to understand that God was a Spirit and that He should be worshipped in spirit and in truth. They were convinced that they should not worship the saints, nor pray to them. The boy read that Jesus said that they should pray to the Father in His name and that the Father would hear."

"So then you showed them what the New Testament says about repentance for their sins and the need of accepting Jesus Christ as their Savior, did you not?" asked Mildred.

"Oh, yes," Carlos assured her, "we did. They know they should accept Christ, but they hesitate to do it, they are afraid that afterwards they might sin and be lost. We showed them that, once they trusted in Jesus, He would not only save them but would **keep** them forever.

"So, what seems to be the problem?" I asked.

"They told us that the boy had read a portion of the New Testament that seemed to say to them that if they should fall into sin after having received Jesus as their Savior, their salvation would be cancelled, and since there was no other way to be saved, they couldn't get saved again, they would be eternally lost. The boy could not remember where he had read such a Scripture nor could we think of any verses that said that. When we pressed them to make a decision for Christ, they said 'No, they would wait until they were sure that they would not commit such a sin.' We told them that we would be back to see them in the afternoon and bring our pastor with us. Do you think that you can resolve their problem, Don Eduardo?"

I thought for a moment, then replied, "The Lord helping us, we will find those verses, and the Holy Spirit will illumine our minds, and make us able to explain the truth to them."

After our siesta, we all went to the Rivera home. We found the couple with their son waiting for us. It was a happy home; they were cheerful and optimistic. I thought, "These people must be saved, but are just confused about the eternal security of their salvation."

Emelio Rivera was crippled in one hand, though he was able to hold the tools of his trade. They did a little gardening, but he earned a fair living for his family by re-caulking the seams of the boats that plied the Cuyuni River between El Dorado in Venezuela and Georgetown in Guyana. There was free trade along that river, although the custom officials kept a close watch on the traffic.

Soon they were talking about their problem. To me, it was quite evident that Emelio, his wife and little boy believed already but were not ready to make a definite commitment to Christ for fear of falling and being eternally lost. To be sure that such was the case, I had Juancito read Romans 3:23; 10:9,10; Acts 16:31 and John 1:12. Then I asked them the following questions:

"Do you recognize that you are lost sinners? Do you believe in your heart that Jesus is the Lord and that God raised Him from the dead? Do you understand that to be pardoned for your sins and be saved eternally, you must receive Jesus into your heart?"

Emelio replied, "Yes, we do, we believe all of that. But somewhere Juancito read that if we receive Christ as Savior and then fall into sin, we would be lost forever because there is no other way to be saved. We don't want to take a chance on that."

"No, you don't, and you won't," I assured Emelio. "Brother Carlos here says that you cannot find the verses which have led you to believe what you have just told us."

"That's right, our boy Juancito, has not been able to find it, try as he will."

"But Christ is God and is able to save you eternally. Don't you believe that?"

"Yes, Christ is able, **but what about us?** We are weak and we could fail to follow the Way and fall into sin. If we do, how can we be saved again? If the Way of Christ can't do it, what other way is there?" anxiously asked Emelio. "The verse says there is no other way."

I began to understand their confusion and silently prayed for the Lord to help me find those verses for it seemed to me that if those verses could not be made clear to them, the quoting of many security verses would fall on deaf ears. But Carlos and Esteban continued to show them verses of assurance while I leafed through the New Testament. At last, my eyes fell upon Hebrews 6:1-11. As I read the verse, I had the answer.

"Emelio," I exclaimed, "could these be the verses that are troubling you?" Finding the verses in the boy's New Testament, I had him read aloud Hebrews 6:4-6. "For it is impossible for those who were once enlightened, and have tasted of the heavenly gift, and were made partakers of the Holy Ghost, and have tasted the good word of God, and the powers of the world to come, if they shall fall away, to renew them again unto repentance, seeing they crucify to themselves the Son of God afresh, and put him to an open shame".

"Yes, those are the verses! You see that they say it is impossible to renew the gift of God if we should fall away. And, if Christ is the only way, we have to be sure to stay in that Way. If we can be sure that we won't stray and get lost, we will gladly receive Christ."

I thought, "How can I explain these verses in a simple way and not get involved in deep theological explanations which they would not understand at this point in time? Lord help me."

Aloud, I began to explain, "First of all, look at it this way. Brother Carlos and Esteban have shown you a lot of verses which teach that it is impossible for a truly born-again person to become lost. Now Emelio, the Bible does not lie, nor does it contradict itself."

Emelio nodded his head in assent and I continued, "So we have to interpret these verses in the light of all the teachings of the New Testament. Therefore, you have to understand that these verses **cannot** teach that it is possible for a saved person to be lost when he sins.

"Son, read verse 6 again. See, it says **IF**, emphasis on the **IF**,... **IF** it were possible to be lost after being saved, which it isn't. I repeat, **IF** such a thing were possible, then yes, it would be impossible to be saved all over again. The sinner would be putting Christ to open shame, implying that Christ was not able to keep him after He had saved him."

I was hoping that my explanation would satisfy the Rivera family. I could not go any deeper with such new believers. I then pointed to verse nine and asked the boy to read it. "But, beloved, we are persuaded better things of you, and things that accompany salvation, though we thus speak."

"You see, the writer of Hebrews declared that **he is sure** that they who are saved will go on to live for Christ and serve Him with all their heart. **You are to trust the Lord to keep you** and not be anxious that you might fall into sin. The Lord wants you to have assurance as the writer says in verse eleven. Read it aloud, Son.

"And we desire that every one of you do show the same diligence to the full assurance of hope unto the end."

I then read verses from chapter five leading up to the problem verses, and then explained, "You, the new believers, having partaken of the milk of the Word for salvation, now go on with the Lord and grow in grace and knowledge of Christ. You begin to eat stronger food, that means the deeper teachings of the Word. You go on to enjoy learning more about Christ and His plans for your life. Of course, you will talk to your lost friends and relatives about sin and repentance, faith and baptism, seeking to get them to accept Christ. But you do not need to think of those things again because you are saved forever and can never be lost again.

"Now there are some people who think that they can lose their salvation. But they don't understand. If the Gospel of our Lord Jesus Christ does not have the power to save you **forever**, then it does not have the power to save you **ever**. The problem that many people have is that they think **they** have to **keep themselves** saved, when in truth it is **Jesus who keeps** them saved. It is true that you, in your weakness, cannot keep yourselves saved, **but Jesus can.** You should try to live a pure life, not to stay saved, but because you love God and want to please Him.

"Look here, Emelio, señora and Juancito. Look at the Gospel of John, 10:28 and 29. After Jesus explains that He is the Good Shepherd and we, the believers, are His sheep, He says that we are safe in His hands and that no one can pluck us out of His hands, nor can any one pluck us out of God's hands. Jesus tells us that His sheep 'shall **never perish**'. Do you hear it, Emelio... señora... Juancito? Jesus says NEVER... NEVER... NEVER. What does that mean, Emelio? If you believe in Jesus and have accepted Him as your Savior, will you ever be lost? Can you be lost, Emelio?"

As Emelio hesitated to reply, I continued, "Let me tell you a little story to help you. A little boy about three years old, went out for a walk with his father one afternoon after a rainstorm. There were puddles of water still on the pavement, so the father suggested that his son let him hold his hand. The little boy replied, 'No daddy, I big boy now, I can walk by myself.' But after just a few steps, the little boy's feet slipped when he stepped in a puddle, and he fell to the ground. The father picked him up and wiped off the mud from his clothes.

"The little boy then said to his father, 'Daddy, I guess I had better hold on to your hand.' So they walked on. But soon the boy slipped in another puddle and as he was falling down, he lost his grip on his father's hand. The father picked him up and again wiped off the mud.

"Again the little boy spoke to his father, 'Daddy, **you had better hold on to my hand**.' As they continued their walk it was inevitable that the boy should again slip on some water on the pavement. But, this time, as his feet beat a tattoo in the air, his father lifted him up high so that the boy never touched the ground. The difference was in the fact that the boy was not holding onto his father's hand, it was the father who was holding onto the boy's hand.

"Don't you see, dear ones, that you are not holding Christ's hand, it is Christ who is holding your hand, and He will never let you go. You are safe in God's hand... Can you believe this, Emelio, that you can never be lost again?"

"Yes... Yes, I do... *gracias a Dios*, I do... I do! I understand it now. God will never let me be lost. Praise God!... Dear wife and Juancito, you see it too, don't you?" asked Emelio as he put his arms about them, drawing them to him in a loving embrace.

Carlos Hernández with Emelio Rivera

"Yes, we do too," the boy and his mother answered as with one voice.

Back at Mr. Brown's place, we sang the *Doxology* as we praised the Lord for the family which had just trusted the Lord for salvation, Emelio Rivera, his wife, María, and son Juancito.

Before we left El Dorado, we had the opportunity of preaching the Gospel in the Federal Penitentiary located on the other side of the Cuyuni River. The officials of the prison knew Emeterio for it was he who sold them much of the fresh fruit and vegetables they wanted for their meals. Thus he was able to make the contact to ask for permission to hold an evangelistic service for the prisoners. One of the officials, a lieutenant of the army garrisoned in the prison to guard against rebellion, was of an evangelical background. He arranged for permission for us to be taken across in the government boat.

The lieutenant also arranged for us to hold a Gospel meeting in each of the two divisions of the prison, one for the hard-core prisoners, and one for those whose good behavior gave them more freedom. The meetings were well attended. Everyone accepted tracts and Gospel portions. We were also permitted to give an invitation for salvation and, under the watchful eyes of the guards, had freedom to deal personally with the men who responded. The guards were present everywhere during the meetings so they heard the presentations of Gospel truth and the testimonies of the brethren. We missionaries could not talk to the soldiers except when they were off duty, but quite a few of them attended the night street meetings held in town.

The lieutenant who arranged the meetings accepted a New Testament and was counseled to return to the Lord in whom he had professed to believe as a youth in the city of Maracay. He promised to follow Christ again. A number made professions of faith in Christ, but these had to be committed into the hands of the Savior, for it was not possible to do any follow-up work.

This first visit to El Dorado was a blessing and a happy time for Mildred and me and for the brethren who accompanied us. We all gave thanks to the Lord for the privilege of preaching the Gospel openly in El Dorado and for the souls that were saved then and on subsequent visits.

Before leaving El Dorado, we were able to get the little group of believers organized into a little mission church so that they would continue to meet under the direction of brother Emeterio. Later on, deacons from the churches in Tumeremo and El Callao, and occasionally a missionary, would visit them to encourage them and to try to win others to the Lord. This was good for Hezekiah's sake. The towns folk used to make fun of him because he would no longer drink and carouse with them. Prior to our visit, he had had no fellowship with other believers, no teaching of the Word nor help in witnessing to the lost. Emeterio's farm was so far out in the jungle that he did not come to town very often. But now the believers met together for fellowship and worship, and to encourage one another. Their unity in the Lord began to win the respect of the people.

After about a year, Hezekiah Brown decided that he was too old to return to his home on Dominica. His few relatives would probably be dead, his friends gone too. So he sold his property "as is" and moved down to El Callao to be among his brethren and, as he expressed it, among his "own kind." While not from his island, he felt that the English-speaking people were his *paisanos* for they came from various other islands of the West Indies with a similar background and culture. Teófilo and others saw to it that all his needs were supplied as Hezekiah grew older and more feeble. Hezekiah Brown lived for about eight years in El Callao before he took up his new abode in heaven with his beloved "Lawd Jesus."

Chapter 27

The William Cambridge Story

"Is It Possible To Know?"

> *"These things have I written unto you that believe on the name of the Son of God, that ye may know that ye have eternal life...."* (I John 5:13)

> *"...for I know whom I have believed, and am persuaded that he is able to keep that which I have committed unto him against that day."* (II Timothy 1:12)

During our **first term**, shortly after I returned from the trip to the Orinoco River Delta, we began our ministry to the English-speaking people. We felt that this was the **second reason** why the Lord brought us back to El Callao after Mildred's illness. When we began our **second term**, we were able to work several English meetings into our regular Spanish missionary work. These meetings continued until the time came for our second furlough. The attendance was good at all the meetings, and a number were saved. After we were gone, others professed faith in Christ. Two of these are of special interest. This chapter relates the story of one of them—**Mr. William Cambridge**.

Mr. Cambridge's story begins on the same evening that we held our **very first** Sunday service in the village of Saint Vincent. We had good attendance and the people seemed to know the hymns we sang and joined in. We had our folding organ with us for Mildred to play. They also listened attentively to the sermon I delivered. But, at the close of the service, something very discouraging occurred. I approached Mr. William Cambridge, the head man of the village, to thank him for allowing us to use the village meeting hall. But he spoke first.

"Mr. Schwartz." Mr. Cambridge said my name rather sternly. I knew by the tone of his voice that, to put it mildly, he was definitely not very pleased about something.

"Mr. Schwartz," he repeated, as he pressed his finger into my chest. "This will be the last time you preach in our village. I have never heard anything so sacrilegious."

I was taken aback. "Why?" I questioned. "What have we said to have made you so angry? We only sang some old hymns, the testimony of our men simply told what Jesus has done for them. I have only explained from God's Word how to be saved."

"What have you done, you ask? You have preached a lie, that's what you have done, and I'll not permit you to do it again here in St. Vincent," Mr. Cambridge assured me.

"Now just a minute, sir. I did not lie nor say anything that is not written in this Bible."

"Oh, yes you did. You said that it is possible in this life to be saved and know it. That is impossible! Everyone knows that we cannot know if we are going to heaven until we die. You have preached a lie, sir, a lie directly out of hell, and I will not allow you to come here again with your false teachings and try to lead my people astray."

Mildred and I were astonished. We could not believe what we were hearing. We had expected an entirely different reaction from Mr. Cambridge, especially since the people in attendance had seemed happy with the service, both with the singing and the preaching.

"But, Mr. Cambridge," I remonstrated, "the Apostle Paul wrote that the Lord whom he knew was able to keep him safe for all eternity. The Word of God assures us believers that when we die we will go directly to heaven to be with Jesus. Mr. Cambridge, if you believe in Jesus with all your heart you are saved, and so you must know that you will go to heaven some day. I don't understand how you can be offended. I simply...."

"Don't say anything more, Mr. Schwartz," interrupted Cambridge. "I cannot accept such teaching. It is heresy! Now, hear me well, you may never again use this building for your religious services." With these final words, Mr. Cambridge turned and stomped out of the building, followed by the few people who had remained to hear the discussion.

Nothing more could be said or done that night, so we gathered our hymn books, folded the organ, got into the car that was waiting for us, and began our return trip to El Callao, bouncing and swaying over the rocky, winding dirt road down the hill. No one spoke for a time, each silently brooding over the events of the night, feeling discouraged over what seemed a defeat in our very first attempt to reach the people of St. Vincent with the Gospel.

Finally Miguel asked, "Now, what? Doesn't the Lord want to save anybody up there?"

"Of course He does, and we will go again next Sunday night," I assured him, as the car swerved around a deep mud hole and then was jerked back to avoid a huge boulder which had slid partly into the road from the hillside.

"We don't let a bad road like this one keep us from going up there as long as these cars will take us. And we won't let Mr. Cambridge stop us from preaching in St. Vincent."

"But, Pastor, Mr. Cambridge said that we could not use the hall again."

"So what? That won't stop us. We'll hold our meeting in the open air, in the little plaza."

Mildred asked. "Don't we have to get permission from Mr. Cambridge for this also?"

"No, we don't have to ask Mr. Cambridge's permission. Here in Venezuela we have freedom to preach the Gospel anywhere, just so we don't encroach upon the freedom of someone else. We already have the okay of the chief of police. Mr. Cambridge has no official authority, he is just a leader of the local community and is in charge of the meeting hall. Since the people do look up to him, I did as Teófilo suggested and talked to him to get his permission to use the hall. Anyhow, Lord willing, we'll drive up to St. Vincent again next Sunday afternoon."

We returned to St. Vincent the next Sunday and held our meeting in the open air. There was no outward opposition, but Mr. Cambridge, his family and a few others did not attend. Meetings were held early each Sunday evening for several weeks, until the road got so bad that the driver refused to go beyond El Chile. So we held our meetings in the little plaza there.

There had been no response to the Gospel in St. Vincent. Some had expressed interest, but were too afraid to voice it. However, a few from St. Vincent walked down to El Chile. Quite a few children attended, so Mildred had a Bible class for them before I preached.

One Sunday evening, sixteen-year-old Edward, one of the Cambridge boys, accepted Christ as his Savior, along with several other young teenagers. Edward's sister, Minerva, wanted to, but she said she would have to ask permission of her father first. Of course, he refused.

Edward showed much interest in Bible study and in a desire to continue following the Lord. But then, we were saddened when Edward informed us that his father had now forbidden the children to attend the meetings. It was all right, Mr. Cambridge said, for them to hear the Bible stories and learn the verses, but he would not allow them "to change their religion."

Finally, the roads became so bad and the condition of the cars so poor that the drivers refused to travel after dark even up to El Perú. So we had to suspend that ministry. We then began a Bible study class one night a week in the homes of the English-speaking people in El Callao, which continued until we left for the States on our first furlough.

During the first year after our return to Venezuela, we had to concentrate all our efforts in the Spanish work. I again became the missionary-pastor of our El Callao Baptist Church. Francisco had served as pastor in our absence, but now, he and his wife Melina went to the Gran Sabana as missionaries to the workers opening up new gold and diamond mines.

Our missionary personnel had been depleted during the war years for reasons already explained. One couple had returned just as we were leaving and another had returned while we were on furlough. Now others were beginning to rejoin us. But until they got resettled on their stations, we had to visit the churches located in other towns. We were able to carry on this work because of the half-ton pickup truck we had brought with us.

We were able also to start up English Bible classes in El Callao on a biweekly basis. Mildred held weekly Bible Clubs in town, and on Friday afternoons, we alternated between El Chile and Chili-Mex in El Perú. The latter was in the home of Mercedes and Whitey, where I also had somc adults to teach. The clubs were in Spanish.

Now, to resume the Cambridge story. Toward the end of our second term, I was teaching the book of Romans in the home of one of the English-speaking members of the El Callao church. A number of these English folk had been saved and baptized, and were anxious that others of their Protestant brethren might come to Christ. Through their efforts, many unsaved attended and were beginning to understand the doctrine of justification by faith, but still hesitated to take a definite stand because of peer pressure from their Anglican relatives.

One evening as Mildred and I arrived at the home for the class, one of the believers met us at the door and whispered, "Wait until you see who has come tonight." We were surprised, but extremely happy, to see William Cambridge, and several other new ones who wanted to enroll. He explained that he was just going to observe, but after several sessions, he too enrolled. To make the class in Romans more important to them, those who wanted to do so, could take a final exam. If they passed, they would receive a certificate of accomplishment.

Mr. Cambridge and his family had moved down to El Callao for economic reasons. You probably remember that the "mother vein" had disappeared and the gold mines had almost closed down. Because of the testimony of some of his friends who had become Bible-believing Christians, Mr. Cambridge was not as prejudiced as he once was. As the class progressed, he came to understand the way of salvation, answering correctly a number of the questions, but he still would not commit himself wholly to Christ.

Then we learned that for health reasons, we would have to leave on furlough six months sooner than the usual four year term expected of our missionaries in those days. In our English Bible class we had just completed the study through the eighth chapter of the book of Romans. Our co-worker, Peggy Degnan, promised to finish the study, but, would be unable to continue the class because of her responsibilities in the Spanish work.

The year before we had sent Eddie home to stay with his aunt Viola in Philadelphia to continue his schooling there. We had home-schooled him through the first year of high school, but did not have the material to take him any further. Besides that, we had to study harder than he did in order to check his work, especially his studies in Latin and French.

One day at dawn, Mildred, Danny and I left for Caracas. The truck carrying us and our baggage paused at the edge of the river Yuruary which flows past El Callao. Again it was our friend Peña who was taking us in his new truck, one of the first to be imported after the War. While waiting in the dim light of the dawning day for the ferry-raft to take us across, we saw three men come walking down the bank toward us.

There had been two farewell parties, one in the church and one given by the students of the English Bible class. Now these three men had come to the river to bid us one last good-bye. One was deacon Noel, another was Ricardo Laptist, a recent convert, and the other... That's right, it was Mr. William Cambridge.

After the first two had embraced us in a fond farewell, Mr. Cambridge approached me, took my hand in his, and said, "Mr. Edward," (most of the English-speaking people now called me by the friendly "Mr. Edward" rather than the formal Mr. Schwartz). "Mr. Edward, I want you to know that you are no longer my enemy as I once considered you. I want you to know that I am now your friend."

"That's great news," I almost shouted as hope was born anew in my heart that Mr. Cambridge would be saved. "And, can you now tell me that you are also a believer, that you have accepted Christ as your only and sufficient Savior?"

Cambridge turned his head away and, gazing across the river as if looking into the future, answered, "I cannot tell you that. At this time, I can only tell you that wherever you go in this world, you will always have a friend here in Venezuela."

On the other side of the river, after the truck climbed the steep bank, Peña paused to let us look back and wave to the men still standing by the river. We wondered whether we would, in the providence of God, ever see the town of El Callao again and the people we had come to love so dearly in the Lord, especially those who had been won during our short ministry there.

But our Father in heaven, in His great mercy and kindness toward His children, does not reveal to us events of the future. Mildred and I would have felt additional discouragement and sorrow had we known that so many years would pass before we would return to Venezuela.

But you do not have to wait as long as we did to hear the rest of the William Cambridge story. We take up the story when, seventeen years later, we went back to Venezuela for the missionary visit mentioned in the story of Whitey and Mercedes.

One evening when the meeting in the Bethel Baptist Church in San Félix was just over, and Mildred and I were standing in the doorway with pastor Francisco talking about old times, a young fellow approached us and spoke to me.

"Pastor Eduardo, I have a message for you from Meestair Gambres. He wants for you to visit him at his home."

I thought, "Meestair Gambres... he says, 'meestair' which has to be his Spanish pronunciation of Mister. It must be an English-speaking man, otherwise the young fellow would have called him Señor Gambres... Gambres, I mentally repeated. Could he possibly mean Cambridge?" Aloud, "Do you mean Mr. Cambridge?"

"Sí, Pastor Eduardo, Meestair Gambres, he wants to see you."

Pastor Francisco, the same Francisco who was one of our students in the El Callao Bible Institute, now pastoring the San Félix church, spoke up. "Brother Eduardo, I know where Mr. Cambridge lives. I will be happy to take you to his house tomorrow."

"But, is this the same Mr. Cambridge who lived in El Callao many years ago?"

"Yes. Long ago he retired and moved here to San Félix with his two single daughters who keep house for him. Minerva comes to our services once in a while," explained Pastor Francisco. "Mr. Cambridge is bedridden and it is doubtful that he will live much longer."

Arriving the next day at the Cambridge home, we recognized the daughter who greeted us at the door, the one who wanted to receive Christ as her Savior back there in El Chile but was forbidden by her father.

"Well, well, Minerva, it is so good to see you. How long has it been? Almost seventeen years since we last saw you in El Callao."

Minerva shook my hand and turned to embrace Mildred. "Thank you for coming, welcome to our home. Father is expecting you. He begs you to enter and to forgive him for not greeting you at the door. You will have to speak loudly, for he does not hear too well anymore."

Mildred and I, along with Pastor Francisco, entered the bedroom. William Cambridge was propped up with pillows to a half-sitting position. When he knew that we were there, he extended his arms toward us and called, "Mister Edward, come close."

I leaned over the bed and Cambridge, in spite of his weakness, strongly embraced me. Then, holding me at arm's length, spoke again. His voice was raspy but strong.

"Mister Edward, you must remember the last words we spoke on the bank of the Yuruary River, as we said good-bye many years ago. I assured you then that wherever you might travel in this world, you would always have a friend to count on in Venezuela."

I did remember, for Mildred and I had prayed for this man these many years. These folk always loved to be dramatic and make the most out of simple statements. So, after a lengthy pause, Mr. Cambridge continued.

"Well, Mister Edward, when you left here, I said good-bye as a friend. Now, as I welcome you back to Venezuela, I greet you as a **brother in Christ**."

I could hardly believe my ears. William Cambridge, a brother in Christ? I thought to myself, "Well, Ed, you have been praying for this to happen, why do you doubt?"

Pastor Francisco, who had remained standing in the doorway, came close to the bedside to explain. "Yes, William Cambridge is now a brother in Christ. I was keeping this as a surprise for you. Three weeks ago, when I visited him, he received Christ as his Savior. He resisted the Gospel truth for a long time, but finally confessed that he has never been able to erase from his mind the lessons in Romans you taught back there in El Callao, that we are justified by faith and faith alone without works. Minerva had called the day before to say that he was ready."

"Praise the Lord," Mildred and I shouted in unison. "We prayed for this, but I guess our faith was weak for we never expected it to happen. Lord, forgive us."

"Yes," spoke Mr. Cambridge with a twinkle in his eyes. "**Now I am saved, and know it**. I once thought that it was a bad teaching, but now I know it is true."

"What about you, Minerva?" asked Mildred. Your father will not hold you back now."

Minerva, still timid Minerva, bowed her head, slowly shaking it from side to side, and almost inaudibly, whispered, "Not yet. Not yet." She did come to Christ sometime later in special meetings held in Bethel Baptist Church in San Félix.

Later, as we drove back to the home where we were staying, we exchanged our feelings. Mildred, in tones of wonder, summed up our thoughts. "Just think, Ed, the seed was first sown in Mr. Cambridge's heart... how long ago was it...? 1943 ...almost 25 years ago. Just now it has sprung up to produce a new life. At last William Cambridge has been born again."

She continued, "How good the Lord is to give us so many years in His service, and allow us to see with our eyes the fruit of plantings done many years ago. Truly the Lord fulfills His promises. This reminds me of what the Apostle Paul said, 'And let us not be weary in well-doing; for in due season we shall reap, if we faint not' (Galatians 6:9)."

I agreed. "Yes, one sows and another reaps. We sowed the seed, and our brother Francisco reaped the harvest. Praise the Lord for you, brother Francisco."

"Well, yes and no," replied Francisco. "Yes, to 'praise the Lord!' But, no to any praise for me. We work together, but we must remember that it is the **Lord who gives the increase**."

Three years later, back in Venezuela on permanent status again, I visited Mr. Cambridge a number of times before he passed on to glory. I had his funeral service to which many members of the family came, including Edward, now a medical doctor practicing in Caracas.

Several times during those visits, Mr. Cambridge made the same statement to me, "I did not lose even one of my children, praise God, I kept everyone. But, I lost them in the end."

These folk have another characteristic, peculiar to "the Islands," they sometimes talk in parables. I carefully probed his mind and gradually understood. He had been a very strict parent, as most of them are, demanding obedience and respect. He had raised them in the "fear of God," and a high standard of moral conduct. Not one of them had forsaken that code. And they took care of him in his old age. They supported their two sisters, his caretakers. He loved his children and they loved him. He lost none of them and had kept them together as a family.

BUT, he lost them spiritually. Now that he was saved, he realized that he had prevented them from responding to the Gospel call when they were children. As far as we know, Edward was the only one, besides Minerva, who ever accepted Christ. All his children were at the funeral, but they were there and gone again so quickly that there was barely time to say hello and good-bye let alone verify their spiritual condition. While it is important to live a wholesome moral life, of far greater importance is the spiritual condition of the soul, not only in this present life, but for all eternity. Mr. Cambridge, with regret, realized this too late.

May we all be forewarned!

Chapter 28

Mrs. Teodora Cudrington

"I will never change my religion"

"...by the name of Jesus Christ... Neither is there salvation in any other; for there is none other name under heaven given among men, whereby we must be saved."

(Acts 4:10-12)

During this second term, the prejudice toward us evangelical Baptist missionaries on the part of the English-speaking Protestants continued to ease. This was because a number of their group had made a profession of faith in Christ. This change accelerated after William Cambridge began to attend my Bible study class. Then, one day Mrs. Teodora Cudrington, a leading member of the Anglican Church, paid a visit to our home.

"Pastor Edward, I have come to invite you to hold an English Bible study class in my home on a permanent basis. In this way my people will always know where it is being held and there will not be the confusion we have experienced in the past." Until this time the class had been held in different homes of the English members of our church.

"Well, Mrs. Cudrington, this is a pleasant surprise, and I shall be very happy to accept your invitation. It is also good in that your home is centrally located. The next meeting, you know, will be, Lord willing, this coming Thursday night."

Prior to this visit, Mrs. Cudrington, had not been too regular in her attendance; in fact, she had not really approved of the classes, and we felt that she only attended to make sure that her people were not being proselytized. Evidently she was now satisfied with our method of simply teaching the Word of God to these people of "another Christian religion" and letting the Holy Spirit do the convincing and the converting. For us, this method has always paid off.

"Yes, Mrs. Cudrington, we'll be happy to continue the Bible studies in your home."

As Teodora Cudrington rose to leave, I added, "Just one more word please, before you go. You have heard me say many times that the most important thing in this life is what you have done about your personal relationship with God and the Savior."

"I know... I know... but I must tell you again that I shall never change my religion. I've been Anglican all my life and I will never change. Please don't try to convert me."

"My dear Mrs. Cudrington, as I too have said many times, I do not ask you to change your religion. Jesus said, 'I am the way', He said **'I'**, not a religion. And then to make it more clear, He added, **'no man** cometh unto the Father, **but by me**....' I pray that you will receive Jesus Christ as your **one and only Savior**. Then He will tell you what to do."

Some weeks later, when it became known that we were leaving Venezuela, Mrs. Cudrington paid us another visit. After the formal greetings and serving of tea and cookies, Mrs. Cudrington expressed the sorrow that she and the class felt upon hearing that they were losing their Bible teacher. Then she asked if there was some way in which they could continue the Bible studies once this course was finished.

"Pastor Edward, we have come so far and many of us feel that God would have us go on with the Bible studies. We feel that the Lord has many blessings in store for us. Even Mr. Cambridge has so spoken to me. We understand that you have to leave and that, after this study in the book of Romans is finished, Miss Peggy cannot continue. Can you suggest something?"

"Well, Mrs. Cudrington, my wife and I have been praying much about this and I think that the Lord has given us a solution to the problem."

Taking a book from my desk nearby, I placed it her hands. "That, Mrs. Cudrington, is what we call a Scofield Study Bible. It is the King James version of the English Bible with study notes written within the text by that respected Bible teacher, Dr. C. I. Scofield. A person can, by following these notes and references in the Bible in consecutive order, study all the major themes and doctrines of the Christian faith. It can be done individually or with others in a class."

Mrs. Cudrington leafed through the pages of the Bible and after I had given a few more detailed explanations, she remarked, "Yes, I see how it goes. It is a bit complicated, but maybe one can learn from it."

"I suggest that the class continue to meet in your home, study together Dr. Scofield's notes, and look up the Bible references, and read them carefully and prayerfully. Never take the notes as Gospel truth until you have checked them with the Scriptures as we have always done."

"But Pastor Edward, how can we do this without a teacher, or at least someone to direct us and make us do the work? I also see the need of some lessons with questions and answers."

"That's where you come in, Mrs. Cudrington. I think that you are the one to take the leadership in the class. You will also have a copy of the book, *Rightly Dividing the Word of Truth*, which I will send you."

"But, how can I do it? I am a woman and besides I have no experience as a teacher."

"Nevertheless, I believe that the Lord wants you to do it. After all, you will not be teaching in the true sense of the word. You will simply be the one to organize the class, exhort the people to study, and make sure that they come to the class and do the work. It will be the Holy Spirit who will lead you into the truth as each of you individually needs to know it, whether for salvation or for growth in the Christian life. If you need help in working out some problem, I am sure that one of the missionaries who remain in El Callao or one of the deacons from the Baptist church will help you."

Mrs. Cudrington finally agreed to do as was suggested. Before she left, both Mildred and I prayed for her and the project. To our great delight and surprise, Mrs. Cudrington also prayed audibly, asking the Lord to take us home safely and bring us back again soon. We concluded that Mrs. Cudrington was very close to becoming a true believer, if she wasn't one already.

Twenty-four Bibles with Dr. Scofield's notes were ordered from the U.S., and delivered into Mrs. Cudrington's hands, who distributed them to those who attended.

During the years that we were away from Venezuela, we never ceased to pray for the people there, remembering especially our Bible class of English-speaking people. From time to time a letter would come from the resident missionary to tell us of the conversion of this or that one, of their baptism and reception into the membership of the Evangelical Baptist Church of El Callao. One young lady, Clarisa Robinson, was saved and went on to Bible college. Then there was the blacksmith's son and his wife. Even the official in the

Anglican church who read the priest's sermons sent in from Caracas, though he did not leave his Church, testified to accepting Christ as his Savior. We had hoped to hear about others, but as those seventeen years went by, letters from the field grew further apart and finally stopped altogether.

Then, at long last we found ourselves back in Venezuela for our two months stay. In almost all of our churches we found at least one or two individuals in which the seed we had planted had produced a new life in Christ. Most of these were Spanish-speaking Venezuelans, but a few were English-speaking West Indies folk.

We especially remember, two enjoyable nights spent preaching in the mission church in the village of El Arrozal. It was a joy to meet Ricardo Laptiste again, one of the three men who had bid us good-bye on the banks of the Yuruary River that dawn when we left El Callao.

When the gold mines around El Callao closed down, and rich deposits of iron ore were discovered in the mountains south of San Félix, many families moved into the area where the men could find employment with the Bethlehem Steel Company that came in to exploit these new riches. Ricardo left El Callao, searched out an area around El Pao, the new village built for the workers, found a fertile piece of land and established himself on a little farm. He made a fairly good living raising vegetables and tropical fruits which he sold to the people settling there.

Ricardo had never married, lived a separated Christian life and testified to everyone of his faith in the Lord Jesus Christ. He, along with several families he had won to the Lord had established a fundamental Baptist church, and erected a small building in which to hold services in the village of El Arrozal. When Mildred and I visited them, they were planning to build a larger building on the same site.

On the first night of the Bible conference, the people were slow in gathering. The meeting had been called for seven o'clock, but as was the custom, the people were not really expected on time and the meeting eventually began about twenty minutes to eight.

"Patience, Pastor Edward," exhorted Ricardo. "We'll have a good crowd yet."

Ricardo had barely spoken when a little elderly lady, whose arthritis evidently was bothering her, came into the church and slowly walked toward us. Her dress, shoes and especially that old-fashioned hat, identified her as one of the English-speaking ladies.

Venezuelan ladies hardly ever wore hats. In contrast, the West Indian ladies never went anywhere without one. As she approached, her face lit up, her eyes sparkled, and a tremendous grin stretched her skin taut, the bright reflected light of the gasoline pressure lanterns highlighting her cheek bones.

"Mister Edward and Sister Mildred... don't you know me?" Her face clouded over, the wrinkles deepened and the crow's-feet again made tracks from the edges of her eyes.

I searched my mind for a clue. "That hat, that dress... Why won't my memory respond? I should recognize her... She has to be one of the ladies from our past life in El Callao."

Then aloud, I said, "You are Mrs... Oh, please forgive me. I see the face of someone I should know, but...."

"I am Teodora, from El Callao. I am the same Teodora Cudrington who took the Bibles with the good Dr. Scofield's notes for the English Bible class."

"Mrs. Cudrington!" we exclaimed together. "Of course, of course, we should have known you, but, after all these years, our memory is not so sharp, and we have gotten some older since the day we left you in El Callao. But, what are you doing here?"

"Well, Pastor Edward, do you remember what you told me the last time we talked?"

"Not really, except that I probably urged you to accept Christ as your personal Savior."

"Yes, you did that," agreed Mrs. Cudrington. "But I told you again that I would not change my religion. Then you said that you were not asking me to change my religion. You said that I should just receive Christ as my Savior and He would tell me what to do."

Mrs. Cudrington paused as if to give more importance to what she was about to tell us. Mildred couldn't wait, and impatiently asked, "So, what happened? Tell us quickly."

"Well," and as she spoke, Mrs. Cudrington, first pointed her finger at herself, next toward the sky, and then spread her arms wide open. And in the excitement of the emotion-filled moment, she forgot her refined way of speaking and reverted to the calypso dialect of the islands. She said, "Well... Ah did... He did... an heah ah is!"

"Praise the Lord!" we both shouted. Mildred embraced Teodora, kissing her on the cheek. "Oh, how wonderful, now you really are my sister in Christ!"

Ricardo, smiling from ear to ear, explained, "Sister Teodora has been a great help to me. Several years ago she moved here from El Callao to keep house for her son who opened up a grocery store in the village. She came to the meetings we were holding in Moreno's house. After a little bit, she accepted the fact that Jesus Christ was the only Way and received Him as her Savior. She has been baptized and is a faithful member of our congregation here in El Arrozal."

Teodora's daughter-in-law, Teodora, two members of the San Félix Church

What joy! What a blessing! Praise the Lord! Again we were seeing fruit from the Seed that we had sown many years before. As in the case of William Cambridge, we remembered that favorite verse, "...in due season we shall reap, if we faint not" (Galatians 6:9b).

VI
Philadelphia Ministry

Chapter 29

How Missionary Work Started in Philadelphia

"Trust... Delight... Commit... Rest in the Lord, and wait patiently for him...." (Psalm 37:3-7)

For health reasons, as related before, we had to take our second furlough six months early. Thus, the summer of 1950 found us at home in Philadelphia. The doctors advised us to spend at least three cold winters in the temperate climate before returning to the oppressive heat and high humidity of Venezuela's interior. For several years after the war, it was next to impossible to find a home or an apartment to rent. In a wonderful way the Lord supplied the means that enabled us to start buying a little house in North Philadelphia.

The first year of this furlough was spent resting and visiting our supporting churches. Then, when Dr. Arthur Fetzer, General Secretary of Baptist Mid-Missions, suffered his first heart attack, we were called into the Home Office in Cleveland to help him in his work. We enjoyed the six months we spent there, receiving and answering mail from our missionaries working all over the world.

We were saddened to think that we might never get back again to our beloved Venezuelan people. We also felt a little confused because we had received such a definite call to missionary work in Venezuela, we thought that field had to be the only field where we could minister. But as we worked with Mr. Fetzer, we began to see and understand that the Great Commission included the entire world, not just the little corner of it where we had served. But the Lord was preparing our hearts to answer a call to another field.

I was invited to continue to work out of our Home Office as a deputation secretary, but the Lord did not give us peace about it. We wondered, "What are we to do? Does the Lord have some other work for us to do?" We did feel, however, that whatever it was, it had to be some work in which we could use Spanish and thus protect the investment time spent in learning that language. We were a bit concerned, not worried, just a little anxious.

We felt very sure that the Lord wanted us to return to Philadelphia. He reminded us of our life-time verses, especially that part which said, "Rest in the Lord, and wait patiently for him." Waiting with patience has always been difficult for me. I like to see where I am going in advance. But this time, the Lord said, "Wait. Wait for the door to open before you try to go through it. Wait, then when it opens, go through."

Back in Philadelphia, we began to help our friend, Dick Ward, in his little Rescue Mission downtown at 412 Green Street. While doing some visitation work for brother Dick, we encountered a number of children playing in the streets who were speaking Spanish. For more information about them, Dick directed us to Domingo Martínez, a believer in Christ, who owned a grocery store in the area. Martínez told us that there were an estimated 6,000 people living in Philadelphia who spoke Spanish, most of whom were Puerto Rican.

We thought, "Could this have a special meaning for us?" I secured a number of Gospel tracts in Spanish from Bob McCarthy who was at that time directing the Scripture Gift Mission, and about the first of October, 1952, began a house-to-house survey to find these people and to determine if a church-planting ministry would be feasible.

Every day that I went out, I found at least one family among the Spanish-speaking people interested in attending a Sunday School and church service where they could understand the teaching and preaching and where they would not be shunned by the church people. We found so many within such a short time that we decided to hold Spanish-language church services on Sunday nights. The first service was held on the last Sunday of December in the little mission on Green Street. Mildred and I began to dedicate all of our time to this new work.

Mildred began to hold Bible clubs after school hours for the children, first in the Mission and then in several homes. This gave us many good contacts with the parents. In addition to the Sunday night service, I held two evening Bible study classes for adults, one on Tuesday and one on Thursday, in various homes of interested families. Open-air evangelistic meetings were also begun on Saturday nights on strategic street corners in the neighborhoods where there were concentrations of Spanish-speaking people. A home visitation program was begun.

The work grew slowly at first. Although many had expressed interest, they attended only spasmodically. We averaged no more than ten to fifteen. About eight of these people were already believers in Christ and had been members of Baptist churches in Puerto Rico. Then, in July of 1952, we answered a call from two pastors in South New Jersey and one in Tylersport, Pennsylvania, to help them reach the migrant farm workers from Puerto Rico with the Gospel. The men of the churches transported the workers to the churches and we conducted the meetings. A number of the men received Christ as Savior that summer.

Bible Clubs

Street Meeting

We questioned the value of that migrant work, especially since we had no way to follow up the converts to help them grow. Our work in Philadelphia suffered because this migrant work took us away three days a week. I planned not to do it the next year, but the pastors begged me to continue. We changed our opinion when some of the converts returned that second summer and told us that they had found and attended evangelical churches in Puerto Rico.

After that first summer migrant work ended, we once again concentrated on the mission work in Philadelphia. The attendance during the summer had been very poor, but a week or so after our return, the work began to grow and soon we had between forty and fifty attending the Sunday night services. The children's Bible club meetings were well attended, and during those fall months, a number of children accepted Christ as Savior. Later, adults also began to come to the Lord. Truly, we were blessed by the Lord as promised by the Psalmist. He gave us the desires of our hearts and brought it to pass.

Pablo Hernández Story - First Adult to Receive Christ

> *"...do the work of an evangelist,... be instant in season, out of season."* (II Timothy 4:5 and 4:2)
>
> *"...have not the faith of our Lord Jesus Christ... with respect of persons."* (James 2:1)

It was the first week of November, and because vandals had broken the street light, it was quite dark as I parked my car in front of the four-and-a-half story post-colonial brownstone. There was only one other car parked on the street. The Hispanic community had not yet reached an economic stability that would make private ownership of cars possible.

I noted casually the dim lights shining from most of the windows of the row houses. Crossing the pavement, I bounded up the white marble steps, stained from the lack of soap and water, the surface worn down by more than a century and a half of feet pressing upon them.

These Franklin Street brownstones had seen much better days when they had been lived in by more affluent upper-middle class families. Now they had been humbled to the status of tenements, "home" to the many Puerto Ricans who had left their beautiful tropical island paradise to seek better paying jobs in Philadelphia. They were willing to sacrifice everything to make a better life for themselves and their children. That included being exploited by the absentee owners of the buildings left decaying from lack of paint and repair, infested by roaches and rats. Although there was still some rent control, the owners could place some small piece of furniture in the apartment, call it "furnished" and charge an outrageously higher weekly rent.

Quite often, Mildred and I were sickened to see the living conditions of some of the families we visited. On one occasion we were greeted by a sobbing mother who let us into her apartment. A nurse, sent by the social service, was working over a little baby girl, cleaning and bandaging a wound in her head that had been chewed on by a rat during the night.

Now, as I entered the house on Franklin Street, I pushed open the right side of the double door. It swung in freely, banging itself against the wall of the vestibule. I thought, It must have new hinges." Usually it took more strength to open these old doors, hanging awry with loose bottom panel scraping the floor. Or one had to grasp the door with two hands, supporting it on broken or missing hinges, guide it open and lean it back in order to enter.

The vestibule and hallway were very dark. I paused to let my eyes become accustomed to it. The bulb in the ceiling was missing but my eyes adjusted to a dim ray of light shining down the stairway from the floor above. A little way down the hall, I could see a thin sliver of light shining under the doorway of the first floor front apartment. I knocked and waited.

As the door opened, a man peered into the dark hallway. "Yes, what can I do for you?" Then he recognized me, and said, "Oh, it is you, Reverendo. Alicia and the boys are not here."

It was Pablo, the husband of a lady who attended services quite regularly. He had come only once to the meetings. I had been advised by some relatives, not to waste my time on him. "Forget it," they said, "we know him from our village in Puerto Rico. He's a stubborn man."

"You say that Alicia and the boys are not here? Has no one else come?" I asked.

"No, no one has come here tonight. Alicia had to take a message to a lady she works with at the clothing factory, who was absent today. Why do you ask about other people?"

"Well, we were to have a Bible class here tonight. Alicia invited us and I announced it in the service Sunday night. I hope you do not mind."

A wry smile on his face, an almost silent "humph" slipping from between his lips, Pablo answered, "It would not make much difference, Alicia usually gets her way... Well, come in and wait, she should not be too long and maybe some of your brothers will yet be coming."

With that he opened the door wider and stepped aside so that I could enter. He then led me into the front room, and invited me to sit down. I marvelled at the very nice furniture. But then, after all, both Alicia and Pablo worked, so they had the means to make the weekly installments.

We sat there in an embarrassing silence. I made some small talk about the weather, his work, his two boys and where they had lived in Puerto Rico. I should have been looking for an opening to speak about spiritual things, but I wasn't. I confess that I was unduly influenced by what his family and friends had told me. They had spoken with such assurance, *Pablo? Qué va!* [expressing disbelief]. "No way will you ever lead Pablo to accept Christ."

My thoughts were also on the Bible study I was supposed to give that night. I was disappointed that no one had come. Even Alicia, who had invited me to hold the meeting in her home, had forgotten. As the minutes clicked by, I felt more and more **sorry for myself!**

I thought, "I wonder if it was worth it to suspend the weekly Bible studies in the homes?" Sunday night I announced that the Bible studies would start again. This was to be the first one and now, even though I had given special emphasis to the announcement, no one had come. By not having the classes over the summer, I had let the people get out of the habit of coming.

In between my thoughts, I tried to keep a conversation going. After almost thirty minutes, the Lord finally got through to me. "Ed... Ed..." I heard a voice in my head, rather weak at first because I wasn't listening. "**ED... ED,.. listen to me**," stronger now, the voice interrupted my thoughts. "What are you doing?...here I have given you the opportunity to talk to this man about Me, and you are goofing off, talking about everything under the sun except that which is most important. Do you not realize that this man is lost?"

The voice continued. "I allowed Alicia to go on that errand and the people to forget about the meeting so that you would have **ample time alone** with this man to give him the Gospel, and you're holding back. Forget the pessimistic remarks of his relatives and friends. Have you forgotten that my Gospel is the power of God unto salvation?"

Now I knew what it meant to be spiritually deflated, humbled. In my heart I thanked the Lord for the rebuke and for reminding me of the work I was supposed to do, "the work of an evangelist." While listening to Pablo give his opinion about some unimportant trivia, I silently prayed, "Thank you, Lord, and forgive me for almost missing this chance to have Pablo alone."

Pablo finished his comment and we remained silent for a minute or two. Again, I prayed, "Lord, you know the kind of person this man is, please give me the wisdom I need."

Aloud, and even yet fearing that I might be rebuked, I began. "Pablo, my friend, we have been conversing tonight about many things which really have little importance in our lives, now or hereafter. Now I would like to talk to you about Christ and His claim upon your soul."

Pablo was silent for a moment or so. I watched him intently, trying to interpret what might be going on in his mind from the changing expressions on his face.

As I watched and waited, Pablo raised his eyebrows in an inquiring expression, then the corners of his mouth began to curl upward in a slight smile. The man nodded his head several times as if making a decision. Then, in a serious tone of voice, he spoke.

"Thank you, Reverendo, I had been expecting, yes, hoping that you would speak to me about God, but I thought that you had decided not to. So, speak, I will listen."

I was surprised! Opening my Bible which had lain beside me on the chair arm all the while, I began with my usual presentation of the Gospel.

Reading Romans 3:23, I asked, "Do you realize, *mi amigo*, that you are a sinner and forever lost unless you receive Christ as your Savior?"

"Yes, I do," Pablo answered without any hesitancy. "You don't have to convince me."

I looked up from my Bible which I had been leafing through to find another passage to read. "You do? You really do?"

"Yes, of course, are we not all sinners by nature and by deed? I have been sorry many times for some things that I have done."

I could not believe my ears. I thought, "Oh... maybe he is just putting me on. Even so, this man must know more about spiritual things than we thought."

Aloud, I said, "Well then, look what it says here in John 3:16." Getting more enthused with my work, I held the Bible so that Pablo could read it for himself, and quoted the verse as he followed with his eyes.

"You see how that God so loved you that He gave His Son Jesus to die for you? Now read here in Romans 5:8." Read it for yourself, Pablo." Pablo read, "But God commendeth his love toward us, in that, while we were yet sinners, Christ died for us."

"You see, Pablo, in your lost sinful condition, God loved you and provided forgiveness for you. You do have to repent, but you can't win God's forgiveness by good works."

"I know that." Pablo replied. "I know that I can do nothing to merit the love of God nor His forgiveness. I found that out years ago, and that is why I gave up religion. My prayers, doing penance for my sins, my good deeds, my church, did not give me the peace in my soul that I wanted. So what good was it to continue? I gave it all up!"

"You're right, but the Bible tells how we can have that peace. See what it says in Colossians 1:20. 'And, having made peace through the blood of his cross, by him to reconcile all things unto himself; by him, I say, whether they be things in earth, or things in heaven.'

"Now, read also what it says in Romans 5:1." Pablo read, "Therefore being justified by faith, we have peace with God through our Lord Jesus Christ."

"So, Pablo, the bottom line is this, and I put it to you in a question,... do you understand that forgiveness for your sins, the salvation of your soul, and peace in your heart, is obtained through faith in Christ?"

"Yes, I do... You do not know it, of course, and neither does Alicia, but recently I have been reading the New Testament which you gave to me that one time I visited your meeting."

"But Pablo, do you believe it?"

"Yes, I do. It is what God says, is it not? How could I not believe it?" affirmed Pablo.

"Well then, let me ask you another question, Are you saved? I mean, do you know that your sins have been forgiven and, if you die, you will go to heaven?"

"That I cannot say. Is such a thing possible? To know for sure?" asked Pablo.

"But you say that you believe that Christ died for this purpose."

"Yes, I believe, but I do not know for sure that God has forgiven me."

"I think I see the problem. You believe, but you have not as yet received Jesus Christ as your Savior. Look here in John 1:11 and 12. Let us read it together....

"You see how Jesus came unto His own. That means that Jesus came to His own people, the Jews, and his own did not receive Him. But as many as **received** Him, to them gave He power to become the sons of God, to be saved, even to them that **believe** on His name.

"You see, the two action words? It says that you have to **believe**. But it also says that you have to **receive** Jesus as your one and only Savior. Have you ever done that, Pablo?"

"No, I have not. No one ever told me that I had to. How do I do it?"

"Well, Pablo, it is such a serious step to take, I want to be sure that you really understand and that you really want to do it, and that you will have no regrets."

"I do, I do. I have wanted to do it for some time now, I mean, I wanted to do something, I did not know what it was. But I was too proud to tell anyone and, I guess, because of the way I spoke to my relatives and friends, they lost interest in me, maybe thought I was hopeless."

"I am sorry about that, truly sorry. But, believe me from now on I trust that I for one will not be influenced by what other people say, and will do the work that I am supposed to do.

"Now then, Pablo, if you are really serious and want to accept Jesus as your Savior, here is one more Bible verse that tells you what you should do. In the book of the Revelation, chapter 3 and verse 20, Jesus says, 'Behold, I stand at the door, and knock: if any man hear my voice, and open the door, I will come in to him, and will sup with him, and he with me.'

"Jesus is standing before the door of your heart. He wants to come in, but He will not open the door. He is waiting for you, He is waiting to hear you invite Him in. When you do, He will come into your heart, He will forgive your sins, and He will give you eternal life.

"You see, Pablo, it is a question of your **will**. God has done it all, Jesus has paid the price. God offers you salvation as a free gift. All that you have to do, all that you can do, is accept the gift. Would you like to receive Jesus as your Savior, right now?"

Without any hesitancy, Pablo bowed his head. We both slipped to our knees. I started to prompt Pablo in his prayer, but the man, with tears running down his cheeks, took over.

"*Bendito Señor Jesucristo* [Blessed Lord Jesus Christ], I am sorry for my sins and for the way I resisted you for so many years. Please forgive me. I invite you now to come into my heart and help me to...." His words trailed off. For a moment, his emotions took over.

I whispered, "You are doing great. Now thank the Lord for what He has done for you."

"Thank you, *bendito* Jesus, for saving my soul. Thank you for keeping the people away so that the pastor could show me the way to be saved. Thank you, thank you, thank you."

I then prayed for Pablo, that he would continue faithful in Christ and that he would be a witness among his many friends and relatives now living in the city.

We rose from our knees and seated ourselves in our chairs, but not before embracing each other as I told Pablo that we were now brothers in Christ.

"Now, there is one other passage of Scripture that I want you to see. Here it is in Romans, chapter ten and verses nine and ten. Here, read it for yourself."

"That if thou shalt confess with thy mouth the Lord Jesus, and shalt believe in thine heart that God hath raised him from the dead, thou shalt be saved. For with the heart man believeth unto righteousness; and with the mouth confession is made unto salvation."

"You see, brother Pablo, now that you have believed and have accepted Him as your Savior, the Lord wants you to confess Him before other people. There are many other verses in the Bible which teach that you must tell others how Jesus has saved you. What a surprise it is going to be when you tell your relatives and friends that you have accepted Christ!"

Hardly had I spoken these last words when the hall doorway opened and in walked Alicia and the two boys. Surprised to see me, and at the same time remembering, she cried, "*Hay, qué pena* [Oh, what a shame], pastor Eduardo, I forgot all about the Bible study tonight." Looking about her, she further remarked, "And it looks like all the others forgot too."

"Yes, they did," agreed Pablo, "but am I ever glad that you and they did forget; otherwise, pastor Eduardo would not have had the opportunity of showing me the way to get saved. You will not believe it, but tonight I accepted Christ as my Savior."

"You what?" shouted Alicia. Then, turning to me, she asked, "Is this true?"

"Yes, it is, praise the Lord! You should be very happy. You are not only husband and wife, you are now brother and sister, united in Christ."

"Well, this in indeed a surprise. I never thought that Pablo would become a believer!"

I bid them good night and drove home, rejoicing that another soul had become a child of God. As I related the experience to

Mildred, she also rejoiced with me. She had not been feeling very well and so had not accompanied me to the meeting.

Well, Pablo was now a *cristiano de verdad* [true Christian]. He was baptized the next year in October and became a charter member of our new church. He found his work in the church as a faithful usher, has always been at the door to welcome the people, and hand them a copy of the church bulletin. To this day, Pablo Hernández is one of the most faithful.

I thank the Lord for being patient with me and for opening my eyes that day to my need of being alert to every opportunity that may come my way to try to win a soul to Christ.

Chapter 30

Social Gospel versus Spiritual Gospel

Teach and Build

"...Not by might, nor by power, but by my Spirit, saith the LORD of hosts." (Zechariah 4:6b)

The missionary work in the City of Brotherly Love was going very well. We had recovered from the summer slump made worse because the migrant work had taken us out of the city too often. The Sunday night services at the Mission were again well attended as were Mildred's weekday Bible clubs. At Christmas time (1952), Mildred prepared a program for the children. Realizing that the little Green Street Mission was too small for the expected attendance, we borrowed the use of a Mission on Fifth Street. In January and February, the work continued to grow, souls were saved and more people attended the services on Sunday nights.

Then, in March, we rented the Sunday School building of the old Fourth Baptist Church on Randolph and Buttonwood Streets. Now we held a combined Sunday School and worship service on Sunday afternoons. Mildred continued the Bible clubs for children three times a week in homes in different sections of the Hispanic colony, and I had two evening Bible studies a week, also held in a private home. We were rejoicing in the growth of the work.

By this time we had 124 names on our Sunday School roll with an average attendance of 85. However, of the total attending, only about 25 adults, plus some of their children professed saving faith in the Lord Jesus Christ. Suddenly our attendance dropped to less than fifty. Inquiry revealed that those we lost had transferred their interest to a religious-social mission where they were supplied with many of the material things they thought they needed.

We were chagrined and saddened, as were our brothers and sisters in the Lord. It was a great concern to everyone that we had lost so many adults and children to a social mission. Our concern was, of course, not so much in the loss of numbers but in the lost opportunity to disciple those people and lead them to a saving knowledge of Christ. The burden of our prayers for quite a few weeks was that the Lord might see fit to supply us with the necessary resources so that we too could offer the poor people some material help, establish a clinic, and be able to do whatever else necessary to retain the people within our group. It was not our desire to get into a social ministry, but we just could not ignore some of the sad conditions we found.

Then we became convicted! Certainly if the Lord willed it, we would already have had the means to do some kind of social work. But the fact that God had not supplied the where-with-all was proof that He did not want us to become involved in such activities. I confessed my fault to the Lord, and asked Him to show me what our program should be for the future.

The Lord answered very clearly. He seemed to say, "Be not concerned that you cannot do the social work that others can, even though you lose some people. I will see to it that you will have ample supply of candidates for salvation and for the establishment of My kind of a church, and maybe, just maybe, later on you may be able to help those in need in a material way. But meanwhile, you are just to **preach My Gospel, leave the increase to Me**. Remember what I have said in My Word: *'Salvation belongeth unto the Lord...'* (Psalm 3:8). Preach salvation and the Holy Spirit will do the rest. Then **teach... teach... teach sound doctrine** to the believers, and get them well established into My church and in sound doctrine."

It was as though I had actually heard the voice of the Lord speaking to my heart, and the instructions were clear and simple. So it was that Mildred and I determined not to be concerned about social work nor about how other religious organizations functioned and seem to prosper. We would dedicate our entire time to seeking the lost, winning them to Christ, teaching them the Word, and, the Lord helping us, organizing them into a strong fundamental Bible church. Much later, it is true, we were able to establish a mission school and day care center. Through that school, Timothy Academy, whole families were won to the Lord.

To emphasize **teaching** in my sermons was not difficult for me, for this is what I like to do most. In fact, I was always afraid that I might go overboard and become lax in evangelistic preaching. In any case, in the two week-night Bible classes I taught doctrine. If some non-believer happened in, I brought in verses to show the need for salvation.

As time went on, I began to doubt a little, wondering if it were possible for souls to be saved under doctrinal teaching alone. But, I continued this practice and, as time went on, the leading of the Lord in the matter was confirmed.

Angel Morales Story

> *"O come, let us sing unto the Lord; let us make a joyful noise to the rock of our salvation."* (Psalm 95:1)

"Pastor Eduardo, if you will permit me, I would like to speak to the class tonight."

I had just arrived, my car loaded with believers, at the home where the Bible class was to be held that night. It was Angel Morales who spoke as I was hanging up my overcoat on the rack. This young man of about twenty had arrived from Puerto Rico several weeks prior to this meeting and was living with his sister, Aleja Ramírez, and her family. Aleja had received the assurance of her salvation after struggling with Jehovah Witness teaching, and was now a faithful member of our congregation. Later she became a teacher of ladies' Bible classes.

Aleja had informed me that her brother and the rest of her family had all been members of a Protestant church in Puerto Rico. But when Angel came to Philadelphia to find work, he determined to escape the strong influence of his parents and not go to church anymore. He was going to get a job, enjoy life for a time, then return to the island to marry Gloria and bring her back to the States. He rejected all of Aleja's invitations to attend our church services.

However, to get his sister "off his back," Angel finally promised to attend at least one service at her new church. He kept his promise, liked the program, especially the lively singing, and continued to attend, even the week-night Bible studies in the homes. The young man had seemed very much interested in the doctrinal studies. I had begun these home Bible studies with the doctrine of the Scriptures, then the doctrine of God, and currently was in the doctrine of Jesus Christ. Tonight we were to study the details of His resurrection.

I wondered what the young man was going to say. Up until that time he had not participated in the meetings. After we had sung a few choruses, I indicated to Angel that he could take a few minutes. He came forward and stood in front of the lectern, and began to speak, nervously at first, then gaining confidence, in a strong firm voice.

"Most of you people are from my area of Puerto Rico and a few of you were members of the same church of which my family are members. I attended Sunday School from the time I was a little boy and learned a lot of Bible verses. I have been active in the young peoples' group and joined the church, but I really never knew what it meant to be saved. I went to the church because there wasn't much else to do in our country *barrio*. Up here, away from my folks, I decided that I would give up church and spend all of my time working to make money.

"I am now glad that my sister, Aleja, begged me to come with her to the Sunday service of her church. I liked the way you sang and so I came back again. At first I did not pay much attention to Pastor Eduardo's sermons. But then, I guess it was the Holy Spirit who spoke to me, for I began to have more interest. I have never heard the Bible explained so clearly.

"I always thought that I was a Christian. Well, I guess I was just like everybody else who says they are Christians. But last week I heard for the first time that Jesus was my **Substitute** who died on the cross in **my place**, and that it was to pay for **MY sins** that He shed His blood.

"I went home to my room and got out my New Testament and looked up again the verses that Pastor Eduardo showed us about the substitutionary death of Jesus. I realized that I had never taken Him as my Substitute. Oh, I thought that Jesus was the Savior in a general sense, but that night it became personal and I told Him for the first time that I wanted Him to be MY Savior. I am now a genuine Christian, I know I am saved."

Many voices were heard with rejoicing and thanksgiving. Several remarked, "That is exactly how it was with me." Of course, Mildred and I rejoiced with the people, and I thought to myself, "I guess it is pos-

Angel and Gloria in Puerto Rico
2 children (a relative on Mildred's right)

sible for souls to be saved through doctrinal teaching, praise the Lord, and thank you, dear Jesus, for leading me in this way."

Story of Lucy Quiñones and her Dad

> *"Be ye therefore ready also; for the Son of man cometh at an hour when ye think not."* (Luke 12:40)

Springtime had come once again to Philadelphia. Thousands had visited the various public gardens as the weather grew warmer, including the great Azalea Gardens at the Friends Hospital on the Boulevard. Easter Sunday morning we held the very first Sunrise Service in Spanish in Philadelphia. The third Sunday in June our church, as most do, celebrated Children's Day.

By this time Mildred had trained several members of our mission church to teach classes in the Sunday School. A young lady, student at the University of Pennsylvania, Lucy Quiñones, taught in the children's church. In the worship service of that day, Lucy was asked to bring a demonstration for the older folk of how she was teaching the children basic doctrinal truths. She was very good at bringing such truths to the children's level of understanding.

The lesson was vividly brought out with the use of a flannel-board. The lesson was on the second coming of Christ. She gave the practical application of the truth with an object lesson which Mildred had prepared for her. It was a box of sand in which some pins were buried. Some pins were made of steel and represented saved people who had died, their souls being with the Lord in heaven and their bodies buried in the earth. Some pins of a non-magnetic substance represented the bodies of people who had died, but who were not saved.

Mary K. Kasler who joined us later, and Lucy Quiñones

Lucy explained that the magnet which she held in her hand represented Christ at His second coming. She held the magnet over the box of sand, and we saw the steel pins rise up and cling to the magnet. The non-magnetic pins remained in the sand.

Lucy concluded: "When Jesus comes again, a shout from the air will be heard by all believers on the earth. The bodies of the believers will rise from the grave and will be united with their souls which have been with Jesus in heaven. Then those believers who are **alive** when Jesus comes, will be taken up from this world to be with Him forever also. But the bodies of those who have not received Jesus as their Savior will stay in the grave until that day when they will have to go to that bad place away from God forever.

"Now we do not know when Jesus is going to come again. That is why Jesus said to the people that they should be ready because He could come back at any time. So, if you have not received Jesus as your Savior yet, boys and girls, mommies and daddies, you should do it now. If you wait, it might be too late. Wouldn't it be sad if, when Jesus comes again, Mommy and daughters would go to be with Jesus and Daddy would have to stay in this old, bad world, to suffer with all the other bad people?" As Lucy spoke those words, her voice trembled, then broke.

Recovering, she repeated very slowly. "The people who are not saved will have to stay in this bad, old world. How sad it will be if sister goes to be with the Lord and brother has to stay, or if children go to be with the Lord and Mommy and Daddy have to stay. Oh, boys and girls, wouldn't it be awful if Mommy went and Daddy had to stay?"

I had not planned to give an invitation for this was just supposed to be a demonstration of how the Bible truths were taught to the children. But, almost at the last moment, I gave an invitation for anyone who would accept Christ as Savior to raise his hand and then come forward to make public confession of faith. I know that I was led of the Spirit.

As the first hand went up, I could not help shouting, "Praise the Lord!"

Everyone knew from my emotion-filled voice that someone for whom they had been praying must have raised his hand. Heads that had been bowed in prayer, lifted, and eyes that had been closed scanned the congregation to see who it was. It was Don Juan, Lucy's father.

Lucy, her sister and mother, had been saved for a number of years. But Juan could not see the need of accepting Christ as his personal Savior. Did he not already believe in God and in His Son Jesus? Was he not a good moral man? Who could accuse him of smoking, drinking or neglecting his family? Everyone knew he came home from work to stay home with his wife and daughters, he did not run around like other men. True, he did not go to church with them, but week-ends he spent fixing up the house. He would take them to church and pick them up again and take them anywhere they might want to go. No, he wasn't a sinner like other men.

His wife and daughters, under the teaching of the Word of God, began to live more consecrated lives, giving up some of the worldly things which had occupied their minds in former days. Juan saw the difference and asked his wife to buy him a Bible, which he started to read. He began to see that it was not religion or a good life that made the difference, but a Person. It was the Lord Jesus who made the difference in the life of his family.

Juan started to attend some of the services on Sundays. I had spoken to him a number of times and urged him to accept Christ as his personal Savior, but to no avail. Seeing the change in his attitude, I took heart and began to speak to him again on the matter. But, for some reason, Juan still resisted with a "not yet" or a "I'm not ready," so I had to let it go at that.

It had to be that Lucy's Bible lesson demonstration struck a responsive chord in Juan's heart. Maybe it was the "Mommy and daughters would go to be with Christ and Daddy would have to stay" that touched him, for he very dearly loved his wife and daughters.

There was much rejoicing that Sunday afternoon, for not only Juan raised his hand and came forward to confess Christ as Savior, but three young persons came with him. One of those was José Figueroa who was president of the Young Peoples' Society.

President of the young people, and not saved, did you say? Yes. It happened

Church leaders - Anibal, Julio, Pastor Ed, Jaun Quiñones, Pedro, Pablo and Julio Morales

this way. There were some fifteen teenagers regularly attending the services. Of these only three professed to be saved: Lucy, her sister Lolín and Pablo Pérez, a Seminary student, son of the pastor of a large church in Mexico City, who came to help in our work. We felt that even though the majority were not saved, they should be organized into a society in order to give some permanency to their attendance. The responsibilities would give some assurance that they would be there. So, with fear and trembling, we organized the young people.

Praise the Lord, it worked out. Then, through continual Bible study, all of the remaining young people of that society came to Christ by the end of the year. We must rely only on God's Word, and that alone. Praise the Lord, His Word "...is quick, and powerful, and sharper than any two-edged sword... a discerner of the thoughts and intents of the heart" (Hebrews 4:12).

The first week in October, at the close of the migrant season, on the invitation of the First Baptist Church of Hammonton, New Jersey, we participated in their missionary conference. We held our first baptism there in preparation for organizing our congregation.

Thus as 1953 came to a close, the *Iglesia Evangélica Bautista de Filadelfia* [Evangelical Baptist Church of Philadelphia], independent and fundamental, was duly organized with eighteen charter members who signed the Articles of Faith and the Constitution, and elected their deacons and other officers. Then, we began to look around for a property we could buy to have a building of our own which would enable us to have a complete schedule of weekly services.

Chapter 31

The Pedro Vázquez Story

"Yes, God can save a truck driver."

"Bring ye all the tithes into the storehouse... saith the LORD of hosts...." (Malachi 3:10)

"Upon the first day of the week let everyone lay by him in store, as God hath prospered him...." (I Corinthians 16:2)

Gregorio Marcano hesitated as he entered the ward on the fourth floor of General Hospital. The patient he expected to see in the first bed was not there.

"Nurse," he called to the lady in white who was making notes on the chart of the patient in the next bed, "where is my friend Carlos?"

"Oh, good afternoon, Mr. Marcano. Your friend Carlos was released just this morning."

Gregorio was well known in General Hospital as he was in others of the city. After he had retired from business, he offered his services to the pastor of a small Evangelical group of Cubans living in the City of Brotherly Love. Pastor Cárdenas had put him to work visiting shut-ins and the sick in nearby hospitals. Gregorio took his responsibility seriously and his prayers and words of comfort were much appreciated by everyone, believer and non-believer alike.

"Perhaps you would like to say a prayer for this man who now occupies the bed your friend had," suggested the nurse. "He was unconscious when brought into emergency about noon. They are now waiting for the results of the tests the doctors ordered. He has been asleep ever since they brought him up. I'm sure that if he were awake he would appreciate a prayer."

"Of course, that is why I am here. What is his name?"

The nurse looked at the chart at the foot of the bed. "Pedro Vázquez, age fifty-two."

Gregorio moved closer to the bedside as the nurse continued her chores of up-dating the charts of the other patients. Bowing his head, he began his prayer.

"*Nuestro Padre que está en los cielos* [Our Father which is in heaven], and Father of our Lord Jesus Christ, I come to thee at this moment in the precious name of our Savior...."

Gregorio Marcano was very fluent when speaking in his native tongue, especially so when exhorting or praying. Some thought that his language was too elevated and too flowery. True, it was beautiful to hear, but it was often wished that he would get to the point. Be that as it may, he was very sincere, and every expression was born in the depths of his heart.

He did not, of course, know anything about the man, Pedro, lying there, but he committed him to the Lord, asking that wisdom might be given to the doctors, that he might be free from pain, and that, if he were not a born-again Christian, this affliction would lead him to seek God and accept His Son as his only and sufficient Savior.

As Gregorio finished his prayer and lifted his head, he saw the man open his eyes ever so slightly and, in a whisper that could hardly be heard, he said, "Gracias, Señor, gracias."

Evidently Pedro had heard and understood the prayer even though he seemed asleep. Now his eyes closed and, as his breathing became more even, he fell into a more restful sleep.

"I too wish to thank you Señor, for the prayers you said for my Pedro." Gregorio heard the feminine voice coming from behind him as he turned from the bedside.

"I am Herminia, Pedro is my husband." The lady, probably in her middle forties, began to sob, "Oh, Señor, my Pedro is so sick and I do not know what to do."

"There, there, Señora, please do not cry, I am sure that they will soon know how to help your husband, and besides, have I not just prayed for him? We must have faith."

"I know that, Señor, I do believe in God. But, what I mean, Señor, is that I am so new here that I do not know anyone to go to for help, and besides, I do not speak English. You see, Pedro came here from Puerto Rico several months ago to get work. He is a good hard worker and makes a good salary. He sent me a ticket to come to him. I just arrived last week, so I know no one. This morning Pedro left for work. Then, about ten o'clock, his co-worker who speaks Spanish came to tell me that Pedro had fainted at his work and, when they could not revive him, they sent him to the hospital in an ambulance. This man was sent to take me to the hospital because I have to sign papers if they have to do something serious to him.

Gracias a Dios, the social worker here speaks Spanish. She interpreted what the doctor had to tell me."

With these words, Mrs. Vázquez began to sob again. "I do not know what to do. I have no family here, no friends, I do not have anyone to whom I can go to ask for help."

"Ah, Señora Herminia, you have me. I thought the Lord sent me here today to pray for my friend Carlos, but now I see that He has other work for me to do. So, tell me, how can I help you? If I cannot do what is needed, we shall ask God to send us to the ones who can. What did the doctor tell you? Trust me, I will be your friend in need."

Herminia dried her tears with some tissue that the nurse handed her as she passed by.

"The doctor told me that my Pedro has not been eating well and that he is very weak from malnutrition. Oh, if only I had been here to cook for him, he would not be in this condition. They will have to keep him here in the hospital to build him up and then they must operate on his hernia. The doctor said that Pedro must have a blood transfusion now and again later on. This is my big problem, Señor. I know of no one who can give blood to my Pedro."

"It is not to worry, Señora. God will provide. Just have faith. I have some brothers in the Lord and I am sure that among them we will find one to give the blood your Pedro needs."

After writing down the address of the apartment where Pedro and Herminia lived, Gregorio took his leave. Already he had in mind to whom he would call to find the blood-donors.

"Pastor Eduardo, it is I, brother Gregorio, you know, Gregorio Marcano from the missionary work of Pastor Cárdenas." I had come to know Gregorio through my door-to-door visitation in the Hispanic community.

"Of course, I know you, brother. How goes your ministry in the hospitals?"

"Very well, pastor. It is about an experience that I had about an hour ago at General Hospital that I am calling you. I went there to pray for my friend Carlos and found a stranger in his bed. *Gracias a Dios*, Carlos is better and was sent home. But I had gone there to pray, and pray I did for the man in that bed. He is one sick man, pastor, and needs some help."

Gregorio proceeded to relate the entire incident, giving me the name and address of the sick man as well as where to find him in the hospital. Gregorio explained that he had suffered at one time from malaria and hospitals would not accept his blood.

"I know what you mean," I commented. "I am in the same condition. I have not had a malarial attack in six years, but the germ may still be in my blood, and so they cannot use it."

"However, brother Gregorio, I will announce this need tonight in our Bible study class and we will trust that someone will be able to donate the blood. Also, I have a brother in Christ, Bill Holeton, a *Norte-americano*, who quite often donates blood. I will call him."

"*Gracias*, pastor Eduardo. I have prayed for don Pedro and his wife Herminia and I am sure that the Lord will supply their every need. So I will leave this special need in your hands, but I will continue to visit the man. We will see how the Lord will not only supply his physical needs, but will also bring him to salvation in Christ."

"I too am sure that He will. The Lord works in wonderful ways to bring sinners to Himself, and I praise Him for men like yourself, brother Marcano, who are faithful witnesses. Keep up the good work and give my regards to Pastor Cárdenas."

I related the conversation to Mildred and then, at our evening meal, we both prayed for Gregorio, his work, and for the man, Pedro Vázquez and his wife, Herminia.

The Lord did supply for the needs of this couple. Gregorio continued to visit Pedro during the three weeks that he was in the hospital. So did I. Almost every time I visited Pedro, I found Herminia there, which gave the added opportunity to speak to her about the Lord.

Don Pedro had been a truck driver back in Puerto Rico, traveling between San Juan and several of the larger cities of that island paradise such as Ponce and Mayagüez. In those days there were no super-highways like those that now cross the central mountain range. Truck drivers would have to spend their nights in the city where they made deliveries. Pedro, in the several conversations I had with him, told of his experiences and admitted that he knew he was a sinner, but he doubted that the Lord could love "this sinful trucker" enough to save his soul.

Herminia was a devout Catholic and was afraid to even talk about the Gospel of the grace of God though His Son Jesus. She insisted that Mary was her intercessor with God the Father, and that she was committed to the adoration of the virgin and the reciting of the rosary.

But, one day, Gregorio was able to get through to Pedro, who confessed his sins to God and accepted Christ as his Savior. Gregorio called me, and we rejoiced together that another sinner had repented and entered the family of God.

In due time, Pedro was home with Herminia in their apartment on Franklin Street, and soon back to work. The church where we held our Sunday afternoon services was located only three blocks from where Pedro and Herminia lived. Pedro insisted they attend regularly on Sundays as well as the night-time Bible classes in the homes. Herminia, was an obedient wife, so she accompanied her husband, but with fear and trembling.

Little by little, Herminia's prejudices and superstitions were broken down. Mildred and some ladies of our congregation visited her. Soon Herminia began to understand the teaching of the true Gospel. One Sunday afternoon, Herminia accepted Christ as her **one and only** Savior.

The reader has noticed how we missionaries always emphasized the "one and only" Savior. This is because with some people, to accept Christ meant simply to add Him to the multitude of saints to whom they were already praying and trusting for spiritual help and possible salvation. Invariably the verse in I Timothy 2:5 would be quoted, "For there is one God, and one mediator between God and men, the man Christ Jesus." Jesus must be seen as the **one and only** Savior. This helps to clarify the truth. Jesus, and He alone, can save.

Now, Pedro and Herminia were united not only as man and wife in marriage, but they also were united in Christ. In due time they were baptized and united with our newly organized Baptist church. Pedro joined Pablo in his ministry and has faithfully served through the years as an usher in our services. In later years, Pedro served as a deacon, and Herminia became a faithful worker. But first, there had to be that spiritual growth that we look for in the lives of the truly born-again. Pedro and Herminia had much to learn.

Pedro and Herminia Vásquez

For example: one afternoon after service, during this time of spiritual growth, Pedro approached me as his missionary-pastor and said, "Pastor Eduardo, I have a good plan for raising the money we need to buy that building uptown you told us about."

Pedro spoke very softly and stood very close to me as if he were afraid that someone else would hear and maybe steal his secret plan before he could even tell it to me.

"I know a man who sells cars and he will loan us a car to put on display so we can offer one like it in a raffle. We can sell tickets, say for $5.00 each. Just in the Hispanic community alone we can sell enough tickets to get twice as much as the car is worth. Then we pay the dealer for the car and use the rest of the money to put down on the building for our church."

I would have been chagrined to hear such a suggestion from a more mature believer, but Pedro was very young in the Lord, recently out of a church organization that considers raffles, bingos and church socials, legitimate ways to raise money for religious purposes. I could not reproach him, but kindly explained how true Evangelical churches support their ministries.

"Brother Pedro, I know that you mean well and have carefully thought out your plan, but we believers do not raise money in this manner in spite of the fact that it is for a good cause.

"The Lord knows we are going to need a lot of money if we are to have our own church building someday. But our work is the Lord's, and we must do it according to the teaching of the Bible which teaches that we should give of our earnings voluntarily. The Lord wants us to bring our tithes and offerings into the church for its expenses and to support missionary work."

"But, pastor, do you really think that our people will give enough money in their offerings for us to get our own building? Down in Puerto Rico even Protestant churches raise money through raffles, suppers and sales of different kinds."

"Yes, Pedro, they will. If the brethren really love the Lord, they will contribute to the work with their whole heart, and they will do it abundantly just like the children of Israel did when God told Moses to build the Tabernacle."

Then, realizing that Pedro would not know that story of the Old Testament to which I referred, I related briefly how Moses asked the Jews to bring offerings of gold and silver, fine linens and other articles for the building of the Tabernacle. I told him how the people with willing hearts brought in so much that finally, Moses had to tell them not to bring any more.

"Brother Pedro," I explained, "our Father in heaven has untold riches, more than enough for us to get our own building. We just have to ask Him in faith, believing that He will put the desire into the hearts of our people to contribute what we need without having to sell lottery tickets or raffle off a car, like the worldly church people do. We will do as Jesus said, 'Ask and ye shall receive.' Do not worry, brother, the Lord will supply all our need through the voluntary tithes and offerings of the believers. God will be honored and the believers will be blessed."

"I'm sorry, Pastor Eduardo, I didn't know."

Pedro looked very disappointed and downcast for he was so sure that he had found a good way to raise money for the church. I tried to speak with love and kindness, so that Pedro would not take offense. And he didn't. He recognized that, as a babe in Christ, he had much to learn.

"Pastor, you must have patience with me. You know I was such a man of the world before I came to know Christ and accept Him as my Savior. I do want to serve my Lord, but I have not had much schooling. I do not ever expect to be able to teach others, but I do have some business sense and have always been able to make a good living. Please, do not hesitate to teach me. I want to learn how to be a good follower of Christ."

"That is good, brother Pedro. I know you meant well, I too want to be a good follower of Christ and to be a good under-shepherd to you and the rest of our people."

Pedro gave me the typical Latin bear-hug good-bye, indicating that he had no hard feelings. As we then left together, I closed and locked the doors.

The believers did become faithful supporters of their church and its mission program. It was difficult at first to teach them their responsibility. For many years the denominations in the United States financially supported the churches they established in Puerto Rico thinking the people were too poor to build and support their own. They failed to teach the people the Biblical principles of giving and thus deprived them of many blessings. Eventually, as we studied the Bible together, our people did learn and have abundantly supported the church and its ministry. The Lord has abundantly **blessed them in return** as you will read in the next chapter.

Chapter 32

Leave the Word to Serve Tables? Never!

"It is not reason that we should leave the word of God, and serve tables... we will give ourselves continually to prayer, and to the ministry of the word." (Acts 6:2b,4)

The Evangelical Baptist Church of Philadelphia, seeing their need for their own place of worship, established a building fund. Much to brother Pedro's surprise, the believers willingly gave so that by the spring of 1956, they had saved enough to make a down payment on a property on Reese Street, west of Fifth Street, just north of Lehigh Avenue. Members and friends worked hard that summer to get it renovated, and by October, we were in our new location.

During those first years of contact with the Puerto Rican families, we learned that the majority had left their beautiful paradise island in order to better themselves economically. To do so, both parents needed to have employment. Thus, there was a need to have someone to look after their little ones during the day. The school age children also needed to be helped over the language barrier until they had mastered enough English to attend public school.

Virginia Forkell who joined us later, and Margaret Tolosa

So, at the time we secured our own building, a combination day care center and school was founded. This project was made possible as we were joined in the ministry by Margaret Tolosa, former missionary to Venezuela, a trained and licensed school teacher. Our school was founded under the name of *Academia Timoteo* [Timothy Academy], based on the Scripture verses of Proverbs 22:6 and II Timothy 3:15. We began with classes for pre-schoolers, kindergarten, first and second grades. Other grades were added later. Mildred and I served as administrators.

It should be noted that this school was not a true Christian day school which requires that the parents of the children enrolled be Christians and sign a doctrinal statement with which they were in agreement. Timothy Academy was a **mission school** whose object was to reach the entire family with the Gospel of Christ, win as many as possible to Him, and bring them into the fellowship as members of our church. Thus it was that for quite a number of years, seventy-five percent of the children came to the school from non-evangelical homes. Nevertheless, all of the children were given Bible lessons every day and the parents had to agree to this. While not required to do so, the parents were also urged to send their children to our Sunday School.

In those days, many of the homes of Puerto Rican families had a placard attached to the front door which read, after naming their family religion, "Therefore, we will not admit into our home, nor listen to any Evangelical worker, nor receive any of their literature." But those who needed the services of Timothy Academy, of necessity, had a change of attitude. When the teachers visited the homes to talk to the parents about their children, they were freely admitted. There were always opportunities to show that the solution to every problem could be found in a knowledge of Jesus Christ. As a result, whole families received Christ and became members of our church, or joined a fundamental one when they moved back to Puerto Rico.

By the fall of 1960, the school had developed both academically and spiritually. A large number of students had graduated from our school, having completed their third or fourth grade work. Some had been with the school from their pre-kindergarten days. The reputation for academic achievement had also been established in the nearby public schools, for many of the children, when transferred from Timothy Academy, after being tested, were advanced to a higher grade. The church was now running about two hundred plus in the combined Sunday School and worship program. There were about seventy constituted adult members.

One afternoon, I gave an interview to the newly-appointed Coordinator of Puerto Rican Affairs of the Camden-Philadelphia area. I gave Mrs. Trinidad a tour of the facilities and a brief history of the work. She explained her responsibility, which was to coordinate the work of all the organizations working with Puerto Ricans so that there would not be a duplication of effort.

"Do you not think it better," she asked, "that we work together and pool our resources? Do we not have the best interests of the people at heart? I am sure YOU do, Reverendo."

"Of course we do," I replied. "And I believe that you do too, as do others that are working to better the conditions of the Puerto Rican people. But, the methods that each group uses are different, and our methods are more distinct. Many of the activities offered to help the people are good and needed. But, there are also activities of which we do not approve,"

"Would you care to explain?" asked Mrs. Trinidad.

"Yes, gladly. But I do so at this time not for the purpose of debate. I do not want to give the impression that I am criticizing other organizations which are trying to help the people. First of all, teaching English is good. It is good also to teach sewing to the girls, carpentry work to the boys and the philosophy of good citizenship to all ages. So is giving family counseling to those who need it. But we would approve only if the highest standard of morality were used in the counseling. We cannot approve of the modern-day so-called family planning counseling."

At this remark, I could not help but notice how the lady's eyebrows arched and her expression indicated that she was about to protest. But I kept right on, not giving her a chance to interrupt because I really didn't have time to debate the issues.

"It is good also to help the people as much as possible by establishing free dental and medical clinics for the poor. Sometimes we wish that we could get involved in such beneficial social activities and maybe we will some day, if God so wills. But we are sure that we have a better way of helping the people. It is by the preaching of the Gospel of our Lord Jesus Christ.

"The Apostle Paul wrote that the Gospel is the power of God unto salvation to every one that believeth. Through believing with the heart and accepting Christ as your Savior you receive pardon for your sins and everlasting life. The Word of God also says that he who has accepted Christ is a new creature, that is, he is born again, and because he received a new nature, he does not want to live the way he did before, but now wants to please the Lord and glorify God.

"What I am explaining to you is this while social work is good to help the people in a material way, the people need something to change the ambitions and desires of their hearts. Social work is temporary, it provides a temporary respite, but the problems recur. When a man's heart is changed, so is his life, and this change is permanent. The Bible says that the heart of man is deceitful above all things, and desperately wicked: who can know it? (Jeremiah 17:9).

"Mrs. Trinidad, look what God promises in His Word here in Ezekiel 11:19,20, '...and I will put a new spirit within you; and I will take the stony heart out of their flesh, and will give them an heart of flesh... That they may walk in my statutes, and keep mine ordinances, and do them; and they shall be my people, and I will be their God.' God was speaking to His people Israel, but the truth applies in a spiritual way to man living today.

"You see, the natural man cannot live a better life though he try with all his might, he needs to be born again, changed by the Spirit of God. The average man, as you well know, lives a poor and sinful life and social work can only give him some relief from the consequences of his sin. But, change his heart, and of his own volition, he will become the kind of a man who cares for his loved ones as he should, and his heart will be filled with peace and satisfaction.

"I could cite you innumerable cases of men and women who lived in immorality and self-satisfaction until they accepted Christ as their Savior. The women became more chaste as well as beautiful in their manner of life. The men became, as we say in Puerto Rico, *caseros* [homebodies]. They ceased to run around, stayed home with their families and took better care of their homes. They no longer spent their money on wine, women and song, but on the needs of their wives, their children and themselves. That change came about because there was a change in their heart. Social work cannot do this. We have the better way, Mrs. Trinidad, and we cannot leave our way to get involved in social work no matter how good it might be. Saint Peter once said, 'It is not reason that we should leave the word of God, and serve tables' (Acts 6:2)."

Mrs. Trinidad nervously fumbled in her purse as she asked, "Is it all right if I smoke?" She began to remove a cigarette from the pack.

"I am sorry, but it is prohibited. First of all, we do not allow it here because the habit is bad for everyone's health, and secondly, the law forbids it here in a school."

"I am sorry too, and I wish I could get rid of this habit, but I guess I am too weak. Maybe I need your religion to help me."

"Not our religion, Mrs. Trinidad, but our Christ. He will help you, not only to give up smoking, but He will help you in everything else, if you accept Him as your Savior."

Mrs. Trinidad hung her head. Clearly she had been convinced that the Way of the Lord was best. Then she asked, "But how can this business of being born again help our people economically? I can see what it can do for their moral and spiritual lives, but what about their poverty, how can it help them better their living conditions?"

"I have explained the spiritual principle that helps the people live so that their material needs are more easily obtained. Now, let me give you some very practical proof. Here is a newspaper clipping from the *Evening Bulletin* of last week. It compares economical conditions between white, black and Puerto Rican families here in Philadelphia. The average yearly wage of the white family is $6,800, that of the black family $4,900, and that of the Puerto Rican family $3,600. Yes, our families are on the bottom, economically, according to this report.

"The report also gives the percentages of the families who have bought or are buying their own homes: white families, 65 percent, black families, 45 percent, Puerto Rican families, 18 percent. I thought the survey was wrong, for I believed that my Puerto Rican families were much better off. Last Sunday morning I took a survey of all present, which showed that 85 percent of the families were buying their own homes, not the 18 percent reported in the newspaper. Included in my survey were families who have not yet accepted Christ as Savior and experienced a change of heart, but are being influenced by the Gospel.

"I thought of writing to the newspaper to correct their misconception. But, as I made inquiry among the Puerto Ricans on the street, I discovered that apparently their figures were correct. Can you guess why there is a contradiction of percentages, Mrs. Trinidad?"

"No, but I am sure you are going to tell me," the lady replied, with a smile.

"I thought you would never ask," I laughingly commented. "As a preacher, I sometimes get long-winded with my explanations. I apologize, but I want to prove to you beyond a shadow of a doubt that the Jesus way produces practical results in the lives of our people."

"I know... I know," Mrs. Trinidad agreed, "and I am interested. Please go on."

"Well, it is true that the average Puerto Rican family is economically way below some of the other ethnic groups. But, having Christ in the heart makes the difference. Our people are living on a much higher level. As further proof, I submit the following story."

I then explained about the services among the migrant farmers in South New Jersey and the baptismal services that were held in the Baptist Church of Hammonton in those first years.

"The first time we did it, we took our people with us, some in my car and some in the car of another family, plus about thirty people in a bus which I borrowed. The next year that we went, I borrowed the bus again, but there were also eight cars owned by our people. The third year, and the last time we did this, I did not have to borrow the bus, our people made up a caravan of some twenty cars of their own to take them to Hammonton.

"You see, the people were getting saved and bettering themselves economically. The Lord helping them, they were now using their money more wisely, buying cars and other good things as well as contributing to the support of their church. They created a building fund, and the following year they had sufficient for a down payment on these buildings in which you are now sitting. And, yes, 85 percent of our people are living in homes which they are buying.

"My dear Mrs. Trinidad, do you now see how Christ makes the difference in lives? Do you understand now why we say that we must dedicate all of our time and effort to the preaching of the Gospel of Christ, and that we do not have time to engage in social work?"

"Yes," the lady admitted, "I understand and admire your position. Keep up the good work." Then, hurriedly grasping her purse and her file folders, she rose from her chair, saying, "I have taken up enough of your time. I have another appointment I must keep."

"Permit me one more word before you go, please... Forgive me the personal note, but, what about you? Do you not see that you too have a need for the Savior?"

"Oh, believe me, Reverendo, I have often thought about it. I have relatives in Puerto Rico who are Evangelical. But I am so busy I really do not have time for much religion. I go to mass once in a while, but I have such a concern for my people that even on Sundays I am running here and there trying to get more cooperation from the different social organizations."

"Well, please continue not only to think about the Gospel, but to do something about it for your own sake. Don't delay too long. The expression, 'Mañana is good enough for me', is cute and laughable when sung, but how tragic the thought that mañana may be too late."

By this time, I had walked Mrs. Trinidad to her car. Thanking me for giving of my time, she promised to consider seriously the message of the Gospel she had heard that afternoon.

"Thank you for your concern, Reverendo. Keep up the good work of saving my people and, please say a prayer for me."

"I will... God bless you, and may you soon receive the blessed Savior into your heart.

I thought, as I walked back to the church office, "We have the best way. We will help the people in any way that we can, but **we must never, never leave the Word to serve tables**."

Chapter 33

Living Water - Part 1

The Beatrice Soto Story

"He who believes in Me, as the Scripture has said, Out from his innermost being springs and rivers of living water shall flow." (John 7:38, ANT)

Beatrice had problems. She, her husband and three children had recently moved to Philadelphia from Puerto Rico. Her husband, Cecilio, found work almost immediately and had rented a small house, and furnished it with the bare necessities. Their funds were limited but relatives living nearby loaned them the pieces of furniture that they lacked. They soon discovered that the wages Cecilio brought home were not sufficient to supply their daily needs.

Beatrice had to find employment. This was not the problem. Her relatives and friends working in the clothing factories readily found her employment, but how could she care for her three children while working? This was the problem, and it was made more acute because the children did not speak English and, worse yet, one of the girls was mentally retarded.

"*Qué podemos hacer?* [What can we do?]" she complained. "Our church school has no program for our children. Carmen suggested that the public schools might have a program. I hate to seek help from the Protestants, but tomorrow I will visit the Franklin Public School."

Beatrice was a very, very devout Catholic and it was actually with fear and trembling that she entered the school office to talk to the secretary. It was difficult also for Beatrice because of her limited knowledge of English. But she found no solution to her problem in the public schools. There was just no program in Spanish to help the retarded child.

"Whatever am I going to do?" Beatrice tearfully asked her neighbor. "I feel that my children must be together. But, neither our parochial school nor the public schools can help me."

The sympathetic neighbor was a member of our church. Even in her predicament, if Beatrice had known, she would not have spoken to her. But God was working in this instance.

The neighbor counseled, "Why don't you try *La Academia Timoteo* [the Timothy Academy]? It is located on Reese Street above Lehigh Avenue. It is run by the Baptist church I attend."

"Run by the Baptist church?," Beatrice almost whispered it, as though she was afraid to speak it out loud. "Oh, I could not do that, I am Catholic!"

"But, my dear friend, they are good people and will help you if they can. Don't be afraid, they love Christ and your children could not be in a better place."

That evening Beatrice talked it over with her husband. He was more liberal in his beliefs, but sympathized with his wife's fears. He suggested that she check it out. That night, after reciting the rosary with so many "Hail Marys" and *Padre Nuestros* [our Fathers], she decided to conquer her fears, swallow her pride, and visit Timothy Academy in the morning.

Mildred had just finished a consultation with a mother whose child was giving some trouble in the school, when Beatrice rang the bell. Opening the door as she bid good-bye to the mother, with a smile and a cheery *Buenos días*, Mildred invited Beatrice into the office.

Mildred listened to Beatrice as she told of her problem and how, when neither the Catholic school nor the public school could help her, she had come to Timothy Academy with many prayers to the Virgin that her children might be enrolled. Mildred agreed, "Yes, you do have a problem. We can enroll the boy and the one girl, but we do not have a program for the retarded child. You say that the children do not speak English?"

"Hardly a word, señora. But please, try to do something for my children. Things are so strange here, that I do not think it would be wise to separate them, especially the retarded one."

Trying to be kind and sympathetic, Mildred explained, "We have no problem with the language as all our teachers are bilingual. We would put the boy and his sister in the same room, in the first grade. When they have learned enough English they will go to the grade where they should be. But what can we do with the retarded girl? We really have no program for her and we could not assign a teacher just to take care of one child."

"Oh, señora, please, please try to think of something. My poor little girl must have somewhere to stay while I and my husband work."

Then, Beatrice got an idea which she immediately voiced. "The social worker in the school in Puerto Rico told me that my little retarded girl cannot learn very much anyway. Could you not let her just sit in the classes with my two others? She is a good girl, she obeys most of the time, and with her sister and brother with her, I am sure she will not cause you any trouble. Maybe, just being there she might learn a little bit. Also, señora, I assure you that she knows how to take care of her personal needs."

Just then some children came down from their classrooms to go out in the yard for recess. The teacher's helper led and Margaret, the school principal and their teacher, followed.

"Margaret," Mildred called, "could you let Delia watch the children for a few minutes? I need to consult with you about a problem. Could we possibly enroll a retarded child?"

Mildred then introduced Beatrice and related the problem. Beatrice, with tears in her eyes, spoke up, "Please, Missy, help me and my children. I will do anything to have my children taken care of." (In Puerto Rico the teachers are almost always called "Missy.")

Finally it was agreed that they would do as Beatrice had suggested. The retarded child could sit in the class with her brother and sister provided she would obey and not disturb the other children. But Beatrice must understand that the teacher could not give the retarded girl any special attention or any special instruction.

Then, before Mildred took down all the information about the children, she explained the purpose of the school and that each child enrolled would have to attend the Bible study period given each day. Knowing of the fear of anything not Catholic, Mildred wanted to make it clear about the religious training the children would receive and that it was obligatory.

Again that fearful look came into Beatrice's eyes. She had heard so many bad things about the Protestants. Trying to allay Beatrice's fears, Mildred went on to explain.

"In the Bible study period, the children do not learn anything bad. They are taught only those truths that are found in God's Word:

stories about Adam and Eve, about Abraham, about Joseph, about David and Goliath, about Daniel in the lion's den, oh, just so many stories from the Bible. They learn about how Jesus was born of Mary, how He cured the sick and calmed the troubled waters. They are things which all true Christians believe."

Beatrice's own interest was aroused and she felt deep down in her heart that her children would not be harmed, but would be helped. She nodded agreement and Mildred proceeded to fill out the information forms. Then Mildred told Beatrice about our Sunday School.

"Now Beatrice, you do not have to agree to this, but if you would permit it, we would like to pick up the children in our school bus on Sunday mornings to bring them to Bible school where they would learn even more about God and Jesus Christ. We would deliver them to your home again about noon. You do not have to pay anything for this additional service."

Mildred was glad to see Beatrice, after a little hesitation, nod her consent. Thus began a relationship which was to result in eternal blessings for Beatrice and her family.

********** ********** **********

"Mama... Mama!" shouted Edna, as she and her brother Freddy followed by their retarded sister, María Eneida, burst into their house. (Many Puerto Rican children are given English names.) It was on a Sunday in late November, just a little past noon. The children were all excited, and as they waved small sheets of paper, all three began to shout.

"Mama, look we have poems to recite for the Christmas program in Sunday School."

Beatrice took the papers, cut-outs from used Christmas and birthday cards. There were pictures of flowers or scenery. Underneath a verse or two was typewritten. Mildred always gave the children the verses they were to learn written on these pretty cards so that they would be more likely not to lose them as happened so many times. Of course, María Eneida's paper had nothing on it except the pretty picture. She would not be able to learn a verse, but she would have been awfully disappointed if she did not get a paper to take home as the other children did.

"And, Mama, here is an invitation for you to attend the Christmas program" said Raquel, as she took a folded sheet from her little purse.

Beatrice's children had adapted themselves very quickly to the new environment. As children have the special capacity to do, they were fast becoming adept with the new language. Even María Eneida, though just sitting in the class with Freddy and Edna, or playing with some simple toy, was learning to express herself and make her wants known.

Then one Sunday when the children came home, Beatrice had been chagrined to hear Edna and Freddy say, "Mama, today we let Jesus come into our hearts, we are saved and we are going to heaven to be with Him someday."

"Oh *Dios mío*, what have I done?" Beatrice said to herself. "My children have become Baptists. The Virgin will take her blessing away from us." Once again the old fears welled up in her heart. Then, she remembered how pleased she had been at the change in their behavior. They never were really naughty children. They just did not always obey right away, and sometimes they fought among themselves. But ever since they began to attend Timothy Academy and the Baptist Sunday School, Beatrice had seen a big change in them. She had to admit, "They are more loving and considerate toward each other and to their father and me."

That evening when Cecilio came home from helping a relative move to another house, Beatrice discussed the situation with him. Cecilio advised his wife to *investigarlo por tí misma* [investigate it for yourself]. He had said, "Why don't you go with the children some Sunday morning and see for yourself what goes on? Go with the children to the Christmas program. The Baptists will not think you are getting interested in their religion since you are just going to hear the children recite their poems."

So the Sunday before Christmas, Beatrice was ready and got in the bus with the children. She was very cordially greeted and ushered to a seat where she could hear and see all that went on. As Beatrice looked over the congregation, she recognized several of the women from the clothing factory where she worked and wondered if they were Baptists too. Some were, some were not. Some had come just as Beatrice, invited to hear their children recite their verses.

Beatrice was much impressed with the service, but felt very uncomfortable when I, as missionary-pastor, gave the sermon after the children's part was over. Beatrice went home from that service very confused. This was certainly much different from what she had been taught.

"So, Beatrice, what did you find out this morning?" asked Cecilio. "Are the children being hurt in any way, are they being taught bad things?"

"Our children did very well when they recited the verses, and I liked the Christmas carols the people sang. But, when the pastor got up to speak, I listened very carefully. He said many things that I have never heard before, like how Jesus came into this world to save sinners. He said hardly anything about the Virgin and the Baby Jesus. He kept talking about Jesus dying on the cross for the sins of the people and that if those sins are to be forgiven, the person must believe in Him and receive Him as his personal Savior. I wonder how you do that."

"Don't sound bad to me. I wouldn't worry about it," her husband counselled her.

As time went on, the fears that Beatrice had concerning the Baptists began to subside. She thought more and more about the peace and security they had. Then there was that change in her children. They continued to be more loving, kind and obedient. She began to go with them to Sunday School, not very frequently at first, but then more often. "I think it is good for me to keep on investigating what they are teaching our children," she explained to her husband.

Then came *La Semana Santa* [Holy Week], and the Baptist church was having a week of evangelistic services with emphasis on the afternoon service of *Viernes Santo* [Good Friday]. The factory where Beatrice worked closed at noon that day, so she decided to go to church with her children. She wanted Cecilio to accompany her, but he excused himself. With a funny little smile, he gave her the now often repeated advice, "Go, investigate what they teach, we don't want our children to learn anything bad."

He thought to himself, "I am afraid that Beatrice is getting more than just interested in what they are teaching the children. I'll bet she is getting personally interested in that Gospel they talk about. But, I must admit that Evangelical women make good mothers and are more attentive to their husbands. Maybe it would not be so bad if the Baptists got Beatrice converted!"

And that is exactly what happened, that is, not that the Baptists got Beatrice converted, but that the Lord did. It happened not on

Good Friday, but on Sunday. Beatrice had been so impressed by what she heard on Friday that she returned to the Sunday morning service to hear the children recite and listen to the message about the resurrection. She wanted to respond to the invitation that morning but again those fears came and, when she would have gotten up, she felt glued to her seat. She just sat there until the service ended, all trembly inside.

All that Sunday afternoon, she paced the floor of her bedroom. Alternately she would resolve to receive Christ into her heart as the pastor had said, then she would tremble with fear and try to put such thoughts from her mind. But she could not get the words out of her mind. The pastor had quoted some verses from the Bible and kept repeating that Jesus had died and rose again to save us from our sins. To be forgiven for our sins and be saved, we had simply to receive Jesus as our only Savior. "How can that be possible without doing something to win God's favor?" she asked herself. "But that is what I heard him prove from the Bible, that it is only by God's grace through faith in Christ, and that there was no other way."

Toward evening, Beatrice prayed, "Oh, Jesus, please free me from my fears. I want that peace in my soul that the pastor talked about this morning. I now know that you are alive in heaven. Oh, Jesus, how long have I worshipped you hanging dead there on that cross." So saying, she removed the crucifix and chain from around her neck. "Oh Jesus, please forgive me. I want to be saved! Please come into my heart, Lord Jesus."

As Beatrice prayed these last words, a peace and a joy flooded her heart and soul so completely that she thought she would burst. There in her bedroom she cried out with a loud "Thank you, Lord Jesus," so loud that the children came running from downstairs to see what was the matter. She embraced them and, with tears streaming down her cheeks, she told them, "Your mother has received Jesus into her heart just like you have." The children understood and sang with her the little chorus they had learned, "Thank you Lord, for saving my soul."

Then that resurrection Sunday night, at the close of the service when the invitation was given, Beatrice went forward to make public her profession of faith in the Lord Jesus Christ. Mildred took her to a room where she showed her verses from the Bible to give her positive assurance of her salvation. After prayer, she showed her Romans 10:9,10, emphasizing the need to become a witness for

Christ. Mildred advised her, "Beatrice, you should start to witness this very night. As soon as you get home you must tell your husband what you have done."

Cecilio was home waiting for his family and received the news very graciously, saying, "I am happy that you are happy. You know you have not been so easy to get along with recently. I knew you were troubled, but I had faith that God would work things out for you."

"He did, Cecilio, and He will do the same for you if you will take Him as your Savior."

"Now, Beatrice, you know that I am not a religious man, neither do I oppose anyone who is. I have always had faith in God and I am sure that He controls the destiny of every man."

"But, Cecilio, God will only bless those who receive His Son into their hearts. We, I and the children, want you to join us in our new life in Jesus."

"Don't rush me, Beatrice. I must have time to think. But when the time comes and God speaks to me, I will do whatever is necessary."

So saying, the matter was closed for the time being. But only for the time being, for there was fulfilled in Beatrice's life the promises which the Lord had made, first to the Samaritan woman at the well of Sychar, and then to His disciples to encourage them.

"But whosoever drinketh of the water that I shall give him shall never thirst, but the water that I shall give him shall be in him a well of water springing up into everlasting life" (John 4:14). And John 7:38 (ANT), "He who believes in Me, as the Scripture has said, Out from his innermost being springs and rivers of living water shall flow."

The Apostle John explained that Jesus was speaking of the Spirit, that those who believe in Him will receive to help them witness for the Savior. This was fulfilled in Beatrice. She could not contain the truth and the blessing which she had received. She had to let it out. She was compelled

Cecilio, Beatrice and Eneida Soto

by the Holy Spirit, dwelling in her innermost being, to witness for Christ at every opportunity. He was in her like a fountain of water that could not be contained, but had to flow continually upward and out. The first one she must win to Christ was Cecilio, her husband.

Cecilio, watching the wonderful changes which had come about, in the lives of Freddy. Edna, even María Eneida and now in the life of his beloved, could not help but be persuaded to seek the Lord also. He began by attending the services at our church. Then, just in a matter of a few weeks, he went forward in response to the invitation to receive Christ as his Savior. Shortly after this, they were both baptized.

But that was just the beginning. Beatrice had read in her Bible, in Acts 16:31, the invitation that the Apostle Paul had given to the Philippian jailor: "...Believe on the Lord Jesus Christ, and thou shalt be saved, and thy house" (Acts 16:31).

Beatrice took the last phrase literally. To her, "and thy house" meant not only her immediate family, that is, her husband and children, but her father and mother, her brothers and sisters, cousins and in-laws. At every chance she got, she began witnessing to them all.

The Lord blessed her faithful witness. Through her testimony, Cecilio's brother Andrés and his wife Estrella were saved. Sometime later, her parents were saved. Then a sister received Christ as Savior. Next came several cousins and her niece, Lillian. Not all came to the Lord right away, but one by one over a number of years. Needless to say, we were overjoyed as we saw the fruit of her witnessing. We do not know how many others are saved as a result of Beatrice's testimony, but we know that the process goes on, for this is how the Lord works. As we witness to the Lord's saving grace, God gives the increase, all to His glory and honor.

Chapter 34

Living Water - Part 2

The Iñor Rodríguez Story

"...and a little child shall lead them." (Isaiah 11:6c)

The Scripture verse chosen to head this chapter is prophetic, and refers to conditions which will exist during the Mesianic Reign of Christ. But the truth expressed in the small portion does apply spiritually as the following story illustrates. It happens time after time when adults are led to the Lord through the salvation testimony of a young boy or girl.

The story is similar to the one just told, but with the following exception, Iñor was not as outgoing as Beatrice. The reader might expect to hear more unusual exploits in soul-winning, but this time the souls were won in a very different manner. In any case, the results were the work of the Holy Spirit, symbolized again by the living waters flowing from the believer's innermost being and demonstrating the changed life. Wonderful things can happen when a new believer, even one young in age, remains steadfast in his faith, come what may.

Dave Warren was working with us in our Spanish Baptist church and school. Dave was a great soul-winner with a special interest in young people. Mildred and Margaret, along with Olga Torres, had founded a Pioneer Girls club in our mission church which proved to be a great blessing. Dave had been encouraged to start a similar work among the boys under the name of Boys Brigade. It was hard work for he had to translate much of the material into Spanish. But he did a fantastic job and soon there was a large group of boys attending, a number of whom, as time went on, accepted Christ as Savior.

One day Dave saw a group of boys tossing a basketball through a hoop fastened to an electric company pole on the sidewalk. He stopped to speak to the boys and invited them to attend a meeting of the Brigade.

Iñor, one of the boys came to the meetings and some time later began to attend our Sunday School. At both places he began to understand the spiritual truths he was learning from the Word of God. Iñor lived outside the area where the mission work was carried on and needed transportation. It was because of this that Mildred and I came to know him. He had come on his own the first few times, but then found it difficult to continue unless he was picked up.

Iñor was a very quiet boy. He had very little to say except to express his desire to know God. At age nine he spoke more like a mature grownup. Perhaps this was because he was left to himself quite often. His father and mother both worked, and his brothers and sisters were older and had their own interests. Iñor had an alert mind, made good grades in school, and began to memorize Bible verses and learn the truths that they taught.

One of the boy's characteristics which we missionaries appreciated very much, was his thoughtfulness and consideration of others. It was very perturbing when a missionary or one of the brethren would be asked to go out of his way to pick up someone to take them to the services and then that person not go, giving an excuse which was not very reasonable nor convincing. Not so with Iñor. It was our responsibility to stop for Iñor to take him to Sunday School. We could always count on him to let us know if for some reason he could not go. He would telephone me on Saturday night or early Sunday morning. This occurred quite frequently during the first six months that we picked him up. Later, his attendance became more regular.

But, it was after one of the sessions of the Boys Brigade that David drove Iñor home and, sitting in the car, helped him pray and tell the Lord that he wanted Him to be his Savior.

It was after this that Iñor took an even stronger stand for the Lord. It is not known just how much he testified to his relatives about his new-found faith, but, having come to know his quiet manner, we suspect that his testimony was a quiet one, that he witnessed for the Lord through his changed life and firm stand in following Jesus. He must have, however, spoken with conviction to his father who was in the military. It was his father who had taken him away on many Sundays when on assignments in other cities. Now his father allowed him to stay at home so that he would not miss his Sunday School and other church activities.

In contrast to Beatrice's verbal witnessing by which many of her relatives were won to the Lord, we missionaries cannot remember ever hearing Iñor testify. Yet many in his family have come to the

Lord, his father and mother, brothers and sisters and in-laws, and grandparents on his mother's side. Then, through the saved relatives' witnessing, quite a number more came to Christ. All because one nine-year-old boy took Christ as his Savior and continued firm in his faith and constant in his attendance at Boys Brigade and Sunday School.

Five years after Iñor's conversion there were fourteen adults from that family who were saved baptized members of our Baptist church. Apparently the living water did not stop flowing even then. Quite a number of years later, Mildred and I were working in Puerto Rico. When we visited a fundamental Baptist church in Levittown, we were greeted by other members of the family who had been saved and had moved back to their homeland. In fact, a number of these were living in an urbanization outside the town and were supporting a Puerto Rican missionary as he attempted to start a fundamental Baptist church there.

One of Iñor's sisters was working as secretary in a large Christian day school established in the church in Levittown. At this writing she is secretary of the Baptist Bible College of Puerto Rico. Another sister serves as secretary in what is now our Christian Day School, Timothy Academy. Iñor's father, Don Ulysses, after retiring from the military, studied at Philadelphia College of Bible. After graduation he moved to Puerto Rico where, for a time, he was pastor of a Baptist church in a village in the western part of the central mountain range. He is now retired.

Iñor's older brother, Ulysses Jr. and his wife, are also active members of Evangelical Baptist Church, which the Lord established through our ministry in Philadelphia.

Chapter 35

A Tribute to a Faithful Prayer Warrior

The Miss Josephine Dodge Story

"Pray without ceasing." (I Thessalonians 5:17)

"Ed," Mildred called, as she was opening one of the letters that the mailman had just left at our home, "here is another letter from Miss Dodge."

"I suppose it is her usual short note?" I asked, calling in from the kitchenette where I was laying some new tile on the floor.

"Yes, and her usual donation of $2.00 for the work. And, of course, she asks the usual question... 'Has Heide received the Lord as her Savior yet?'" we both intoned in unison.

This story has its beginning while we were still personally active in migrant work. We dedicate it to Miss Josephine Dodge, in memory of this faithful prayer warrior.

********** ********** **********

"Brother Eduardo, when we go to the meeting for the migrants in Runnemede tonight, may I take my niece, Heide, with us."

I had been spending the morning visiting in the homes of some new families that had recently come to Philadelphia from Puerto Rico. Don Julio Morales had been truly saved a number of years before he immigrated to the States. He had been a great help during the first days in our work. He knew a lot of the families from the island paradise and would accompany me to help make the first contact. As I dropped him off at his apartment, he asked this favor.

"Oh, Julio, I do not know if it is wise to take a young girl with us to these meetings. You know how the men are," I remonstrated.

"But Pastor, my sister also wants to go tonight, and there will also be in the meeting those American women from that church who serve us refreshments. I think it would be good. Besides, my niece is new here and is getting bored staying in the house all day. She has not been able to get a job since her working papers have not come through. She is not saved and I would like for her to hear the Gospel from someone else besides me, her uncle."

"Well, okay," I agreed, "but we do not want to make a practice of taking just anyone. We want our men to go, and some of the women too, providing they can sing or give a word of testimony. We do not want to fill the cars with people just going for the ride."

"I agree, Pastor, but for Heide I have a great burden. I have long been praying for her."

There was an elderly lady in the church at Runnemede, a retired school teacher, who played the piano in Sunday School. She had come to me at the beginning of the first migrant meeting in that church and volunteered to play for the service. Mildred always played for those services, but she gave up her ministry of music in those meetings so that a member of the local church would have the experience of serving in this way.

Miss Josephine Dodge could not understand a word of Spanish, but she was such a nice person and had such a winning smile that the migrant workers took a particular liking to her. She was just a tiny lady but very vivacious in spite of her seventy plus years. She was especially attracted to Heide and tried to make friends with her as best she could. When she understood that Heide was not saved, she covenanted with the Lord to pray for her until she would come to the Savior.

Heide had no particular interest in the Gospel and the meeting was very boring for her. She only went once or twice again, but Miss Dodge would always ask for her, "Is Heide saved yet?" Upon hearing the negative answer, she would smile and assure us that she would not give up praying for Heide and that some day the girl would come to the Lord.

During that summer season, Miss Dodge began to place two one dollar bills in my hand as I bid her good night. Knowing that Miss Dodge was living on a small pension, I did not want to take her gift, but she insisted that she wanted to have a part at least in helping to pay for the gas used in coming down from Philadelphia. When fall came and most of the men went back to Puerto Rico, the meetings were suspended. Miss Dodge began to mail her two dollar donation to us each month, "to help pay for your gas," she would write. And always a short note, questioning... "Is Heide saved yet? I am still praying for her."

This continued for eight years and I would write to Miss Dodge to thank her for the gift and tell her that we were sorry to say, "No, Heide is not yet saved."

Then one day, Mildred opened the envelope from Runnemede, and read aloud, "Dear Rev. and Mrs. Schwartz, I am sorry to tell you that my sister Josephine went to be with the Lord last week. In going through her things, I found this note written to you along with two dollars. Please find same enclosed. We will miss my sister very much, she always gave comfort to the rest of us when we did not feel so well, although she herself was suffering too. Please pray for me. Yours in Christ."

The envelope also contained the usual note received monthly from Miss Dodge. She had written it in anticipation of mailing it, probably in the next day or two. Mildred and I were sorry to hear of her homegoing but happy to know that Miss Josephine was now with the Lord. We were saddened also to think that after eight years of praying, she went to heaven without realizing the answer to her faithful prayer for the young Puerto Rican girl.

But the story does not end there. Two weeks after we received our last letter from Miss Josephine Dodge, evangelistic services were held in our church in Philadelphia. Brother Mike Casillas, a student from Bob Jones University, was doing the preaching. Uncle Julio was able to get Heide to attend. Of course, he had never ceased to speak to her about the Lord and her need for salvation. When the invitation was given, Heide was one of those who went forward to make public profession of faith in the Lord Jesus and accept Him as her Savior. Her husband had received Christ as his Savior just a few days before.

There was much rejoicing, of course, in the souls that were saved during that evangelistic campaign, but especially for Heide. There was a kind of sadness in our thinking too. "If only Miss Dodge had lived two weeks longer we could have written to tell her that her prayers for Heide were finally answered."

"What a shame!" commented Mildred as she expressed our thoughts in words. "If only Miss Dodge had not died, she would now know that Heide is saved."

"Yes, it is a shame," I agreed.

A few moments of thoughtful silence passed, then: "But, Ed, did not the Lord say...."

"I know exactly what you are going to say, I am thinking the same thing."

Together, we quoted the words of Jesus from Luke 15:10: "...there is joy in the presence of the angels of God over one sinner that repenteth."

Then Mildred questioned, "Miss Dodge is with the Lord, so then, would not Jesus tell her that Heide, the one for whom she prayed so long, was now saved?"

"I believe He would," I agreed. "The angels are rejoicing, so why would He keep Miss Dodge from knowing and rejoicing too? I can't give you chapter and verse, but, yes, I believe you are right. Miss Dodge must be as happy as we are that Heide has finally accepted Christ as her own personal Savior."

Missionaries working on a foreign field or in the homeland, appreciate their faithful prayer partners who continue through the years to intercede for them and for the people with whom they are laboring. Souls are saved and victories won because of their prayers.

Miss Josephine Dodge is a perfect example of just such a prayer warrior. She "prayed without ceasing" (I Thessalonians 5:17) as the Apostle Paul exhorted, for she had faith in God and His promise that "in due season we shall reap, if we faint not" (Galatians 6:9b).

VII
Dominican Republic Ministry

Chapter 36

Robert and Lena Meyer
The Baptist Embassy, Santo Domingo

"Faithful is he that calleth you, who also will do it."
(I Thessalonians 5:24)

"...he which hath begun a good work in you will perform it...."
(Philippians 1:6)

"Well, Ed, what do you think of our mission work here in the capital of the Dominican Republic now that you have been in it for several months? Do you think that there are possibilities for some day getting a church established?"

"Do you want my honest opinion?" was my question to Bob Meyer's question.

"Yes, of course, but I hope that your opinion is not the same as that of my co-workers." Bob's expression changed from smiling to serious. He hoped that I had caught the same vision that he had for a ministry among the more affluent people in the city of Santo Domingo.

I thought to myself, "I do not want to say anything to dampen Bob's enthusiasm for his work, but I must be honest." After a brief pause, I said, "Frankly, if **I** were you, I would forget the whole idea. I know **you** feel that **God has called you** to minister here in Gazcue among the professional people, so what can I say, really? Who am I to deny that God has called you?"

"No, you can't," answered Bob. "But I would like some idea as to how others feel."

So I continued. "Some day you may succeed in establishing a church among these people, but I think that it will take a long, long time. Now there are also many poor people living nearby and I believe that if you were to work among them you could have a church started much sooner. True, everyone needs the Gospel, including the more affluent, but I think you would have a bigger response, and more quickly, from the poorer community."

"But, Ed, I feel sure that the Lord has called Lena and me to work here in Gazcue. These **up-and-outers** need to know the Lord also and no one ever tries to reach them."

"Now don't get me wrong, Bob. I say that if the Lord has really called you to work among this upper class people, **go for it**. I just know that it would not be for me. While you were away, we tried to hold on to those you had, but I am afraid that we made no progress.

"We did get some new children, but they are from the two urbanizations where Mildred held Bible clubs. Beulah was a great help to us in every phase of the work, especially in the DVBS. But, I am afraid, Bob, that I lost the high school young men. I just could not put up with their disrespect in the services. I hope and pray that you can win them back."

This conversation took place a few days after Bob and Lena Meyer returned from their short furlough. Mildred and I had responded to their invitation to substitute for them in the work which they were establishing among the upper class people of Santo Domingo.

We were free to do this, now that our Spanish church in Philadelphia had called its own pastor. We could have left them on their own a long time ago, but no one of our doctrinal position was available to take the pastorate. Then Fidias Echevarría, a young member of our church, felt called to the ministry after graduating from High School. In three years he graduated from seminary and came to help me in the church work.

Bob and Lena Meyer, Richard, Jeannie, Anita

During Fidias' second year with me, he was examined by a council of Baptist pastors, and with their recommendation, the church ordained him to the Gospel ministry and called him to be their pastor. Later that year, I performed his marriage to Georgina Morales, a beautiful and gifted young lady who had grown up in our church. Rev. Echevarría became pastor officially January 1, 1968. He has had a successful ministry there for now almost 28 years.

Mildred and I then felt called to offer ourselves to temporarily take the places of missionary families during the time of their furloughs. During the first year we served in Puerto Rico when Charles and Molly Cook took their furlough vacation in England. This second year found us in Santo Domingo, capital of the Dominican Republic.

We moved into the Meyer's home, a large and prominent dwelling on Bolivar Avenue in the section known as Gazcue. A very large room at the rear of the building, with an entrance from the side street, was used as a chapel for services. The front of the building, with its tall Corinthian columns and wide porch shaded by tall trees, made for a rather pretentious appearance and caused it to be facetiously called "The Baptist Embassy" because of the constant activity created by the home, church and MK (missionary kid) school located on the property.

Baptist Embassy, 105 Bolivar Avenue

The people with whom the Meyers were working were indeed an interesting population. All were not wealthy, indeed some were on a lower financial level. But all were considered "high society" because of their profession, or their family background. Religion was practiced routinely; by upbringing and custom, it had become an inseparable part of their lives and culture. Most women were devoted to the "Mother Church," but the men participated in religion mostly because it was the **politically correct** thing to do.

There must have been some opposition to the preaching of the Gospel, but we did not encounter any. Most of the people we met had an apathetic attitude, a sort of indifference. There was much misunderstanding as to the meaning of the Gospel. Some we met even reacted to our conversations about the Gospel as though it was an unimportant fringe tradition of Catholicism.

A Priest's Blessing

Bob and Lena Meyer already had a group of believers meeting with them. In the group was a retired Christian medical doctor, Dr. LaMarche, and his wife. Because he was a semi-invalid, he and his wife were brought to the services in the missionary's car when he was able to attend. His wife's maiden name, strange to say, was the same as the doctor's. She had been raised in the parish house by Padre LaMarche, supposedly her father. The doctor, when a student, had been befriended and aided by the priest. The priest did not seem at all offended when at some later date, the doctor and his wife embraced the Gospel; rather he gave them his blessing.

Victory and Assurance

In the group there was a man and his wife who were licensed insurance salespeople. They both attended the services regularly. Mrs. Cocco had a problem. She said that she believed in Christ, but could not get the positive assurance of her salvation. She thought that, because she could not give up the cigarette habit, she was still lost. We showed her assurance verses in the Bible, she finally got the victory over her doubts and later over her habit.

A Message of Hope

There was a young married lady who lived with her father and mother just across the avenue from the Mission Home. She visited the Meyers one day, hoping that perhaps they could help her resolve some of the spiritual problems she was having. The Meyers led Dolly to the Lord. Having more confidence in her father than in her mother, she told him what she had done and how she now had peace in her heart. Don Ricardo Molinari then confessed to his daughter that when he was a young man he too was Evangelical in his faith. He and his brother had come over to Santo Domingo from Puerto Rico and had become wealthy founding a very prosperous import-export business. He had forsaken his faith and married a very Catholic high-society lady. After Dolly's confession of faith, he began to accompany his daughter to the services and became reconciled with his Savior.

While Mildred and I were serving in the Meyer's absence, Mr. Molinari, suffered a severe heart attack, and went to be with the Lord. We had endeared ourselves to the family, praying with them and just being with them in the very room where the doctors worked to try to save Mr. Molinari's life. So, in spite of her devout Catholicism, Mrs. Molinari, at Dolly's insistence, gave permission to hold an Evangelical service during the viewing.

The service was held in the large reception hall of the spacious home an hour before the priest came. There were at least seventy of Mr. Molinari's former business associates, bankers, government people and friends and their wives present. They listened attentively to the "strange" service being held, a first for the majority. Dr. Balaguer, then President of the Republic, could not attend but sent his representative.

A few of the believers were there to sing a number of hymns. The portable organ was brought over from the Mission Home. Edith Weber played the organ, and she and Beulah Hager sang duets. Surprise was written on the faces of those people who had never before heard such songs of cheer and hope at a funeral. In my message I emphasized the fact, that although Mr. Molinari had not lived for the Lord for many years, his return to the true faith in later years proved that he was really saved and that his soul at that very moment was happy in the presence of his God.

At the close of the service, and just before the priest arrived to go through his ritual, a number of the men came to me, all with just about the same comment.

"I have never in all my life heard such a message of hope at a funeral. Our priest only talks about damnation in the fires of hell, and the need to purchase prayers for the dead to get them out of purgatory. But you have preached assurance of eternal salvation for our friend Ricardo Molinari, declaring with such confidence that right now he is in heaven with God." Many of the women present spoke similar words to Mildred and our co-workers, Beulah and Edith. Some even expressed a desire that they too could have such a "beautiful" faith.

In Santo Domingo there is a Catholic custom to hold a service for the departed dead one week after the burial and another service thirty days later. We missionaries took advantage of this custom, and planned memorial services for Mr. Molinari at the same time periods. Dolly sent invitations to all of their friends. Their culture demanded that everyone be present, for it would be a terrible breach of etiquette not to attend unless one had a very, very good excuse, written and sent to the family with a plea for forgiveness.

The services were held in the chapel. A clear Gospel message was preached and time alone will reveal the spiritual impression made upon those affluent people, some of whom for the first time in their lives sat through an Evangelical service.

Hatred Produces Poverty of Soul

Attending the regular Sunday morning service was a lady named Martha and her aged mother. Martha was a very sad person and at the same time very angry. While she was a professing believer in Christ, she was hindered in her spiritual life by the hatred she had for General Trujillo, the former dictator of the Dominican Republic. She just could not get the victory, resulting in an "up and down" kind of Christian life.

Martha's husband had been a civil engineer who had refused to falsify some documents which would have enabled the dictator to "legally" possess himself of some more public property. One day Martha's husband came home and excitedly told her that a friend had informed him that Trujillo was so angry that he had ordered his "execution." She hurriedly packed a small suitcase for him, while he gathered together some of his important documents to take with him into hiding until the dictator cooled off.

After a hurried kiss and an embrace, he flew out the door to run to the car that was waiting to carry him into seclusion. He got only to the curb when a car with several men in it screeched to a momentary stop. Shots rang out and Martha saw her beloved fall. Stunned for the moment, she remained paralyzed in the doorway of her home. As the car sped off, she ran to her husband's side. The briefcase had burst open and its documents were scattered upon the pavement. Her husband's body was sprawled upon them, and his blood, spurting from numerous bullet holes, was already staining the papers and the pavement. Martha kneeled, then sat beside him, raised his head to her lap, all the while speaking endearing words and calling his name. But one of the bullets had found his heart. He died almost instantly.

This had happened a number of years before Mildred and I arrived in Santo Domingo, but Martha was still holding great hatred in her heart in spite of the fact that the Dictator had long since been assassinated and her husband vicariously revenged. We visited

Martha from time to time to try to help her win victory over her feelings, showing her from the Scriptures that such hatred was only hurting her soul as well as grieving her friends and fellow believers as they saw her remain so long unhappy and spiritually defeated.

Martha appreciated our concern and always welcomed us into her home. When the Meyers returned and we were preparing to leave, Martha had us in her home for a meal. We had always admired the beautiful paintings which she had done. As we left her home she presented us with her painting of a scene at Boca Chica, a beach resort, where we missionaries went from time to time for an afternoon of relaxation. It hangs in the hallway of our home. Whenever we see it, we are reminded to pray for Martha, and to once again thank the Lord for the blessings we received in our short time in the Lord's service in Santo Domingo.

The High School Students

The high school students with whom Bob was working lived in the neighborhood. He held a meeting planned especially to attract such young men, usually on Saturday nights. Bob preached his heart out and tolerated many indignities from these young men in an effort to reach them for Christ. There were occasions when **even he** was compelled to close the meeting, only to have them hang around outside to torment him with their catcalls. On one occasion, at the close of a film Bob was showing, eggs were thrown inside the chapel. Once they twisted his eyeglasses when they tussled with him in an attempt to re-enter the building.

But Bob persisted in his attempt to reach these young high school students for Christ. I believe Bob must have the patience of a saint. After his return from furlough, Bob was again able to assemble a group of these young men for weekly meetings. Only eternity will reveal the results in many of their lives, but it is known that a few came to know Christ as Savior and one, in particular, pastored the church for awhile. He now lives in Miami, Florida, where he is serving the Lord by helping to plant a new Spanish-language church.

How good and wonderful it is when a believer, called to missionary service, knows for certain that the Lord has called him to a specific place and ministry. He can be sure that the Lord will also enable him for it. Bob and Lena Meyer were sure that the Lord led them to establish a church among the upper class people of Santo Domingo. They were as **confident** as the Apostle Paul was when he said, “Being confident of this very thing....” The Lord called them, and the Lord performed it, brought it to fruition.

Time has vindicated Bob and Lena and proved their calling. The Lord has blessed them for their faithfulness and obedience in following His leading even under adverse circumstances. There are now five churches of mostly upper class people established in Santo Domingo. Bob and Lena are at present serving as missionaries in Cuenca, Ecuador, where their ministry is again being blessed of the Lord.

Chapter 37

A Retired Italian General

Pietro Torres

"Fight the good fight of faith, lay hold on eternal life... endure hardness, as a good soldier of Jesus Christ."
(I Timothy 6:12; II Timothy 2:3)

During the six months we spent in Santo Domingo, we came to know and love Mitzi Torres, a very vivacious Spanish lady whose personality was described as "bubbly." Being such an avid reader, and anxious to learn as many Bible truths as possible, Mitzi literally "gobbled up" every piece of Christian literature we missionaries gave her. Almost every day Mitzi would phone to ask some question about doctrine or prophecy. Actually, we almost had to adjust our daily agenda so as to allow at least an hour a day for her call.

Mitzi greatly desired to be baptized, but her husband, Pietro Torres, would not hear of it. Bob and Lena Meyer tried to explain the Gospel truths to him, but he refused to listen. Sometimes he would forbid Mitzi to attend church services, then later, he would relent.

During our stay in Santo Domingo, Mitzi invited us to visit her of an evening. "Come by as if you were making a casual call," Mitzi suggested. "Such a visit is normal procedure, in fact, is expected of nice people who have recently come to live in our community. My husband is an austere man but correctly polite, and he must treat you courteously on your first visit."

Bob Meyer had, of course, alerted me to the situation, so Mildred and I made our first visit with some trepidation. However, we were pleasantly surprised to find Pietro Torres quite sociable. He greeted us politely, escorted us into the living room and invited us to be seated.

After some small talk, Pietro turned to his wife. "Mitzi, let us have our coffee in here."

Turning to Mildred and me, he remarked, "Surely you drink coffee. You must join me now as I have not had my usual after-dinner cup."

"Of course... We have spent many years in Venezuela and learned there how good coffee can be. In fact, if we had not cared for coffee, there would have been many times in the interior of Venezuela when we would not have had anything to drink."

Pietro's interest was immediately aroused. He and Mitzi had spent several years in Caracas, Venezuela's beautiful capital city and could not imagine a scarcity of drinking water.

"In Venezuela, eh," he remarked. "Ah, yes, their coffee is excellent. But, how is it that sometimes you would have had nothing but coffee to drink? We always found drinking water readily available. Besides, there are also the good wines and liquors. So who needs water?" This with a hearty "Ha... ha... *sí señor,*" and with the customary Italian smack of the pursed lips and the throwing of a kiss heavenward to show how much he savored his good wines and liquors.

"Yes, of course, but we lived in the interior, in the State of Bolivar, on the far side of the Orinoco River. We arrived there in 1941 when the roads were only wagon trails. We were located about six hundred miles interior from Caracas, in the gold mining town of El Callao."

Pietro's interested silence encouraged me to go on. "For about a year we lived in the town of Tumeremo, close to the border of what was then British Guiana. There our life was even more primitive as far as modern conveniences were concerned. We had no motorized transportation, so often, when we visited out in the country, we did so on foot. Walking under the hot sun with very few trees to shade us, we would get very tired and thirsty. Soon the water in our thermos bottles would be gone, and what little water there was out there in the semi-jungle would not be fit to drink. The folk we visited would offer us a cup of their very sweet, very black and very thick coffee. Oh, how good it tasted and how reviving it was."

That did it. Mr. Torres asked many questions, and I tried to answer them as well as I could. As a civil engineer, he was interested in anything even remotely related to his profession, like road building, bridges, commercial and residential buildings and mining. He wanted to know all about the gold mines as well as about the great deposits of iron ore. He wanted to know how the gold was extracted and refined. He wanted to know about the houses the missionaries lived in, and about the culture of the people in the jungles and on the plains.

I watched for opportunities to speak of the Lord and His Gospel, but none seemed to open up. I bided my time, silently praying that the Lord would open the door for some spiritual comment. Meanwhile, Mildred and Mitzi visited, the latter showing off her beautiful apartment and talking about things of mutual interest. They left us two men alone, while silently praying for me. Then, not wanting to overstay our welcome, I mentioned that we ought to take our leave, but Pietro insisted that we have some refreshments. Mitzi was already prepared, hoping that this would happen. She served us crackers and cheese, and more of the delicious *cafe con leche* with a flavor all its own, imitated but not equaled by the modern "cappuccino."

It wasn't until we missionaries were being escorted to the door that I had an opportunity to speak a word. Mr. Torres's expression then changed from a pleasant smile to a rather stern frown. But the smile came back on again, ignoring my comment, as he spoke.

"You must visit us again. I have many more things I would like to ask you. I too have had some unusual experiences, so maybe I will do some talking also."

He then turned to his wife. "Mitzi, invite our friends to come back again. I want them to enjoy with us one of your delicious dinners. You set the date. Any time is all right with me."

Mitzi could hardly contain herself. The next Sunday she told us, "It is a miracle for which I have long prayed. I have to pinch myself to see if I am dreaming that it is happening. *El viejo* [the old man, an endearing expression in Hispanic America] even said I could come to church every Sunday and maybe some Wednesday nights for Bible study, as well as the weekly afternoon ladies' meetings."

Very wisely, Mitzi did not invite us right away for a meal. She allowed several weeks to go by. Then one evening, Pietro asked her, "Eh, Mitzi, what about your missionary friends, don't they want to visit us again? Have you invited them as I said you should?"

"Oh, *cariño* [my dear], they certainly do want to come again, but, you know, they have many obligations, other people to visit and sick people to pray with." She wanted her husband to think it would be a special favor and even a sacrifice for missionaries to visit just to socialize.

"Ah, yes, I suppose you are right. But do not delay any longer. They must come soon again," insisted Pietro.

One day I remarked to Mildred, "What is it with Mr. Torres? How is it that we seem to have made a hit with him? It seems inexplicable, doesn't it? Maybe it has something to do with that personality chemistry the social psychiatrists talk so much about."

"Be that as it may," Mildred commented, "I think the Lord is answering our prayers, and we had better take advantage of this strange and unexpected friendliness Don Pietro is showing."

For our second visit, Mitzi indeed prepared a banquet. Pietro was jovial and almost servile as he passed the different platters of food, urging us to fill our plates. Really, we needed no second invitation, being encouraged also by the delightful aroma coming from the platters. The food indeed was "out of this world," I complemented, to the delight of both Mitzi and Pietro. After the meal, came the delicious coffee, served on the balcony.

Then there was again the animated conversation between us as we exchanged experiences. This time Pietro did most of the talking. He wanted to tell of his life as a major general in the engineer corps of the Italian Army during World War II. He showed me a newspaper clipping, a picture of himself and other officers standing with Mussolini in the center. After the war, he had traveled to other countries, including Venezuela. He met the vivacious Spanish lady who became his wife. They seemed to be quite compatible, though Mitzi was some years younger than Pietro. After their marriage, they settled in Santo Domingo where Mr. Torres was now working as a civil engineer.

During this second visit, I did have several opportunities to speak of spiritual things. The Lord seemed to give perfect leads in the midst of our verbal exchange. Each time this occurred, however, Don Pietro became silent. Watching his facial expressions, I could see nothing to indicate resistance to what I said, nor did I detect any interest, nothing except a polite patient waiting on the part of this old general. During the slightest pause, he would quickly change the subject by relating an experience of his own or by asking me a question about secular matters.

So the evening moved on until the time came for some last refreshment and a polite good night. I felt that I had made some progress, but did not want to overdo it and chase the general away. During our six months' stay in Santo Domingo, Mildred and I visited the Torres two other times. Each time, Pietro listened a little bit more attentively as I explained the Gospel. The man was still a long way from considering the claims of Christ upon his soul, but at least he was listening. Once he even held the Bible in his hand and followed along as I read.

Then Bob and Lena Meyer returned to the field, and Mildred and I made our plans to take up another ministry. Before we left the Dominican Republic, there was a farewell service for us. As the good-byes were said, Mitzi thanked us for having "sort of neutralized" her husband's distaste for the evangelical faith, and begged us not to forget to pray for her and Pietro. We assured her that it was the Lord who was at work in his heart.

There must have been a breakthrough that only the Lord knew about. During the next couple of years, Pietro became more tolerant and gave Mitzi freedom to attend all of the services of the Baptist church. The time finally came when he allowed her to be baptized. Not only that, but he attended the baptismal service and, as time went on, other meetings. Mitzi was overjoyed and so encouraged that she began to believe that some day Pietro would also be saved.

Six years went by and Mildred and I were back on our beloved field of Venezuela. Since our boys were both grown up, married and on their own, we did not have to plan our furloughs around the school year. We were permitted to take short furloughs of a few months every two years. In this way the believers on the field would not be left alone for the usual furlough year and there would be better continuity to the work.

During our trips home to the U.S., going and coming, we were invited to stop off in Puerto Rico or the Dominican Republic to hold evangelistic campaigns. Easter week in 1975 found us once again with Bob and Lena Meyer in Santo Domingo. The Meyer's work had made considerable progress. I was to preach in Gazcue from Wednesday through Sunday.

For the few days before the mini-campaign, Bob and I visited a number of professional men to give them a word of testimony and to invite them to the services. One of those men was Pietro Torres who greeted us very cordially. Don Pietro was very busy trying to complete some architectural drawings for a construction firm about to build a large office and apartment complex, but he sat and listened to our plans for the special meetings.

"Surely you will take time off on *Viernes Santo* [Holy Friday] afternoon," I suggested, hoping to appeal to his early religious background. It will be a good time to bring Mitzi to the service in memory of the crucifixion of our Lord. Not only will you have a little rest from your important work, but I am sure that you will be blessed in your heart and soul."

Mr. Torres began to protest. He had to meet a deadline. But I did not want to give him a chance to think up any more excuses, so I interrupted, "Remember, Don Pietro, the many pleasant conversations we had together in your home. You became almost interested in the Gospel story and the claims of Christ upon your eternal soul. Now you must come to hear me preach. I will consider it a great honor to have the former General Pietro Torres in my audience."

I continued to speak rapidly without a break. I knew from our previous conversations that the old general was proud of his service in the Italian army. So I began to emphasize the military aspects of the true Christian faith.

I made quick reference to several verses in the New Testament that speak of the Christian warfare, how the Apostle Paul exhorted Timothy to "war a good warfare" and to "fight the good fight of faith," and that he should endure hardship as "a good soldier of Jesus Christ," and to remember that it was Jesus who had "chosen him to be a soldier." I also showed him where the Bible speaks of the "weapons of our warfare."

It seems to be part of the Italian culture as well as the Hispanic that the men leave religious matters up to their women. There are some exceptions, but I wanted Mr. Torres to realize that men also are spiritually responsible, so I spoke of the many soldiers whose conversions are related in the Bible: the military officer who testified before the cross of Christ, saying "Truly this was the Son of God": Cornelius, a centurion of the Italian band, recorded in Acts 10, and then the jailor of Philippi, Acts 16.

The expression on Mr. Torres' face indicated interest. The idea that Christians were really soldiers engaged in a spiritual battle was all new to him. I explained how that he, Pietro Torres, needed more than anything else in this world to surrender to Christ by accepting Him as Savior. Christ would then make him a soldier in His army.

"The Christian life is not easy. It is a warfare against Satan and his army. You need Christ to be your Commander, and Christ wants you to be one of His generals. This is a commission, not for weaklings, but for strong men who are willing to sacrifice all and even to lay down their lives, if necessary... Now, my friend, think about these things, please."

We stood up to take our leave. I extended my hand to the old general. "Will you promise to come to at least one of my services... for friendship's sake?"

Mr. Torres was silent for a moment. Then, with a serious expression on his face, he took my hand with a strong bone-crushing grip, glanced at the pile of papers on his desk and at the drawings on the board, and then said to me, "I cannot promise, but I will try."

As Bob drove us away in his car, we were silent for a time, each with our thoughts about the general and his half-hearted promise "to try." I was silently praying, and I knew that Bob was too, that the man would come to one of the services. Finally, "What do you think, Bob? Will he, or will he not? Did he brush us off, or will he honestly try to come to a service?"

"Only the Lord knows, Ed. We'll have to pray harder during the next few days, not only for him, but for all the others with whom we have made contact."

The services on Wednesday and Thursday nights went well. The audience was small, mostly believers in whom the spirit of believing prayer was evident. The Good Friday afternoon service would be well-attended for, to the Hispanic American, that is the most important religious day of the year. Even people who show absolutely no interest in spiritual matters, become "religious" on that day. This interest may even last through Easter Sunday.

On Friday afternoon, there was very good attendance, Mitzi was there, but Pietro Torres was not. On Saturday night, he did come. It was plain that at first he felt very uncomfortable. He followed the words in the hymn book as the believers sang, and then listened attentively to the sermon. Mitzi was overjoyed that he had consented to accompany her. When we missionaries welcomed him, he was cordially polite and even promised to return the next morning.

On resurrection morning, the crowd was even larger and filled the chapel from wall to wall. All the believers were present, of course, seated with a few of their interested friends. Pietro Torres was there right up front seated beside his wife Mitzi.

I felt great liberty in preaching. Then, remembering how Mr. Torres had once remarked about the difficulty of "believing without seeing," I pointed out that so many times we look at things but do not really see them. I referred to the Apostle John, who, when he had kneeled down to look into the empty tomb, did not really see what he was looking at, that is, he did not understand the meaning of what he saw.

"Just so," I explained, "many look at the exterior ceremonies of the Christian religion, the rites of the church, but do not understand the true meaning of the Christian faith. They know about Calvary and the resurrection of Christ, but do not comprehend what it really means.

"Then John entered the tomb and saw with his understanding. He saw the burial wrappings, still intact but flattened because there was now no body inside. He saw the head cloth, folded and lying to one side. John, himself, testified that it was when he looked this time, he understood, and understanding, he believed. He believed then that Jesus had risen from the dead as He had promised. What he saw was indisputable proof that Jesus was indeed the Son of God, and that His finished work on the cross was sufficient to save all who believe."

The message finished, I had everyone bow their heads. Before finishing my prayer, I gave an invitation to all who wished to accept Christ as personal Savior to indicate it by raising a hand. Several hands immediately were raised, among them was Pietro Torres's.

For the moment I was overcome. My eyes filled with tears of gladness and thanksgiving to the Lord. I could only utter an emotional, "Praise the Lord!" Then I choked up.

Bob Meyer stood up to continue the invitation. All told, there were eleven souls that responded, eleven more who had entered the Kingdom of our Lord Jesus Christ. There was great rejoicing that morning among the believers. Mitzi's heart was filled to overflowing with joy and thanksgiving that her Lord had seen fit to save her husband. Her Pietro was born again! They were not only united as husband and wife, but were now brother and sister, united in Christ.

Later, Pietro was baptized and became a member of the Baptist Church of Gazcue. When they moved to another part of the city, they became members of the church founded by Jay and Jean Nauta. After about ten years of faithful testimony, the Lord called Don Pietro home. Mitzi misses him very much, but continues to serve the Lord with all her heart and strength.

Pietro Torres and Mitzi

VIII
Venezuela Ministry - Part 3

Chapter 38

Mildred and Her Ministry to the Children

"...Jesus... said..., Suffer the little children to come unto me, and forbid them not; for of such is the kingdom of God." (Mark 10:14)

One year after our service in Santo Domingo, Mildred and I were back in Venezuela on special assignment. There was a shortage of missionaries there, and we were to spend our time visiting a number of the churches without pastors. We traveled every weekend, and we often visited two different churches. On week nights we visited other churches, where I would teach Bible classes to the adults and young people, while Mildred was having classes for the children. The deacons would often ask us to counsel with them about church problems.

Inner-city children visit country estate

All through our missionary years, Mildred has had one very strong anxiety, an eager desire, if you will. She expressed it with the words, "We have to win the little children to the Lord before sin and a wicked life can get a hold on them." In contrast to her love for the children was her almost violent feeling toward anything or anybody who would endanger or harm one of "these little ones," a feeling of repugnance and contempt.

In the tropics there is a little beetle that burrows into the ground near the trunk of small trees to lay its eggs. When hatched, the larvae eat the tiny tendrils which send the food from the ground into the plant.

We had a young hybrid lime tree in our patio that had been growing nicely and had already given us two small harvests of large juicy limes. One day, Mildred and I noticed how the leaves were turning yellow. We gave it plant food and cultivated the area around it, but the leaves continued to turn yellow and some branches became dry and brittle.

"Something must be eating at the roots," I suggested to Mildred. "I'm going to dig down around the trunk to see if I can discover what." So with a small garden trowel, I began to carefully clear away the dirt near a small hole in the ground. I had dug only a few inches when I found three dried up beetles and then seven very much alive grub worms. They had eaten away all of the tiny tendrils from the main roots and it was impossible to save our lime tree.

When Mildred saw the grub worms and what they had done, she exclaimed, "Such little beetles, but look what their worms have done to my baby lime tree."

"Yes, what a shame. They would not have affected an older and larger tree for its roots would be deeper in the earth and spread out over a larger area. If we had only known sooner, we might have been able to save our little tree."

Mildred stamped her foot in anger. "That's just like the old devil and sin. It begins like a little beetle, lays its eggs of sin and then multiplies until it destroys everything. But the worst of it is, the old devil likes to get the little ones. And that is why I will never stop working with the children. Maybe some will get saved before sin and a wicked life can get a hold on them."

Ladies' Missionary Society, Philadelphia Church

While Mildred has always been dedicated to a ministry for children, in her missionary work, she also had to take supervision of women's societies, help in the organization of Sunday Schools, take part in visitation programs, and the like. But she was always extremely happy, and competent as well, when she was holding children's neighborhood Bible clubs, and teaching the younger children in Sunday School and in junior church services.

Mildred observed that whenever a general invitation was given to accept Jesus as Savior, though they were told to keep their heads bowed and their eyes closed, they would peep and then raise their hands just because another child raised his. This is why she would just invite the children to talk to her privately if they wanted to take Jesus into their heart.

Mildred never urged the children, but waited for the children to respond on their own accord. When they did respond, it was more likely be the work of the Holy Spirit. The change in their lives was proof that they were truly saved. There are whole families in our churches today as a result of the testimony of a child saved in one of Mildred's Bible clubs.

But, there were some children saved in her ministry about whom she knew nothing until years later. This chapter, and the following two, tell stories about three such children.

The Story of Cristobal of Tumeremo

This story begins near the close of our second term in Venezuela. Mildred and I, along with our fellow missionaries, were attending a quarterly business meeting of our field. We held these meetings in different towns so that the believers would benefit from the mini Bible conference we would hold in the evening in the local church. This time we were in Tumeremo where we first served as missionaries.

Since it was school vacation time, Mildred and Ruth Hege held a Bible club each morning. One of the boys who attended was six-year-old Cristobal. He was a very intelligent boy and learned all the verses that were taught. From the nice clothes he wore, it was evident that he came from a more affluent family. On the very first day he expressed a desire to invite Jesus into his heart, so Mildred took him aside to show him more verses that would give him assurance of salvation. He was awfully young and she wondered. "But then... the Lord is able."

On Friday morning Cristobal did not attend. He had learned all the verses from memory and he was to get a prize on that day. Maria, one of the older girls, said that Cristobal told her that his father had come home from a business trip and forbade him to attend.

That afternoon Mildred and Ruth went for a stroll. They saw Cristobal sitting on a log in front of a store. "Cristobal, we missed you this morning. What happened?"

Cristobal told them what they knew already. He said that his mother was pleased when he told her that he had let Jesus come into his heart, but his father was furious and said he must not go to the club anymore. Cristobal had argued with his father, "I have to go. The teacher has written my name in her book and I will get a prize for being there every day."

"No, you don't have to go anywhere," shouted his father. "And if you see that teacher again, you tell her that she has to rub your name out of that book. You don't belong to any religion except that of our 'Mother' and her church."

Cristobal knew that he had to obey. His father was a hard man who demanded blind obedience from everyone in the family, including his wife. So it was that Cristobal told Mildred that she had to rub his name out of the book. Mildred sat down on the log alongside of Cristobal, opened her Bible and quietly spoke to him.

"Cristobal, you are just a little boy and you have to obey your father. But, tell me, Cristobal, when you prayed and asked Jesus to come into your heart, did you really mean it?"

"Yes, I did... I did, *Señora* Mildred. I meant it with all my heart."

"Well then, did He come in?"

"I... I think so... I feel like He did."

"Cristobal, do you remember that verse we learned? How Jesus said, 'Behold, I stand at the door, and knock...'" She showed him the verse in Revelation 3:20.

"Yes, I remember," and Cristobal continued... "if any man hear my voice, and open the door, I will come in to him." That was the part he had learned.

"Now, Cristobal, Jesus would not tell a lie, would He?

"No, *Señora*, God cannot tell a lie," answered Cristobal as he raised his eyes to meet Mildred's and his expression assured her that he understood.

"Well, then, Jesus is in your heart and nobody can take Him away, ever. Will you remember that always, little one?"

"I will, *Señora*, I will."

"Another thing I want you to remember, Cristobal... see what it says here in Revelation 21:27... The Apostle John, who wrote this book, is talking about heaven, where God lives and He says that whoever has his name written in the Lamb's book of life will go to heaven some day to be with God. Now Cristobal, when you asked Jesus to come into your heart, He did and you are saved. When you did that, Cristobal, God wrote your name down in His book that is called the Lamb's book of life. Remember that you learned that Jesus is the Lamb of God.

"Now, Cristobal, I have to rub your name out of my Bible club book because your father says that I must. But, remember, your name is written in God's book of life and nobody can ever rub it out of that book. Will you always remember that?"

"Yes, I will, *Señora* Mildred, I will always remember."

"Cristobal... Cristobal... " A lady's voice was heard calling from down the street.

"It's mamá, *Señora*. I have to go now."

"Good-bye, Cristobal. Remember, you have Jesus in your heart."

"I'll remember. Good-bye, *Señora* Mildred."

A few months later, when we were in Tumeremo again, Mildred made inquiries about Cristobal of the children who had attended that Bible club. She learned that, because of changes in his business, Cristobal's father had moved his family to Caracas.

********** ********** **********

Twenty years later, we were back in Venezuela on that special assignment. Early one evening, a street meeting was held in the Bella Vista area of San Félix, where our missionaries wanted to plant a church. The believers were gathered in a semicircle in front of the acreage that the government had allocated to our Mission, expecting that on it we would build a chapel and a day school. We were singing a number of hymns, interspersed with testimonies.

A young man, probably in his early twenties, came from in back of the group and stood beside Mildred and me. Supposing him to be one of the young people of the church, Mildred nodded to him and offered to share her hymn book. The young man smiled as he took hold of one corner of the book. But it was obvious that he did not know either the words or the music. The hymn ended, and one of the men stepped forward and began to give a word of testimony.

Then the young man whispered to Mildred. "You will not remember me, *Señora*. I was too little the last time you saw me. But I remember you, *Señora* Mildred."

"No, I can't place you. Should I be able to?" Mildred whispered back.

"No, not really, it has been too long a time and since we last met I have become a man."

"Well then, who are you?" Mildred asked.

"I am Cristobal. I lived in Tumeremo when I was a boy."

Mildred's memory bank began to function, stimulated by the words "Cristobal of Tumeremo," and she remembered.

"CRISTOBAL... CRISTOBAL..." Mildred almost shouted, as I cautioned with a "Shush." But everybody had heard and turned to look.

Whispering again, "Well, I declare! I never expected to see you again this side of heaven, and I always prayed that I would see you there."

Smiling broadly, Cristobal responded, "That's right, *Señora*. I have never forgotten you nor the Bible club."

"Nor I, you, Cristobal, I have often prayed that some day we might meet again. And here it has happened. I'm so glad that you recognized me and that you remembered. But, Cristobal, do you remember anything else?"

Again smiling broadly, Cristobal assured her, "I sure do, *Señora*. My name is written in the Lamb's book of life. I will never forget that. I still have the New Testament you gave me, it is in my suitcase."

Mildred wanted to take the young man aside to continue the conversation. She wanted to know so many things: what had he been doing all those years, where did he live, did he go to church somewhere? But, at that moment, a car stopped on the other side of the street. He raised his hand and waved to the driver, another young man like himself.

"I have to go, *Señora*. I have been on spring break from college in Maracay and that is my friend, also a student. We plan to spend the night in Ciudad Bolivar and then drive on to Caracas and Maracay tomorrow. Classes begin soon."

Cristobal wanted to say more, but his friend was getting impatient and beeped the car's horn twice. Then with a gentle hug and a kiss on Mildred's cheek, Cristobal was gone.

"Did you hear that, Ed?" she whispered, as one of the group was playing a special number on his trumpet.

"I sure did, that is, most of it. Praise the Lord, your Cristobal is apparently a saved person... It's almost my turn now to preach, so we'll talk later."

This term in Venezuela was bringing to Mildred and me many blessings for which we continue to thank and praise the Lord. It was a joy just to have fellowship once again with many of our children in the Lord. As we served in the different churches, every now and again we would meet someone we did not recognize but who would tell us that he or she had first heard the message of salvation in Jesus Christ, and in Him alone, in one of Mildred's Bible clubs, in one of my sermons, or through reading a Gospel tract which I had handed out. The seed planted, sooner or later, sprouted and brought forth fruit to the glory of God.

Chapter 39

The Story of Jesús "Chuíto" Manuel

"...Behold, a sower went forth to sow; and when he sowed, some seeds fell... into good ground, and brought forth fruit...." (Matthew 13:3-8)

We routinely visited our churches for about a year, until a missionary couple, Don and Betty Girton, had to return to the States unexpectedly because of sickness. They had been working in the church-planting ministry that had been started by Steve and Martha Green in Bella Vista, a new urbanization of the rapidly expanding city of San Félix. We were asked to take over this work. As already mentioned, the government had given our Mission a fine piece of property on which we were to build a church and an educational building. A small cottage had been built on the property, but if we did not show more progress, the government would take back the land. When we took over the work, there was also a small portable office building, donated by the Bethlehem Steel Company, in which we held services.

Bella Vista Mission
Portable shack donated by steel company

One Sunday morning, we arrived at the property a little early to set up things for Sunday School. Mildred and I were carrying a small organ to the church from a house across the street where it was stored when no service was being held. No one was living on the mission property at the time. As we crossed the street, a pickup truck slowed down to let us pass. The truck then started up again, but immediately skidded to a stop as the driver jammed on the brakes.

"Doña Mildred! Don Eduardo!" the driver shouted as he jumped from his truck.

We set the organ down in the entrance of the church and turned to face the man hurrying toward us. I judged him to be in his late 30's, or maybe even 40. He wore a broad smile.

"You are Doña Mildred, right? I would know you anywhere... and you are Pastor Eduardo," he said, as he took my hand and began to shake it. Then reaching for Mildred's hand, he drew it to his lips and kissed it.

"But, who are YOU, my friend?" I asked. "You have named us rightly, but I can't place you. Can you, Mildred?"

The man replied, "Of course not, it is now so many years... oh, how many? I was just a barefoot boy. It has to be thirty years ago in El Callao. I am Jesús Manuel, *señores*, but you could not possibly remember my name either. And, *señores*, I am not just a friend, I am now your brother in Christ, and have been for fifteen years."

Mildred slowly repeated his name, "Jesús Manuel," "No, I do not remember that name."

Addressing Mildred, he explained, "No, you cannot remember, because everybody called me 'Chuíto,' that's a nickname for Jesús. But anyhow, you maybe can't remember me because I did not go to the Bible club you had in your home very often, hardly at all. I lived down that little side alley, alongside the house of Doña Collette. I used to come by your house to play with some of the other boys and your son Eddie when he would bring out some of those box games from the United States, mostly in the afternoon when he had finished his lessons for the day.

"Sometimes when you had the Bible club I came by with my friend Joey. When we saw the other kids we did not want to stay, but you would grab us and make us sit down on the floor and listen to the story. We liked the pictures you made up on that board. We liked the cookies and Kool-aid you served. I would hide my cookie in my shirt and pretend I didn't get any so you would give me another. Ha...Ha.

You probably thought I was a lost cause, but you cannot know how those stories and the lessons impressed me... By the way, how is Eddie, your son?"

"Oh, Ed is fine, he is now a major in the U.S. Air Force," I informed the man. "But, Chuíto... Chuíto... I don't remember that name either."

"No matter, Don Eduardo and Doña Mildred... what's in a name? After all, I have a new name now, and it is written down in heaven... hallelujah! I am now a child of God through faith in my Lord and Savior, Jesus Christ. Amen!"

"Well, yes... praise the Lord," I agreed. "Tell us how it happened, how you got saved."

Still smiling broadly, Chuíto began. "After you folk moved up on the El Perú road, I didn't see you very often. I saw Eddie quite a lot in the market when he would come down into town early in the morning to buy meat. But I always remembered the Bible stories, and the one thing you always mentioned, Doña Mildred."

"What was that?," Mildred asked with renewed interest.

"You always said that for me to go to heaven, I would have to let Jesus come into my heart. I don't remember much else besides the Bible history stories... Anyhow, the years went by and I managed to get through primary school. Then a friend of the family in San Félix took me into his machine shop as an apprentice. Now, after almost twenty-five years, I have my own shop out in Unare on the other side of Puerto Ordaz (twin city with San Félix across the Caroní River). That is my pickup," he said, as he pointed to the large, heavy, full-ton pickup truck.

"Then I got married. We have four children, three boys and a little *señorita*. One day my wife told me about a preacher who was opening a small mission in our *barrio*. The invitation gave the hours of service and had a message on the back. What hit me was a sentence that said that Jesus was knocking at my heart's door and wanted to come in to save me, and if I wanted to get to heaven some day I had to accept Him as my Savior. My memory came alive and took me back to my childhood in El Callao. I remembered the Bible club and what you always said.

"For some time I am thinking... what am I doing? It is work... work... work. Is that all there is to life? Is there nothing more? Maybe there is a better life hereafter, no sickness, no badness like here on earth. It seemed like God was already speaking to me.

Anyhow, we went to the meetings and the Lord spoke to both of us. At the invitation, my wife and I went forward. That was fifteen years ago and I have never regretted receiving Jesus Christ as my Savior."

"This is great news." Mildred exclaimed, "Chuíto and his wife got saved together, just like we did, Ed... Well, praise the Lord! You are saved, and after all these years... But how did you recognize Ed and me as you drove by?"

"Well, actually, I was looking for you. About a month ago I was talking to Esteban John... He's an El Callao boy... remember him?"

"Do we ever! He's a deacon in our Baptist church in Puerto Ordaz."

"Yes, of course. Well, we were talking about our boyhood days in El Callao. I asked about you folk. He told me that you had come back to Venezuela a couple of years ago and were starting a church in Bella Vista. I wanted to come by and see you, but I never got over on this side of the river until today. I had to bring something over to one of my wife's relatives who lives down by the ferry. On my way home, I came up this street hoping to see you.

By this time, the people were gathering and it was time to start Sunday School.

"Can you stay for the meeting?" I asked.

"I'd like to, but I have to pick up my family. We'll be late for our own Sunday School, but I'll be there in time to teach the men's class. Anyhow, I have wanted to tell you about the part you had in my final conversion. I never could get those Bible stories out of my mind."

With hugs for me and Mildred and a little kiss on her cheek, Chuíto jumped up into the cab of his pickup, revved up the motor, and, with a wave of his hand, sped down the road.

"How wonderful! What a blessing! Oh, how I thank God for these little bits of news the Lord has sent us. Sometimes I am not sure when the children come to me and say they want to accept Christ as their Savior. Then here comes one who only came once in a while to Bible club. To hear his testimony encourages my heart to keep on with the children's ministry."

"Yes," I agreed, "we need this encouragement, especially when the work gets heavy and we are not seeing immediate results."

Chapter 40

The Story of Rosa Pagán

"But he that received seed into the good ground is he that heareth the word, and understandeth it, which also beareth fruit...." (Matthew 13:23)

Mildred and I continued to work in Bella Vista and before long there was a breakthrough, souls were saved and grew in the Lord. One Sunday afternoon, I had the honor of baptizing twenty believers in the Caroní River, under the shadow of the bridge connecting old San Félix with the new city of Puerto Ordaz. Then a duly constituted Baptist church was organized, and named *La Peña de Horeb* [The Rock of Horeb], their theme song was a chorus by the same name.

By this time, we had outgrown our portable office meeting place, so we made plans to build a church auditorium to seat at least two hundred. We had faith to believe that we would at least win some of the thousands that were moving into the area.

At this time, Larry and Pat Groat, with their two children, joined us, taking up residence in the little home on the Mission property, and gradually adding more rooms. It took months to work the plans for the church through the various departments of the city government and obtain the building permits. When the permits came through, the building program began in earnest.

The first thing Larry and I did was move the little meeting hall to a cement slab that had been poured in the area where the main auditorium would be and we enlarged the hall to twice its size. Eventually this would be used for Sunday School rooms.

Ground breaking ceremony

Then Larry took over the supervision of the major part of the construction, doing a lot of the hard labor himself, as he worked with the contractor, Mr. Lira, a believer from a sister church. Later, Larry became missionary-pastor of the church, and Mildred and I were free to return to those pastorless churches.

But it was on a Sunday morning while we were still working with the Bella Vista church and holding services in the enlarged office building, that the third incident occurred about which we want to tell you. Sunday School had been dismissed and during the short intermission period, a lady who never had attended before came in with Eunice, one of the young girls in our youth group. Eunice lived with an aunt in San Félix so she could attend high school. The little town, El Arrozal, where the family lived, had schooling only through junior high.

Eunice and the new lady visitor walked toward Mildred. "Doña Mildred, I would like you to meet my mother." As is the custom, they touched hands, and each repeated her own name. The lady was smiling as she repeated her name, "I am Rosa Pagán."

To Mildred's surprise, Rosa Pagán continued: "Doña Mildred, I am so glad to see you again. I would know you anywhere, you haven't changed a bit."

"Well, thank you. I am very pleased to meet you too. But you say 'again'. Do you mean that we have known each other before?"

"Yes, indeed we have. I was a little girl in your Bible club many years ago up in El Chile, up the mountain beyond El Perú."

"Oh, my, that was a long time ago, more than 20 years—24 or 25 years, in fact."

"That is right," agreed Rosa, "A long time ago." And then Mildred heard the same words again which always thrilled and blessed her heart.

"But I never forgot those Bible lessons with the pictures you made right before our eyes, with those pretty backgrounds of scenery and the figures of people. It was so fascinating to see the pictures grow. It helped us so much to understand the stories."

"Well, Rosa, and did you receive Christ as your Savior in the class? I must confess that I do not remember."

"No, I didn't. But I am a believer now, and I believe that it is because of the influence that those classes had upon me."

"Tell me how it happened, please."

"Well, I grew up in El Chile and married. I had four children, all girls. Then the work at the gold mines almost stopped and my husband decided to move to El Arrozal, the little village near the El Pao iron mines. Having worked as an auto mechanic at the gold mines, he got work right away in El Pao.

"There was a man living in El Arrozal, who also had moved there from El Callao, his name was Ricardo Laptiste. He and the missionaries from San Félix, I think their names were James and Darlene Russell, were starting a church in El Arrozal. They held Bible clubs for the children and Eunice here, my oldest, asked permission to attend. At first, I said 'no,' but then I remembered how I had enjoyed those Bible club meetings up there in El Chile, so I gave permission. Eunice and the three other girls attended regularly.

Ricardo Laptiste,
The El Arrozal church he built

"About that time, my husband left me for a younger woman and went to El Tigre in the oil fields. Thank goodness we had a little farm and the girls helped me keep it clean and cultivated. They told Ricardo about our plight, and he rallied the believers of the church to help us. I started to attend the services and as I listened to the messages my memory brought to mind again those Bible stories. It wasn't long before I knew that I needed the Savior and Eunice and I accepted Christ in the same service. What a blessing it has been to know the Lord, and I want to thank you for giving me the first lessons about God and His Son Jesus Christ."

"My, how wonderful it is to know how God works, and we praise the Lord with you. What are you doing down here in San Félix?"

"Well, I came down to arrange with my sister to take care of my other girls and to enroll them in school here. I am selling the little farm and the money will keep us going for a little while. I am good at planting so I expect to get work up on the plains on the other side of the Orinoco River where the government is going to plant tropical pine trees for a paper-making industry. They say they expect to plant a million trees. I'll be here in San Félix for a couple of months, so I'll see you again in the church services before I leave."

Rosa worked out her plans and did attend for several months and then went up to work in the pine tree planting project. We saw her occasionally when she came to San Félix to visit and to give her sister funds for the upkeep of the girls. She always attended church in Bella Vista and told us that she attended the church in Temblador whenever she could get into town.

Once again, Mildred and I had reason to praise the Lord for the evidence of a fruitful ministry throughout the years, though some of the fruit was not seen until many years later. Mildred is especially satisfied, happy that her ministry among the children has been honored of the Lord. Many times I have heard Mildred, when encouraging our women to get interested in winning the children to the Lord, give the following logical argument.

Rosa Pagán with Ana María, licensed midwife

"I remember how displeased Jesus was with his disciples when they tried to keep the little children away from Him, and how He then took them up in His arms and blessed them. I also remember how Jesus seriously cautioned the people of the danger of mistreating little children. On the other hand, Jesus must be very pleased when He sees little ones come to Him and receive Him into their hearts as their Savior. I rejoice continually that the Lord gave me that ministry and thank Him for it. All praise to the Lord and to Him alone. You too will be honored and blessed if you get into the work of leading little children to the Lord."

"And whoso shall receive one such little child in my name receiveth me." (Matthew 18:5)

IX
Puerto Rico Ministry

Chapter 41

The Living Word - Part 1

"And the things that thou hast heard of me among many witnesses, the same commit thou to faithful men, who shall be able to teach others also." (II Timothy 2:2)

During those seven years in Venezuela, I saw, as never before, the great need of the men who are serving as *encargados* [those in charge] of the churches we were helping. These are men employed in some secular occupation to support themselves, men who have no formal training for the ministry, yet serving in the place of the pastor. Statistics show that, throughout Hispanic America, ninety percent of the "pastors" work under just such a handicap.

In recent years a plan to educate such men has been developed and called Theological Education by Extension. Combination textbook and work manuals have been designed to be studied at home, and then checked periodically by a missionary or a trained area pastor. Prepared using a method called *programmed writing*, the textbook takes the place of a classroom teacher, in fact, it **IS** the teacher. I used the program with some thirty men, deacons of our churches, to try to give them a better understanding of Bible doctrine and church organization. Written examinations taken occasionally by the men proved to me that the system works. There was only one problem at that time, our program was limited to only five textbooks.

Baptist Mid-Missions' Spanish Literature Division, Editorial Bautista Independiente, located at that time in Puerto Rico, was publishing such textbooks. The work of writing, proofreading, testing and revising is exacting and takes a long time. The team working on this program consisted of only six persons, help was needed. I felt that I would better serve our pastors in Venezuela and on other fields by joining the team and perhaps helping to prepare textbooks covering more doctrinal subjects. I received permission from our Mission's administration to join the team, and we took up residence in Puerto Rico, January 8, 1978.

Our work with the publishing house kept us busy all week but left us free on weekends. Many believers from our church in Philadelphia had moved back to their homeland. Many calls to preach or teach came from the churches they were now attending. I had prepared a series of studies which gave a positive biblical refutation of the charismatic movement. Since this false teaching was becoming a problem to many of the churches, I was kept busy almost every Sunday and some week nights presenting those studies.

********** ********** **********

Georgie Colón and Family

> *"Being born again, not of corruptible seed, but of incorruptible, by the word of God, which liveth and abideth forever."* (I Peter 1:23)

We had been in Puerto Rico for almost two years when our friend of many years, Dr. Miguel Casillas, introduced us to Jorge and Ada Negrón. Upon their invitation, we started a Bible study class in their home on Sunday nights. They had been saved in the church in Fajardo, founded by Dr. Casillas. Later they moved to Río Piedras in order to make contact with relatives and attempt to win them to Christ. The first convert was Jorge's mother, Antonia. As the class grew, we started a Sunday School, then regular morning and evening Sunday services.

Jorge and Ada Negrón, Samuel and Jorgito

Jorge, his mother Antonia
and older brother

One afternoon, my telephone rang. The call was from brother Ortiz, senior deacon of the church in Fajardo. I knew him from one of the times that I preached in his church.

"I'm glad I caught you in, Pastor Eduardo," said the voice on the other end. "I just arrived home from the funeral of an uncle of mine, and I wanted to pass on some information to you without delay. There is a man and his wife that need a visit from you."

"Glad to do it, if I can, brother Ortiz. Give me their names, address and telephone number as well as any information you may have so I may know how best to approach them."

Ortiz told me, "My cousin, Margarita, is quite broken up over the death of her father and needs some spiritual help. You know, there is little comfort in the Catholic religion. I didn't get a chance to talk to her, but during the morning *velorio* [wake], while waiting for the priest to come, I spoke to her husband, Georgie. He is an executive in the Puerto Rico Water Company.

"As I testified to him about the Savior, of life after death, and of the assurance we Evangelicals have that our sins are forgiven, and that when we die we go directly to heaven to be with Christ, he expressed interest in hearing more. Right after the funeral they had to get back to San Juan so we did not have another opportunity to speak. However, I asked him if I might contact a missionary who could go to his house to explain more fully these Bible truths.

"From what Georgie said to me at the wake, I can see that this death has made him think more seriously about his own spiritual condition. He was very anxious to hear more and readily consented to your visit. I gave him your name so he will know who you are when you call him. Pastor Eduardo, call him as soon as possible, it is always good to strike while the iron is hot."

"Right you are, brother Ortiz, I will call him right away. Be sure to pray that the Word of God will penetrate their hearts. Pray too that there will be nothing to hinder our visit."

Immediately upon finishing the conversation with Ortiz, I called the number he had given me. A woman's voice answered the phone. After identifying myself and telling her of my conversation with her cousin, I asked if a visit would be convenient.

"Not tonight," was her reply. "We just got home from my father's funeral and I am just too upset to receive visitors."

I could hear a voice in the background asking if it was the Evangelical pastor on the line. Then the voice, a bit louder now, said, "Let me speak to him."

The masculine voice took over, saying, "I am Georgie Colón. I have been expecting your call. Ortiz said that you would not delay in contacting us. Good... good... I like people that you can depend upon. When can you come to see us?"

I was a bit surprised at the business tone and abruptness of the man's voice, but encouraged because he seemed anxious that I visit. "I am free to visit you almost any time if I know beforehand so that I can arrange my schedule to avoid interruptions."

"Can you come tonight?"

"Tonight? But your wife said she did not feel up to a visit so soon after the funeral of her father. I can make it tomorrow night or the next."

"If you are free, I would like you to come tonight. Whatever you will have to say, if it is anything like Ortiz was telling me, it will do my wife a lot of good. I would consider it a personal favor if you could come over tonight, let's say, about seven-thirty. Can you make it?"

"I'll be there. Give me your exact address and an idea of where your street is located. I know Villa Andalucia, for that is where we have been holding Bible classes."

That night Mildred and I talked for about two hours with Georgie and Margarita. Two of their daughters were also present. We thoroughly explained the way of salvation, answering all their questions about sin, punishment, repentance, life after death and many others, showing them verses from the Word of God to substantiate our answers.

Georgie had been the one to ask most of the questions. They all seemed interested, but from their facial expressions, I could not determine if they were being impressed or not. But, because it was now the right thing to do, and not wishing to belabor the issue, I asked, "Now that you have heard what the Word of God says about your spiritual need and what you must do about it, would you like to accept Jesus Christ as your only and sufficient Savior?"

To our great surprise, Georgie immediately, without any hesitation, replied, "I will right now accept Christ as my Savior."

I thought, "Oh, how little faith we sometimes have. Truly the Word of God is quick, and powerful, and sharper than any two-edged sword. Tonight the power of the Word to enter the soul and bring those who seek to a saving knowledge of Christ has again been demonstrated."

To the little family, I spoke, "Well, praise God for your decision, brother Georgie. I can now call you brother, you see you have now been born into the family of God because you have received Christ as your Savior. And what about you, *Señora* Margarita?"

Margarita, was struggling with the many questions and doubts that had been raised. Her eyes filled with tears welling up from a heart now made to realize that her father and many others of her relatives and friends who had died without a true faith in Christ were eternally lost. She bowed her head as if to pray, but instead, in a barely audible whisper, said, "Not tonight, I need more time to think."

The little family was seated in a circle, dad and mom on chairs, the two daughters seated on pillows on the floor between their parents. Margarita began to cry softly. Mildred put her arm around her shoulder and, wishing to console her and at the same time encourage her to trust in Christ, whispered, "Doña Margarita, trust in Jesus, He will sustain you. He will be a Friend, closer than a brother. When you have Jesus, you have everything."

But Margarita shook her head. "Not yet," she repeated.

I turned to the daughters. The older was a freshman in the pre-med school of the University of Río Piedras, the younger one was soon to graduate from high school. The older girl, Marjorie, immediately nodded her head "yes," but Yolanda followed her mother's example with a single word, "Later."

I led Georgie and daughter Marjorie in a prayer of acceptance after which they both added their own words. After their prayers, we showed them verses of assurance. Then the girls served us coffee, cheese and crackers in typical Puerto Rican fashion. One just cannot get up and leave after a visit. The visitors must be treated with refreshments.

Georgie bought Bibles for each member of the family. Although his wife and one daughter had not received Christ as Savior, he insisted that they attend all the services of our church with him and Marjorie.

Then, on the second week, after the Bible study, and before the prayer part of the service, Margarita spoke: "I am ready. I want to have Jesus as my personal Savior also."

"Praise the Lord," was heard from every voice present, as I turned to Yolanda.

"Yes, I too want to accept Christ as my Savior."

About the same time, a third daughter and her boy friend, students at the University of Mayagüez, accepted Christ as savior through a Christian campus group.

The Colón family - Yolanda, Georgie, Luis, Margarita, Wanda and Marjorie

The Lord continued to bless our ministry with souls saved. These were baptized and organized into a local church. A commercial building was purchased and remodeled. The sign upon its roof read: "The Evangelical Baptist Church of Trujillo Alto, Independent and Fundamental."

Georgie Colón became an avid student of the Word and gave evidence of having the gift of teaching. He became the teacher of the adult Sunday School class and, often taught the Wednesday night Bible class when I had to be away.

Georgie loved to testify to the power of the Word of God in his life. "What a difference there has been in my life since Jesus came in. Many things never would have happened if I had known then what I know now. Now I want to spend as much of my time as possible witnessing for Christ and teaching His Word."

Georgie Colón continues, "It is through that Word, the incorruptible seed, and the work of the Holy Spirit that we are saved. It is true what Peter says in his first letter, chapter one and verse twenty-three, 'Being born again, not of corruptible seed, but of incorruptible, by the word of God, which liveth and abideth forever.'"

Yes, the Bible is the LIVING WORD of God.

Chapter 42

The Living Word - Part 2

Gilbert and Margarita Graciani

"Then they that gladly received his word were baptized...." (Acts 2:41a)

"...took bread... Take eat... in remembrance of me." (I Corinthians 11:23,24)

"...as oft as ye drink it, in remembrance of me." (I Corintians 11:25)

"But, my love, why won't you take me to the Baptist church? We could go to that new one on the highway, the one we pass on our way to the mall," Margarita begged her husband. (This is another Margarita, not to be confused with the one in the last chapter.)

"No... no... **NO**," Gilbert denied her. "Those Baptists are crazy. They used to carry on their services decently and in order, but now they aren't much different than the Pentecostals. The last time we went to the big one in Carolina the music almost drove me crazy. It sounded more like a dance than a church service."

"Well, I would rather have it that way than the way the service is conducted in that dead church your family goes to," argued Margarita. "The music puts me to sleep, and the liturgy isn't much different than in the Catholic Church."

"Oh, come on, Margarita, you know it is not the same. We don't celebrate the Mass like they do. Our teaching is much different. We believe like Luther taught, that the just shall live by faith." Gilbert started once again on one of his favorite theological dissertations.

"I know, I know," Margarita interrupted. "I've heard it a hundred times already. But, I don't see why you want to go to your old church, you're not one of their pastors anymore."

"Well, my parents and grandparents were Lutherans, I was raised a Lutheran and I studied in the Lutheran Seminary. I feel more comfortable in a Lutheran Church. I can't stand the hand clapping and the hollering that goes on in many of the Evangelical churches today."

"But, dearest," and Margarita began to pout and whine, "why can't we go just once to that new little church? Please take me, please, Gilbert, it just might be different. The sign on the roof says it is fundamental. What does that mean, Gilbert?"

Evangelical Baptist Church of Trujillo Alto (Independent - Fundamental)

But before he could answer, Margarita continued, "It also says it is independent. Maybe that means that it is different from the other Baptist churches. Please, Gilbert, let's go there tomorrow. We won't know until we go there at least once. Please, Gilbert? That time you went with me to my friend Gloria's church, you admitted that it was not so bad."

"But that wasn't a regular service," Gilbert protested. "It was... what did they call it? Children's Day service... the recitations were nice, but I didn't appreciate that woman's preaching. The Bible prohibits a woman from being a pastor. No, Margarita, I will not take you to another Baptist church. Now, don't start to cry. It won't do you any good. That's final. Tomorrow we will go to my church. Anyhow, we haven't visited my parents for several weeks, so we will go to their house after morning worship."

Margarita knew her husband well enough that, when he used that tone of voice it was better not to say anymore. It would only end in another bitter quarrel, and they would say things for which they would be sorry. She would bide her time. She couldn't explain her feelings, but she just knew that God wanted them to visit that Baptist church on highway 846.

Now, see how the Lord works! In Chapter 30, you read how Angel worked and saved money in order to go to Puerto Rico to marry his fiancée, Gloria, and bring her to Philadelphia. She was a nominal Christian, but became a true believer in Christ under our ministry and was baptized in our church. After their first child was born, they moved back to Puerto Rico where she opened a beauty salon in Río Piedras. During our service on the Island, Gloria was Mildred's hairdresser. It was this same Gloria who first introduced Margarita to the Gospel.

A number of weeks after that conversation. Margarita and Gilbert, with their baby girl, Anamar, were shopping at the Carolina mall when Gilbert remembered that Margarita had a birthday coming up. "Let me see," he thought to himself, "oh my, it's the day after tomorrow."

To Margarita, he said, "Since we are here in the mall shopping, what would you like me to buy you for your birthday?"

She had been thinking about that and had planned what she was going to say. She was just waiting for him to ask. "Gilbert, my love, this year I do not want you to buy me anything."

"What! Oh, come on now, Margarita... Do you feel all right? Are you feverish? You must want something. What woman wouldn't have something in mind when her husband asks, 'What do you want for your birthday?' God has been good to us recently. I'll buy you anything... within reason, of course." Gilbert thought that he had better add that condition.

"No, Gilbert, I don't want you to buy me anything," Margarita repeated. "I just want you to take me to that little Baptist church on Sunday."

She looked at her husband to see his face going through a number of contortions. "I've been tricked," he thought to himself. But he was a fair man and would give her what he promised. After all, it wouldn't cost him anything—a few dollars in the offering.

He allowed a smile to creep across his face. "OK, Margarita, my love, you win. We'll go to that little Baptist church on Sunday morning. Just this once though," he quickly added.

I was teaching the Sunday School lesson to the adult class when the couple walked into the chapel. The man was pushing a small baby carriage and his wife carried the customary utility bag. They took seats on the back row, arranging the coach with the baby by their side. The man looked up and I nodded a greeting of welcome, then continued to teach the lesson.

After the lesson, the children with their teachers marched in from the rooms behind the chapel, and the young people came up from the basement where they held their class. With hardly a break in time, the children by classes, and then the young people, recited the Bible verses which they had learned. Then came the celebration of birthdays, followed by the offering and the announcements. New visitors were also welcomed as deacon Jorge read off their names from cards filled out by the Sunday School secretary, Miguel Ramos, Sr.

Gilbert and Margarita with baby Anamar, were the only new visitors that day. As was my custom, I had taken mental note of their reaction during the various parts of the program. On the visitor's card there was no indication as to their religious affiliation, if they had any. In our church the singing was lively but decently done and I noticed that the man sang lustily, especially during the hymn "A Mighty Fortress Is Our God." He had given his undivided attention to the message of the morning, letting his wife attend to the needs of their baby.

When the worship service ended, Mildred and I stood at the door to speak to the people as they departed. A few of the women gathered around Margarita to welcome her and to see the baby. As the number of people thinned out, the man approached me and introduced himself more formally. Repeating his name, he told me that he was sorry that they had arrived late, and then assured me that he had thoroughly enjoyed the service and that they would be back again.

Gilbert told me, "I liked what I heard of the last part of the Sunday School lesson as well as your sermon. You have a way of teaching the Bible as you preach, I like that... By the way, I must tell you that I was a Lutheran minister for twelve years, but I am always interested in hearing sermons even though they are based on other theological persuasions."

"Did you say that you **were**—past tense—a Lutheran minister?" I asked.

"Yes, I have been out of the pastorate for some years now. I graduated from the Lutheran Seminary. I served as a pastor of one of our churches in the Spanish community of Brooklyn, and then for a number of years in Ponce, here in Puerto Rico... But, it is a long story, Pastor Schwartz. Suffice it to say, that I am no longer in the ministry. At present I am a business management consultant."

Margarita was pushing the coach toward the doorway and Gilbert turned to help. She was surprised, but pleased, to hear her husband say, "Good-bye, for now. We'll be back sometime soon"

"Yes, please come again. You will always be welcome. Here is my card with my home address and telephone number. Any time that you would like to talk, give me a call. Again, let me say that I and our church people are *a sus órdenes* [at your orders]."

Two Sundays went by before the couple returned to morning worship. After that they hardly missed a Sunday morning service. Gilbert participated quite often in the question and answer time of the Sunday School lesson. But, being accustomed to attending church services only once a week as is the practice, sad to say, of the majority of church people nowadays, they did not start attending Sunday or Wednesday nights until some time much later.

They were very friendly and quite hospitable, so before long Mildred and I were invited to their home for an evening meal. After the meal, there followed several hours of animated theological discussion as we exchanged and compared opinions. Gilbert and Margarita lived in the suburbs not very far from the church, in a large home, which they were remodeling.

During these conversations, Mildred and I came to know the couple better and to understand their problems. They were very open and willing to listen to counsel. Gilbert had graduated from the Lutheran Seminary in Germantown of Philadelphia. In fact, we discovered that we had mutual acquaintances, one of whom had been his professor of Greek and Hebrew, Dr. Charles Sigel. The professor and his wife Lois once lived close to our Spanish church.

The walls of Gilbert's den were covered with diplomas and certificates of honor from universities in Puerto Rico. He had degrees for teaching, degrees for management in the business world, a real estate license, and, of course, his earned doctor's degree in theology.

Gilbert told of his experiences as pastor of Lutheran churches in Brooklyn and Ponce. He told of problems which resulted in his first marriage ending in divorce. He then got into business. He was in real estate and taught in the University of Río Piedras, where he met

Margarita. In time they were married. Their little girl was about a year old when they began to attend our church. Besides being a business management consultant, he was also into computers.

Gilbert told me that he had never had Bible studies of the kind that he was enjoying now in our church. Nor had he ever thought so deeply about the Bible way of salvation. His thinking had always been limited by his church's theological position, and he was having difficulty reconciling that with what he was now hearing. He did, however, believe that the Bible was the inspired Word of God and without error, and he was willing to listen if I could give him verses from the Holy Scriptures that would prove the truths that I was claiming.

So we discussed many doctrines, sitting there on the sofa in the living room, with our Bibles open before us. One of the first references that I showed him was II Peter 1:20, "...no prophecy of the scripture is of any private interpretation."

Gilbert **agreed** that a Bible doctrine (teaching) should not be established on the interpretation of one or two verses; that a verse, and even portions of Scripture, should not be **isolated** from the context and interpreted by themselves. We must compare Scripture with Scripture.

I believe that Gilbert had truly received Christ as his Savior, but was confused as to the true meaning of baptism and the Lord's Supper. When this was cleared up, he came into full assurance of his salvation. He had always preached that salvation was by pure grace through faith in the redemptive power of the shed blood of Christ, without works, but still taught, without realizing the contradiction, that the ordinances were a means of obtaining God's grace.

It would be impossible, my dear reader, for me to remember all of the conversations we had as, week after week, we exchanged opinions. Nor could I possibly repeat the words with so many quotes of "he said" and "I said." Neither is it the purpose of this book of memoirs to give you detailed Bible studies, in order to show how Gilbert came to the correct conclusions. (If such studies are ever asked of me, I am always willing and happy to oblige.) The major object in our writing is to bring glory to God by illustrating how His Word, the Bible, is "powerful and sharper than any two-edged sword" and will clarify our thinking and affirm our beliefs. Regarding Gilbert and Margarita, the following two paragraphs should suffice.

As we studied the Bible together and compared Scripture with Scripture, Gilbert finally understood that the Holy Spirit indwells the believer at that moment when Christ is received as Savior, and at that same moment the Holy Spirit **baptizes** the believer into the body of Christ. He saw clearly that water baptism has no power to save and that it is simply a visible **testimony** of the believer's identification with Christ in His death, burial and resurrection. He understood also that **only believers** are to be baptized, and that innocent babies are already saved and will continue in that state until they reach the age of accountability. Therefore, it is necessary that believing parents instruct their children in the Christian faith so that when they reach that age of responsibility, they will, of their own volition, choose to receive Christ as their Savior and follow with baptism.

Finally, Gilbert also understood that the Lord's Supper is simply a **memorial,** and that the partaking of the bread and wine is neither a means nor a renewal of salvation, not even of purification. The Lord's Supper helps the believer to remember His death, and to better understand the communion and divine relationship that exists between the members of the local church as members of the Lord's spiritual Body. The Lord's body is not physically present to strengthen and deepen our personal relationship with Himself as Gilbert previously believed, but is the work of the indwelling Holy Spirit as the believer obediently grows "in grace and the knowledge of our Lord and Saviour Jesus Christ" through Bible study and prayer.

Now that Gilbert understood the truth concerning baptism and the Lord's Supper, I thought it was time for him to make a decision. I said, "Well, Gilbert, after all our Bible study, and comparing the various religions in the world, you must see that, based on their beliefs about the ordinances, there are but two kinds of Christian churches, sacramental and confessional. The sacramental churches follow the Roman Catholic Church in her teaching that salvation is obtained through participation in the sacraments. The confessional churches believe that salvation, offered by God in His grace and mercy, is obtained **solely** by a genuine **confession** (profession) of faith in the finished work of Jesus Christ. So then, the bottom line is that you, Gilbert, must make the decision. Which kind of church will you choose?"

"No question about it, brother Eduardo. I choose the **confessional,** for I am now convinced that this is the kind of church that our Lord Jesus Christ is building."

A short time after this final discussion, both Gilbert and Margarita received believer's baptism and became members of Evangelical Baptist Church of Trujillo Alto, Puerto Rico. After a time, he served as treasurer of the church, and Margarita as a teacher in the pre-school department of our Sunday School. She is a gifted designer of floral arrangements and blessed the church from time to time with beautiful floral decorations.

Gilbert, Margarita and little Anamar

Gilbert loves to give his testimony. He speaks of a certain satisfaction he experienced in serving God as a pastor. But he gradually became uneasy, and was concerned about his own spiritual condition. He did not have the peace and assurance he knew he should have, consequently he lost confidence in the effectiveness of his ministry to help others.

"When I was a pastor, I knew many Scripture passages for I used them in the liturgy Sunday after Sunday, but they meant very little to me. I had my doctor's degree in theology, I knew what my church taught, but I did not know what the Bible taught. After I came into full assurance of my salvation, the Word of God took on new meaning. Now when I read the Bible it speaks to me, it **LIVES**. The Bible is indeed the **LIVING WORD OF GOD**."

In time, Gilbert became a great help to us, advising us concerning the management of church finances. By means of the computer, he made the financial reports more understandable. When the computer business became too competitive, he re-opened his real estate office, and managed the sale of our home, enabling us to move north sooner than expected.

Our ministry in Puerto Rico was concluding, the church which the Lord enabled us to establish was about to graduate into autonomy and would be calling its own pastor. One day in conversation with Gilbert, Mildred and I thanked him for all the help he had given us. He replied, "My dear ones in Christ, are you thanking me? It is I who must thank you. Margarita and I owe you our very lives for had it not been for your patience and perseverance in teaching the Bible, we would not yet be sure of our salvation, and that we are on our way to heaven.

"Not only that, but our lives have been changed completely. Before we genuinely knew Christ, Margarita and I used to fight like cats and dogs. Not any more. We always really loved each other, but now we prove it by our actions. Oh, we do have some disagreements... don't we all? But it is very different since we allowed the Lord to come into our hearts.

"Thank you again, Pastor Eduardo and Doña Mildred, for your faithfulness. We will miss you tremendously. It makes me sick when I think of your leaving us, but we know that you are obeying the Lord's calling and pray God's blessing upon you. We will never forget you."

Needless to say, as in all our other experiences, we give the glory to God, our Savior, the Lord Jesus Christ, It is with gratitude that we realize that it is ALL of God. We never cease to give thanks to Him for using us in His service. We have only sown the SEED. We have cultivated it when given the opportunity to do so, and we have watered it with our tears and our prayers. **BUT IT IS GOD THAT GIVES THE INCREASE!**

A holy joy fills our heart and we rejoice as we experience the fulfillment of the promises of Psalm 126:5,6.

> *"They that sow in tears shall reap in joy. He that goeth forth and weepeth, bearing precious seed, shall doubtless come again with rejoicing. bringing his sheaves with him."*

Chapter 43

Epilogue: Memoirs Up-Date

"Even the youths shall faint and be weary, and the young men shall utterly fall, but they that wait upon the LORD shall renew their strength; they shall mount up with wings as eagles; they shall run, and not be weary; and they shall walk, and not faint." (Isaiah 40:30,31)

If we may apply this promise to ourselves, we praise and thank our "everlasting God, the LORD," because **it is HE who gives power** when we faint and **strength** when we have no might. (See verses 28,29.) We acknowledge once again that whatever success we have experienced in our missionary work, as related in our memoirs, was not because of our ability, but because our Lord saw fit to accomplish it in spite of our weaknesses and failings. We have often repeated this statement, not in an attempt to create a feeling of false humility, but because **to our Lord Jesus Christ alone belongs all the honor and glory!** This will also apply to whatever our Lord allows us to continue to do in our retirement. He will give the health and the strength.

To you dear believers who are named in our memoirs, who were won to the Lord during our ministry, we rejoice to point out the wonderful truth that you are our **hope**, our **joy**, our **crown of rejoicing**, "...in the presence of our Lord Jesus Christ at his coming... For ye are our glory and joy" as expressed by the Apostle Paul in I Thessalonians 2:19,20.

********** ********** **********

In Chapter 41, I explained that the reason for our move to Puerto Rico was to join the team of Editorial Bautista Independiente (Independent Baptist Spanish Publications), the Spanish Literature Division of Baptist Mid-Missions. I wanted especially to help in the writing and publishing of study material to prepare pastors who could not enroll in a regular Bible institute or seminary, and who were already in charge of local churches.

We found a house that we could afford to purchase. The cost of renting was too expensive and our support budget would not allow it. We sold our house in Philadelphia to get the down payment. We then moved all of our furniture and household items to Puerto Rico—"burned our bridges behind us," so to speak. But, by the time we were settled in, we found that the missionaries we expected would be our co-workers, had planned to return to their former fields of service, and the ministry of Independent Baptist Spanish Publications was to be suspended temporarily. When others might be called of the Lord to continue its operation, it could be reorganized.

What to do? As we prayed about the situation, we saw that orders from many fields were still coming in for the Theological Education by Extension manuals. It would be a shame, if not a sin, to close down the operation. We felt that to do so would not be the Lord's will and that somehow we should keep it in operation. Rev. Charles and Dr. Mary Cook, who were planning on retiring, then decided to stay with us until we had learned the functions of Independent Baptist Spanish Publications.

When we saw the stock of books was getting depleted, I learned to operate the master burner and the press. Merle Watkins, formerly one of our missionaries to Africa, who was pastoring an English-language church in the San Juan area, was of great help to me and I am forever grateful. Mildred learned to collate the pages, punch the holes in them and install the plastic binders. Then she had to check each book to make sure that the pages were there. Most of the binding and checking was done at night in our home. I received the orders, filled them, packaged and mailed them out with their invoices and kept the ledgers.

We continued this work for almost two years, at the same time working with Jorge Negrón to get a Gospel testimony started. Then we were joined by Rev. Otis and Beulah Pinkston, missionaries to Mexico, who felt called to this work in which they already had some experience. This enabled us to take a six-month furlough in the States, resting as well as reporting to our supporting churches. The Pinkstons kept the publishing operation going as well as carried on the church-planting ministry with Jorge and Ada Negrón. During this time it was decided to move the publishing house to Florida and reorganize it there. We were beginning to hear of others who had expressed interest in joining this ministry.

When we returned to Puerto Rico, the Pinkstons moved to Deltona, Florida, and Mildred and I began to package and send the stock of books to them there. We were able to sell most of the heavy equipment in Puerto Rico and ship the smaller things to Deltona. We were invited to join the work in Florida, but we could not leave the infant church which had just been organized. As the congregation grew, a building was purchased and remodeled to provide a meeting hall, class rooms for Sunday School and a social hall in the basement.

By early spring of 1986, our church was ready to become autonomous. There were three faithful deacons, Jorge Negrón, Raul Moreno and Miguel Ramos. Jorge Negrón, employed by the U.S. Postal Service, was asked to be pastor. He attended night classes of our Bible Institute in our church in Caguas, founded by our missionaries Jim and Janet Stinedurf, and now pastored by Dr. Emilio Suárez, a medical doctor.

We began to make plans to take an active role in writing for Independent Baptist Spanish Publications. By that time, I had a computer and was already using it in writing study material for our local church. We began to pray about where we would live. We finally decided that it would be wise for us to move to South New Jersey where we could take over a house that our son Dan had purchased on a property next to his. It was not necessary for me to be in Florida because my completed work could be sent from anywhere to my co-workers who would transfer it to their computer, make corrections or additions, and format it to conform to the material already published. Our age became a prime factor in the decision. In New Jersey, we would be where we would be taken care of in case of a debilitating sickness. We moved in July.

As our supporters and prayer partners already know, we have been very comfortable here. We continue to write during the week and are quite often called to substitute for pastors in area churches, either on vacation or incapacitated because of illness. On a few occasions, I have been asked to bring some special Bible study.

December 31, 1994, we officially retired and were given emeritus status by Baptist Mid-Missions. In August of 1995, we completed 55 years with our Mission. On October 17, 1995 Mildred and I celebrated 65 years of marriage. Recently, we have taken some time off to finish the final revision of this book of memoirs.

We have two major tasks to complete as the Lord permits and gives health and strength. The current one is to assemble all the source material that I can find on doctrinal and other subjects usually taught in Bible institutes, copy it and send it to Florida to file away for future use by writers we are praying that the Lord will send to help us. There is so much yet to be done that we could not possibly do it in our lifetime. Next, we want to work on a factual and pictorial history of Baptist Mid-Missions' work in Venezuela.

We request, dear readers, that you pray for us and for these projects, and that the Lord will be glorified in all that may be accomplished. We terminate this book of memoirs with the following pictorial report on the present status of our Christian day school and church in Philadelphia.

Facade of the Evangelical Baptist Church, located on the corner of Rising Sun Avenue, 7th Street, and Erie Avenue, Philadelphia.

Interior of the Evangelical Baptist Church, Philadelphia

Rev. Fidias Echevarría (pastor) and wife, Georgina

Timothy Academy Elementary School on 4th Street, south of Lehigh Avenue

Timothy Academy Middle School on Lehigh Avenue at 3rd Street

"Praise ye the LORD!"

Yours because Jesus Christ **LIVES!**

Die Geschichte des Ikebana

Die Geschichte des Ikebana reicht weit zurück. Sie läßt sich kaum in einigen Sätzen zusammenfassen. Ich möchte deshalb hier nur die wichtigsten Etappen nennen und kurz erläutern.

Bis 6. Jahrhundert
Naturreligiöse Opferpflanzen

Vom naturreligiösen Volksglauben her pflegte man der Gottheit bestimmte Pflanzen (u. a. immergrüne Zweige) als Opfergabe oder symbolische Verkörperung darzubringen. Diese Riten sind teilweise heute noch überliefert wie z. B. *Yorishiro* (gottweilender Gegenstand). Die Japaner damals hatten ein inniges Verhältnis zur Natur, welches die geistige Heimat des Ikebana ist.

6.—14. Jahrhundert
Buddhistische Kuge (Opferblumen)

Der Buddhismus kam im Jahre 538 nach Japan und wurde durch Tennos und deren Hofadelstand besonders gefördert (ab 594).
Der buddhistische Kult samt *Kuge* drang nach der kaiserlichen Verordnung (685) in die Privatsphäre der Oberschicht ein. Nach der vorherrschenden *Jōdo*-Glaubensvorstellung (Erlösung bzw. Wiedergeburt im westlichen Paradies) nahm das Kuge seine erste Form an: *Sanzon-Kuge* (Dreierbuddhastatuen). Die typischen Merkmale, z. B. die aufrechtstehende Gestalt, der zusammengebündelte Fuß und die dreieckige Konstruktion, gelten als Grundlage des späteren Ikebana.

14.—16. Jahrhundert
Tatehana (huldigende Blumen) als Vorläufer des Rikka

Das mit der Kriegerklasse aufsteigende Zen begann seine Einflüsse auch auf das Ikebana auszuüben: *Mitsugusoku*-Stil (Dreiergegenstände), der aus Leuchter (Licht = Weisheit), Weihrauchdose (ununterbrochen aufsteigender Rauch = Fleiß) und Blumen (= Geduld) bestand.
Shoinkazari (Ausschmückung des Studier- und Gästezimmers) und dessen *Tatehana*, die durch die mönchische *Ami*-Künstlergruppe des Shogun und durch die neu aufsteigenden *Ikenobō*-Ikebanameister entwickelt wurden.

15.—17. Jahrhundert
Nageire (lockere, schräg fließende Form)

Mit der Entstehung von *Wabicha* (eine stark geistesorientierte schlichte Teezeremonie) wurde *Nageire* u. a. durch Kaufleute in Sakai entwickelt. Da Sakai eine Hafenstadt für Außenhandel war, wurde Nageire anfänglich in schiffsförmigen Hängegefäßen und später auch in Vasen gesteckt.

Es war durch das schlichte Gefäß und entsprechend bescheidene Materialanwendung gekennzeichnet und ist heute noch als *Chabana* (Teeblumen) beliebt.

16.—18. Jahrhundert

Rikka (aufrechtstehende formelle Blumen im grandiosen Stil)

Inzwischen wurde das *Rikka* als eigenständige Kunst entwickelt. Es diente der feierlichen/festlichen Ausschmückung des herrschaftlichen Saals, um die Macht der Daimios, den Reichtum der Großkaufleute, die Autorität der Tennos zu demonstrieren. Es bestand aus neun Elementen und spiegelte den Kosmos wider. Mit der Vollendung des *Rikka* erreichte das Ikebana seinen technischen Höhepunkt.

Sunanomono (informelle Rikka im sandgefüllten Gefäß)

Diese wurde für Regale entwickelt. Von der flachen Schale her erinnert es an den heutigen *Moribana*-Stil.

Ab 18. Jahrhundert

Ikehana (lebende Blumen)

Das *Ikehana* wurde als Zwischending zwischen *Rikka* und *Nageire* entwickelt, um das bürgerliche *Tokonoma* auszuschmücken. Es entstanden sehr viele Schulen, die meistens ihre Form auf dem erwähnten *Sanzonkuge* und ihre Theorie auf dem vorherrschenden Konfuzianismus aufbauten, um das eigene *Ikehana* allgemein verständlich und gleichzeitig beherrschend zu machen. Die heute noch oft gehörten Bezeichnungen „Himmel, Mensch und Erde" stammen von damals. Dieser Stil wurde so populär, daß der Name als Inbegriff für alle Blumenstile benutzt wurde. Das Ikehana selbst wird seitdem *Shōka* bzw. *Seika* genannt.

18.—19. Jahrhundert

Bun-jin-ike (Literatengesteck) als Vorläufer des Moribana

Die Intellektuellen — vor allem Literaten — eiferten dem Leben der chinesischen Literaten nach, indem sie sich musischen Beschäftigungen wie Poesie und Malerei widmeten. Dabei schufen sie auch das Ikebana nach ihren ästhetischen Grundanschauungen, was dann als *Bun-jin-ike* benannt wurde.
Obschon das *Bun-jin-ike* keine bedeutende Position in der Ikebanageschichte einnimmt, lieferte es wertvolle Anregungen zur Bildung der heutigen *Moribana*- und *Nageire*-Stile.

Ab 1868

Die Welt des Ikebana erlitt ihren verheerendsten Rückschlag in den zwanzig Jahren nach der *Meiji*-Restauration (1868), wobei die traditionellen Schulen beinahe eingingen.
Doch mit der Ernüchterung des japanischen Volkes, nach der blinden Verwestlichung und mit der Wiederentdeckung der eigenen Tradition und Kultur, konnte sich das Ikebana wieder beleben. Vor allem nach seinem Einzug in die Mädchenschulen!

Moribana (Arrangement in der Schale)
Man begann die flachen Schalen zu benutzen um das Ikebana auch westlichen Materialien anzupassen. Daraus entstand